Policy Papers
in International Affairs

NUMBER 24

D1563931

Power-Sharing in South Africa

Arend Lijphart

**Institute of
International Studies**
UNIVERSITY OF CALIFORNIA • BERKELEY

In sponsoring the Policy Papers in International Affairs series, the Institute of International Studies reasserts its commitment to a vigorous policy debate by providing a forum for innovative approaches to important policy issues. The views expressed in each paper are those of the author only, and publication in this series does not constitute endorsement by the Institute.

International Standard Book Number 0-87725-524-5

Library of Congress Card Catalog Number 85-82195

CONTENTS

LIST OF TABLES/FIGURE

Tables

Figure

ACKNOWLEDGMENTS

This book represents the culmination of my research on and thinking about the South African problem since my first visit to this beautiful and troubled country from March to May 1971. I am very grateful to the cultural exchange program between the Netherlands and South Africa which made this trip possible. I gave lectures and seminars at the University of Cape Town, the University of Natal campuses in Durban and Pietermaritzburg, the University of Pretoria, the Rand Afrikaans University in Johannesburg, the University of South Africa in Pretoria, the University of Stellenbosch, and the Jan Smuts Institute of International Relations in Johannesburg. I benefited a great deal from the comments I received in response to these presentations and from the many other exchanges of opinion with academics, politicians, and civil servants holding a wide variety of political views.

I should also like to thank the organizers of and the participants in the conferences and meetings on South Africa that I have attended in recent years which have given me the opportunity to discuss, and to receive reactions to, my ideas concerning the prospects of a power-sharing solution: the biennial meeting of the Political Science Association of South Africa on "Adaptation and Change in South Africa" at the Rand Afrikaans University in Johannesburg in September 1977; the conference on "The Prospects for Peaceful Change in South Africa" organized by the Arnold Bergstraesser Institut in Titisee, West Germany, in June 1978; the July 1978 conference in Rustenburg, South Africa, on "Options for South Africa and Implications for the West," organized by the World Peace Foundation in Boston and the South African Institute of International Relations in Johannesburg; the October 1978 "Conference on Southern African Affairs" in New York, organized by the Institute for Plural Societies of the University of Pretoria; sessions of the Buthelezi Commission in Durban in February 1981 and Pietermaritzburg in July 1981; the conference on "Prospects for Peaceful Change in Southern Africa" at the Center for the Study of Democratic Institutions in Santa Barbara, California, in April 1982; the workshop of the European Consortium for Political Research on "Violence and Conflict Management in Divided Societies" in Freiburg im Breisgau, West Germany, in March 1983; the seminar of the Arnold Bergstraesser Institut on "Education and Consociational Conflict Management in Plural Societies" in Metzéral, France, in March 1983; and the conference on "Perspective on Intergroup Relations" of the Human Sciences Research Council in Pretoria in September 1985.

I should also like to express my appreciation for the encouragement in the preparation of this book that I received from Carl G. Rosberg, Director of the Institute of International Studies in Berkeley, California, and for the research assistantship of Diane R. Stanton that the Institute made available. Ms. Stanton's interest in writing a master's thesis on political reform in South Africa gave me the impetus to get this book under way in 1982-83. I also thank her for the stimulating discussions we had in this year and for her assistance in compiling the bibliography.

I presented the book's main findings at seminars in the Departments of Political Science of Rice University in February 1985, the Ohio State University in April 1985, and the University of California, San Diego, in June 1985. I am grateful for the useful comments and criticisms that I received at these meetings. I am also indebted to several wise and kind scholars—Heribert Adam, Laurence J. Boulle, Edward Dew, Theodor Hanf, John A. Marcum, Kenneth D. McRae, Gerrit C. Olivier, Edward Reynolds, Nic J. Rhoodie, Donald Rothchild, Richard L. Sklar, Newell M. Stultz, Albert J. Venter, Klaus Baron von der Ropp, and David Welsh—who read the first draft of this book and provided extremely helpful and valuable advice. Finally, I should like to thank Bojana Ristich for her thorough and conscientious copy-editing.

A.L.

La Jolla, California
October 1985

Chapter 1

INTRODUCTION: THE ROAD TO PEACE
AND DEMOCRACY IN SOUTH AFRICA˙

This book is based on the conviction that peace and democracy in South Africa are a realistic possibility—although by no means a certainty or even a high probability. Nobody who knows South Africa can be an optimist, but few would completely deny that a peaceful and democratic solution can be found. Even if there is only a tiny chance of success—and I believe that the chances are considerably better than that—it is worth a strong effort to turn it into a reality. Moreover, we must try to discover which particular solution maximizes the probability of success.

SOUTH AFRICA AND INTERNATIONAL PEACE

A peaceful and democratic South Africa is important for many reasons. The most important gain would be the replacement of racism and oppression by democratic justice—the greatest boon that South Africa could receive and a dramatic moral victory for all mankind. In addition, South Africa's racially exclusive political regime, the racial policies it has followed, and the opposition that it has provoked are now a grave threat to the domestic peace of South Africa and to the international peace of the southern region of the African continent. Most observers predict that unless drastic improvements are effected in South Africa, a violent revolution will be inevitable. Nobel laureate Bishop Desmond Tutu warns of an impending "blood bath" (quoted in Cowell 1985a), and Hilary Ng'weno, editor of the Nairobi *Weekly Review*, speaks of an "explosion that many people ... fear will destroy the country" (1984:12). Other commentators foresee "an escalation of violence" (Gutteridge 1981:2) and an "all-out racial war" (Parker 1983:xi). And the Study Commission of U.S. Policy Toward Southern Africa reaches the conclusion that violent upheaval is inevitable, either in

1

the form of a "sporadically violent evolutionary process" or as a "much more violent descent into civil war" (1981:xxiv).

Racial tensions in South Africa have already had repercussions in the entire southern African region, and a civil war in South Africa could easily become a regional war. One book on the role of South Africa in southern Africa (Callaghy, ed. 1983) is appropriately subtitled *The Intensifying Vortex of Violence*, and Sanford J. Ungar describes the region as a "tinderbox" (1984). Jennifer S. Whitaker, associate editor of *Foreign Affairs*, writes that an "undeclared war" is being fought in southern Africa and that it "threatens to draw both superpowers into a protracted, region-wide conflict" (1983). Two German social scientists similarly foresee the danger of a "confrontation between the superpowers" (Blenck and von der Ropp 1976:310) and even "a new global war" (von der Ropp 1981: 158; see also Puschra 1981:4). And John Webster writes, "If racial war erupts, it will not confine itself to South Africa, and the world ignores at its peril this possible trigger of a Third World War" (1982:13).

All of the above predictions of serious crisis in and around South Africa are well founded, but the danger is not as imminent as the various authors imply. Tensions are undeniably increasing, but the South African government still appears to be firmly in control, both domestically and in its relationships with neighboring countries. It did not even have to call upon army troops to assist the police in maintaining internal order during the long period between the state of emergency following the Sharpeville massacre in 1960 and the crackdown on renewed unrest in black townships in October 1984. Moreover, the Nkomati Accord on mutual non-interference in internal affairs, signed by South African Prime Minister P.W. Botha and President Samora Machel of Mozambique in March 1984, symbolizes South Africa's predominance in the subcontinent.

Specific time-bound predictions about the intensification of conflict in South Africa have all proved wrong. For instance, the South African Communist Party was far off the mark when it stated in its 1962 program that "the vicious type of colonialism embodied in the present Republic of South Africa cannot long endure. Its downfall and the victory of the South African demo-cratic revolution are certain in the near future" (quoted in Bunting, ed. 1981:315). Judy Seidman quotes a South African admiral as follows: "Time is running out ... I don't think we have five years to play with" (1980:5). This statement was made in 1978, but by 1983 no startling changes had taken place. Pierre L. van den Berghe's prediction that "once the colonial territories to the north of South Africa will have become independent . . . , the collapse of White supremacy will be imminent" (1965:262) may not have been implausible in the mid-1960s, but after a decade of independence for Angola and Mozambique and half a decade for Zimbabwe, it has also turned out to be incorrect. More recently, however, van den Berghe has again argued that "the end of white domination is in sight" (1981a:174). Such predictions reflect "ill-informed, wishful thinking," as Heribert Adam points out, and they are also "counterrevolutionary because they lead to dangerous underestimation of the opposing forces" (1983a: 143).

IS TIME RUNNING OUT?

The above discussion should not be taken to mean that the time factor is working in favor of the South African minority regime or in favor of the chances of peace in the country and the region. The opposite is true. The danger of large-scale violence is all too real, and it increases as time goes by without significant changes in the status of the black majority.* The Study Commission on U.S. Policy Toward Southern Africa entitled its 1981 report *South Africa: Time Running Out*. It is especially important to realize that only a limited time is left for an agreement by peaceful negotiations. In particular, it is becoming more and more difficult for moderate black leaders to remain moderate and accommodating. Black newspaper editor Percy Qoboza puts it this way:

> We have seen how the credibility of leaders preaching nonviolence and patience is beginning to be questioned. . . . Unless the government, and whites in general, do something dramatic toward seeking an accommodation with the rising expectations of our

*In accordance with the widely accepted contemporary convention, I shall use the term "black" to include the three groups that are officially designated as African, Coloured, and Asian (or Indian). In 1983 South Africa's total population of about 31.5 million was made up of 73.4 percent Africans, 15.1 percent whites, 8.8 percent Coloureds, and 2.7 percent Asians. These figures include the so-called "independent" homelands of Bophuthatswana, Ciskei, Transkei, and Venda (Hare, ed. 1983:17).

people, then we would be destroying the hands of those men of goodwill and moderation and strengthening the hands of those—black and white—who are abandoning all hope for a peaceful transformation of our society (1980:147-48).

Fortunately, and perhaps surprisingly, it appears that the time for compromise has not run out yet, and that the 1980s still offer an opportunity to find a just solution. For instance, at a news conference in January 1985, Bishop Tutu emphasized his continued commitment to peaceful change: "Are they [the white minority] not amazed that we can even at this stage say we don't want to drive whites into the sea, but want to build a better tomorrow?" (quoted in Cowell 1985a). In general, Thomas Karis argues, if the white government should show a genuine willingness to accord full citizenship rights to blacks, a "surprising amount of black patience and goodwill may become evident [and] many major issues may be negotiable, for instance, the structure of government . . . , constitutional guarantees, the role of free enterprise, and the timetable of change" (1983:230).

Is there any chance that the white power-holders will move toward a just solution? Two indicators that justify a measure of optimism in this respect are the considerable pragmatism of the white leadership—in particular the top leaders of the ruling National Party—and the leeway that they enjoy to go against the wishes of their electorate and even of their backbenchers. The Afrikaners, both leaders and rank and file, are sometimes depicted as completely rigid and ideologically committed, but this judgment is mistaken. For instance, the most negative interpretation of the new constitution, adopted in 1983, is that it does not entail a true sharing of power with Coloureds and Asians and that it is merely an opportunistic and cynical means of holding on to white power. Without going into a detailed discussion here, I should like to point out that this interpretation is at variance with the view that the National Party leaders are ideological diehards. Cynicism and opportunism are the pejorative equivalents of pragmatism and flexibility. It is easier to move from a short-sighted opportunism to enlightened pragmatism than from ideological purism to pragmatism of any sort. (The question of how the 1983 constitution must be judged—as a step in the right direction or a mere reaffirmation of white supremacy—will be discussed further in Chapter 3.)

PROPOSALS FOR REFORM: A BRIEF OVERVIEW

The gravity and urgency of the South African problem have stimulated a host of proposed solutions. The major purpose of this book is to critically review the most important of these proposals and to recommend an optimal solution. The proposals can be classified into four broad categories: (1) majoritarian, (2) non-democratic, (3) partitionist, and (4) consociational.

In Chapter 2, I shall argue that all proposals in the first three categories must be rejected. Majoritarian democracy—that is, a democratic political system without special autonomy and protection for ethnic and other minorities and without guaranteed minority participation in governmental decision-making—is both unfair and unworkable in a society that is as deeply divided as South Africa's. Majoritarianism will inevitably lead to the violation of the rights of minorities, both black and white, to ethnic and racial polarization, and to civil war and/or dictatorship. As Robert H. Jackson and Carl G. Rosberg state, in deeply divided societies generally "the rule of the majority can result only in the minority being tyrannized. Majority rule is undesirable and even unjust . . . if, as frequently happens, it constitutes the permanent domination of smaller groups by those that are more populous" (1984:181).

Most of the proposed reforms that I term non-democratic try to limit the suffrage of black citizens in order to maximize the whites' relative share of voting power and thus to appease their anxiety and opposition. To be sure, the proponents of a limited franchise usually regard it as a temporary measure and advocate the gradual expansion of voting rights. Such non-democratic plans must be rejected for at least two reasons. First, by today's standards limited suffrage is no longer an acceptable method for democratization; perhaps as late as the 1950s the gradual enfranchisement of South Africa's black citizens could have been regarded as a legitimate path to full democratic rights, but such a policy now is widely felt to constitute a denial of democracy. Second, the only way in which limited but expanding voting rights could possibly be acceptable to South Africa's blacks and to the world community would be if the temporary denial of these rights were of extremely short duration. However, very little can be gained from a short delay, and it is better to institute universal suffrage at once.

The principal appeal of the various partitionist plans is that they try to divide South Africa's plural (that is, deeply divided)

society into two or more separate sovereign states, each of which
is ethnically homogeneous, or at least has a greater degree of homogeneity than South Africa as a whole. Currently prevalent opinion
is much too critical of the idea of partition. Samuel P. Huntington
writes, "The twentieth-century bias against political divorce, that
is, secession [or partition], is just about as strong as the nineteenth-
century bias against marital divorce. Where secession is possible,
contemporary statesmen might do well to view it with greater
tolerance" (1972:vii). Although partition does not deserve to be
rejected as a general principle, several prerequisites must be fulfilled
if its practical application is to be accepted. Partition must be fair to
all groups concerned, and it must be effected with their full consent
and participation. Moreover, partition as a solution for a deeply
divided society makes sense only if it results in separate states that
are substantially *less* deeply divided. All of the partition proposals
for South Africa—from the government's grand apartheid scheme to
plans for a radical partition along a north-south boundary—fail one
or more of these requirements. Finally, even if a completely fair
partition into homogeneous states could be drawn up, it would
require such a drastic, large-scale, and painful resettlement of people
that it can only be thought of as a solution of the very last resort.

The fourth category, consociational proposals, includes the
various consociational, semi-consociational, and quasi-consociational
plans; these will be discussed in Chapter 3. The four basic elements
of consociational democracy are (1) Executive power-sharing among
the representatives of all significant groups; (2) A high degree of
internal autonomy for groups that wish to have it; (3) Proportional
representation and proportional allocation of civil service positions
and public funds; and (4) A minority veto on the most vital issues.*
I shall use the term power-sharing mainly to refer to government by a
broadly inclusive coalition, but as the most important consociational
principle, it may also be used as a synonym of consociational democracy. This is its meaning in the title of this book.

Consociational democracy is the antithesis of majority-rule
democracy as prescribed by the Westminster model. The majoritarian

---

*An extended treatment of consociational theory may be found in Lijphart
(1977a) and in my other writings listed in the bibliography. See also the analyses
by other scholars belonging to the consociational school: Daalder (1971, 1974a,
1981, 1984); Hanf (1980); Hanf, Weiland, and Vierdag (1981); Huyse
1984); Lehmbruch (1967, 1974, 1975); Lorwin (1971); McRae, ed. (1974);
Nordlinger (1972); Powell (1970); and Jurg Steiner (1971, 1974).

interpretation of "government by the people" is "government by the *majority* of the people," and that the minority may be excluded from power. The Nobel Prize-winning economist Sir Arthur Lewis has correctly pointed out that majority rule can be regarded as undemocratic. He argues that the primary meaning of democracy is that "all who are affected by a decision should have the chance to participate in making that decision, either directly or through chosen representatives." Its secondary meaning is that "the will of the majority shall prevail," but if this means that the minority will be barred from making or influencing governmental decisions, it violates the primary principle (1965:64-65).

Most majoritarians assume that the exclusion of the minority is not permanent and that there will be alternation in government: today's minority may become the majority in the next election. They also assume that Westminster-style democracy operates in a homogeneous society in which the majority and the minority are not very far apart in their policy preferences and in which, consequently, the opposition's interests are reasonably well served by the government's policies. In deeply divided countries such as South Africa, these two assumptions do not apply: the interests and outlooks of the different groups diverge much more markedly, and the voters' loyalties tend to be much more rigid, reducing the chances of a regular alternation in power. Hence Lewis's primary principle of democracy demands that executive power be shared among all significant segments in a plural society. Power-sharing may take various institutional forms, such as that of a grand coalition cabinet in parliamentary systems, a grand coalition of a president and other top officeholders in presidential systems, and broadly inclusive councils or committees with important advisory and coordinating functions.

The second consociational principle, a high degree of autonomy for each of the segments in a plural society, complements the power-sharing principle: on all issues of common interest, the decisions should be made jointly; on all other issues, each of the segments should be allowed to decide for itself. A special form of segmental autonomy that is particularly suitable for divided societies with geographically concentrated segments is federalism. If the segments are geographically intermixed, segmental autonomy has to take a mainly non-territorial form. This kind of non-territorial autonomy may be called "corporate federalism" (Friedrich 1968:124; see also Prinz 1978; Glaser 1980; Kriek 1978:197-98; Cloete 1981:150-80).

Like power-sharing, segmental autonomy violates the Westminster principle of majority rule, which does not recognize any geographical or functional areas that may be the minority's exclusive concern. Majoritarian democracy entails unitary—that is, non-federal—and centralized government. Conversely, as M.J.C. Vile states, federalism "involves a rejection of majority rule across the whole area of the federation on all matters" (1977:4).

Third, proportionality as a consociational standard eliminates the sharp distinction between winners and losers evident under majoritarian democracy. The basic majoritarian electoral rule is the plurality system, in which the candidate with the largest number of votes wins and all other candidates are excluded. With proportional representation both majorities and minorities can be "winners" in the sense that each group is able to elect candidates in proportion to its electoral support. In practice, the plurality rule has the effect of exaggerating the representation and power of the majority. It may be called "*dis*proportional representation" in favor of the majority. Proportional representation treats majorities and minorities equally and fairly. Proportionality is also the operational definition of fairness in the distribution of public funds and appointments to the public service.

There are two extensions of the proportionality rule that entail even greater minority protection: (1) The overrepresentation of small groups, and (2) Parity of representation, when all groups are represented equally, regardless of size. These are also methods of *dis*proportional representation—but now in favor of minorities. In federal systems the upper houses are often constituted on the basis of overrepresentation or parity of the smaller units.

Finally, the minority veto is the ultimate weapon that minorities need to protect their interests. Even when a minority's representatives participate in a power-sharing executive, they may be overruled or outvoted by the majority. This may not present a problem when only minor issues are being decided, but when a minority's vital interests are at stake, the veto provides essential protection. The obvious danger of the veto is that its too frequent use may paralyze the government. However, the fact that the minority veto is a *mutual* veto, which can both protect a minority and hurt its interests when used by others, is an incentive to reserve its application to truly vital matters. It goes without saying that the minority veto is again antithetical to majority rule. A basic feature of the Westminster model is an "unwritten" constitution which can be amended by normal majority vote. This means that the majority has the right to change even the most fundamental rules of government. The consociational minority veto restricts the power of the majority to overrule the minority when constitutional or other important issues are at stake.

Virtually all of the recent serious proposals for constitutional reform in South Africa are or claim to be consociational. The most important of these are the two reports of the Constitutional Committee of the South African President's Council (1982a, 1982b) and (based on these reports) the government's proposal for constitutional reform, which was approved with slight modifications by the white parliament and by a referendum among the white electorate in 1983 (South Africa 1983b; Boulle 1984:231-66); the constitutional proposals adopted by the principal white opposition party, the Progressive Federal Party—PFP (1978); and the report of the multiracial Buthelezi Commission (1982), which was instituted by the legislature of the black homeland of KwaZulu and on which I served as a member. In addition to these, I shall also discuss the report of the Study Project on Christianity in Apartheid Society—SPROCAS (Randall 1973a, 1973b), which paved the way for much of the thinking about constitutional reforms along consociational lines in the 1970s and early 1980s; the constitutional proposals of the New Republic Party (NRP—a smaller white opposition party), which do not diverge very much from the government's plan and from the 1983 constitution—the NRP advised its voters to vote yes in the 1983 referendum—but which contain a few notable differences; and two reports which, like the Buthelezi Commission's proposal, concern only parts of South Africa but have significant implications for the country as a whole—the Quail Report on the Ciskei (Ciskei Commission 1980) and the Lombard Commission report on KwaZulu and Natal (Lombard et al. 1980).

In Chapter 3 I shall test the 1983 constitution and the reform proposals against the four basic consociational criteria and discuss their strengths and weaknesses. I shall also try to spell out as specifically as possible what the optimal consociational form would be that a new, genuinely democratic South African constitution could take. Of the three most important reform plans, those of the PFP and the Buthelezi Commission can be regarded as fully consociational, but the rules and institutions introduced by the 1983 constitution fall short of a true consociation. The major failings of the constitution are that it completely excludes the African population, that in the final analysis it preserves white dominance and gives only a very limited share of power to the Coloured and Asian populations, and that it is based on a fourfold racial classification—for the purpose of setting up separate white, Coloured, and Asian electorates and chambers of parliament and excluding the Africans from national decision-making—which has become anathema to most blacks and to many whites as well. Hanf, Weiland, and Vierdag have characterized it as a "sham consociation" (1981:408-19).

The case for a truly consociational solution to the South African problem rests on two logical arguments. One is that since all other alternatives must be rejected, it is the only realistic possibility left. Several authors have stressed this argument. For instance, Lawrence Schlemmer, who is by no means uncritical of consociationalism, reviews and rejects all competing approaches and therefore concludes that "We are brought back to the alternative of a consociational accommodation" (1978a:393). Similarly, Robert A. Schrire states that the absence of viable alternatives "constitutes perhaps the strongest argument in favor of power-sharing" (1978a:11).

The second logical argument is that a consociational solution is the only one on which the major antagonists in South Africa are likely to agree. The first choice of most whites may be the continuation of white predominance, and most blacks may prefer unconditional majority rule, but since these preferences are incompatible, power-sharing is their obvious second-best solution. The Study Commission on U.S. Policy Toward Southern Africa appears to recognize this argument, although it does not say so explicitly. It states that for both sides "certain positions are nonnegotiable": blacks must have "a genuine share in political power," and for whites "a winner-take-all form of majority rule" is unacceptable. This, the Commission argues, is "both the core of the problem and, *because the nonnegotiables are not necessarily irreconcilable, the key to its solution*" (1981:xxiv; emphasis added). This conclusion can be stated much more strongly: the nonnegotiables are perfectly reconcilable, and the logical key for reconciling them is the compromise solution of power-sharing.* This argument is supported by the empirical evidence of public opinion polls, which show "a majority on both sides in favor of, or at least prepared to accept, some kind of consociational solution" (Hanf, Weiland, and Vierdag 1981:441; see also Buthelezi Commission 1982, 1:259-64, 302-4).

---

*Similarly McNamara states that a solution for South Africa must do "two absolutely essential things: It must assure the blacks full participation in genuine political power. And it must protect the whites against a winner-take-all form of majority rule" (1982).

THEORETICAL CONSIDERATIONS OF CONSOCIATIONAL DEMOCRACY

Since its initial formulation in the late 1960s, the theory of consociational democracy has been, in G. Bingham Powell's words, "among the most influential contributions to comparative politics" (1979:295). This means that it has been widely discussed—and widely criticized. To what extent do these criticisms weaken the case for consociational democracy as a solution to the South African problem? In Chapter 4 I shall carefully evaluate all significant objections that have been raised to consociational theory, and I shall conclude that they fail to damage its strength as a normative model. Most of the criticisms are based on misinterpretations or erroneous arguments. Those that have some validity affect only the purely theoretical aspect of consociationalism, and they are at most only barely relevant to consociationalism as a policy recommendation.

The two most prevalent and potentially most damaging criticisms of consociational theory are that the type of democracy which it recommends for deeply divided societies is neither genuinely democratic nor a stable and workable system. Van den Berghe puts it this way: "The success stories are few; the problems are many; and the democracy is largely a fiction" (1981b:349). While these criticisms will be discussed in detail in Chapter 4, they are so fundamental—and fundamentally wrong—that it is desirable to preview the most important counterarguments.

The characteristic of consociational democracy that the critics appear to worry about most is executive power-sharing because it means that the leaders of the different groups cooperate in governing the country instead of dividing themselves into a government and an opposition. This looks like an "oligarchy" or an "elite conspiracy" to those who prefer the competitive and adversarial style of majoritarian democracy. However, there is nothing in the basic concept of democracy as "government by and for the people" that prescribes adversarial instead of accommodative behavior by the political leaders. Indeed the opposite is more plausible: as I have argued above, majority rule is a principle of exclusion, and hence it may well be argued that power-sharing is more instead of less democratic than the government-versus-opposition pattern of Westminster-style democracy.

The same can be said about proportional representation (PR). Compared with the plurality rule and other majoritarian electoral methods, PR is far more prevalent among contemporary democracies. In countries with plurality systems there tend to be many PR advocates, whereas in PR countries there is virtually nobody who wants to shift from PR to plurality. Moreover, the proponents of plurality make their case on a variety of grounds *except* that plurality is the more democratic method; they usually concede that PR is at least in principle more democratic.

In democracies that are organized as federations, group autonomy and minority overrepresentation are entirely normal and unquestioned principles of government. In elections to the United States Senate, for instance, a vote cast by an Alaskan voter has more than a hundred times the weight of that of a Californian voter. The principle of the minority veto is recognized in all democracies that have written constitutions which can only be amended by extraordinary majorities. Consociational democracy clearly adheres to the rule of "one person, one vote" but, because of the special rights accorded to minorities, not always to the rule of "one person, one vote, one value"—but neither do most other democracies (Bull 1980:182).* The major examples of consociational democracy in the Western world are Switzerland, Belgium, the Netherlands (especially from 1917 to 1967), and Austria (from 1945 to 1966). Can anyone seriously argue that these countries are not fully respectable democracies?

The critics who maintain that consociational democracy cannot work well in deeply divided societies tend to focus on the examples of consociational "failures." In particular, Lebanon is often invoked to "prove" that consociationalism is fundamentally flawed: consociational democracy was established in Lebanon in 1943, but it collapsed in 1975, when a civil war broke out. However, it is important to recognize that the principal cause of this crisis was the intrusion of external forces: substantial Palestinian involvement in Lebanese politics followed by Syrian and Israeli interventions. In addition, a number of internal weaknesses in Lebanon's consociational government must share part of the blame for the 1975 breakdown. But the only reasonable conclusion to

---

*The Ciskei Commission's equation of the American and British models of government and its statement that both models emphasize "adversarial politics in which an elected majority enjoys absolute, though temporary, power" (1980: 110) are seriously mistaken.

be drawn from the latter argument is that the consociational arrangements should have been improved—not that the entire consociational system deserves to be condemned and abolished. Short of partition, there is really no alternative to consociationalism for a deeply divided country like Lebanon. It is utterly inconceivable that majoritarian democracy would work in Lebanon—or that anyone in his right mind would even propose it. The choice is not between consociational and majoritarian democracy, but between consociational democracy and no democracy at all.

In addition to the critics of consociational theory, there have been many critics who have argued that although the theory may be valid, it is not applicable to the case of South Africa because South African society is too deeply 'divided and because the background conditions favorable to consociational democracy are lacking. In Chapter 5 I will evaluate these arguments and compare South Africa with several other plural societies. My conclusion will be that South Africa cannot be said to offer a very fertile environment for consociationalism but that the prospects are by no means decisively unfavorable either. It is also important to emphasize that unfavorable background conditions do not necessarily present insuperable obstacles; rather they are problems that creative and constructive statesmanship may be able to solve.

THE RESPONSIBILITY OF DEMOCRATS
IN SOUTH AFRICA AND ELSEWHERE

My recommendations in this book are addressed to all democrats who have any influence on the course of events in South Africa. The effectiveness of foreign pressures on the constitutional development of South Africa should not be exaggerated. Efforts to *force* the South African government to change its ways by economic sanctions of various sorts will be difficult if not impossible to implement and unlikely to succeed—quite apart from the question of whether they would hurt instead of help the interests of the disenfranchised majority (Adam 1983d; Özgür 1982; Foltz 1980). But it is at least somewhat helpful, and it cannot hurt, to keep international attention focused on what is happening in South Africa and to be ready to give both criticism and advice.

Because the South African government and its supporters tend to reject any external attempts to influence developments in the country as illegitimate interference in purely domestic matters, it is important to establish clearly on which grounds outsiders have the right, and even the responsibility, to "interfere." First, as Foltz states, South Africa presents a threat to international peace "not so much because of its external behavior, but because of its internal policies" (1980:71). This consideration gives outsiders a legitimate interest in these internal policies. Second, it makes no sense to say that political reform in South Africa should be exclusively the South Africans' concern as long as the vast majority of South Africans do not have any effective voice in the matter (Bull 1978: 15). Third, if Foreign Minister Pik Botha states that his government is tied "to an extremely democratic system of accountability" quoted in Starcke 1978:71), or if Deputy Foreign Minister D.J. Louis Nel claims that "South Africa's working democracy is the oldest in Africa" (1984), non-South African democrats have the right to point out how undemocratic South Africa actually is and how it should democratize itself.

After a critical speech by Lawrence S. Eagleburger, U.S. Under Secretary of State for Political Affairs, in 1983, Prime Minister Botha responded as follows: "In criticizing the South African Government's policy, he did not indicate how the U.S. would handle a complex situation such as ours without creating large-scale conflict" (statement made in South African parliament; reported in *South African Digest*, 8 July 1983:4). This comment can only be interpreted as a direct invitation to discuss the democratization of South Africa and to spell out which kind of democracy would be best.

Foreign pronouncements on democratic reform in South Africa will do the least good if they are mere denunciations of the current regime and its policies. It is also not helpful to call for the establishment of majoritarian democracy. Although I strongly disagree with Ernest W. Lefever's preference for a hands-off policy toward South Africa, I agree that the Western countries should not be "demanding impossible changes" (1978:26). An example of such counterproductive rhetoric is former President Jimmy Carter's reference to a need for instituting "majority rule in those areas of the world [where this goal has] not yet been attained" (1978) such as South Africa. It would have been much better to call for democracy in the terms in which he proudly described elements of American democracy: "the right of every individual to speak out, to participate fully in government, and to share political power" *(ibid.)*.

But why not appeal for democratic reform in South Africa in even more positive and specific terms? Eagleburger stressed the U.S. commitment to "strengthening the capacity of black South Africans to participate in their country's society as equals— economically, culturally and politically" (1983). But he continued: "We do not presume to offer a formula to South Africa for resolving its unsettled political agenda other than to state that all South Africans must have a say in determining their political system." I believe that the United States and other Western and democratic countries should explicitly and specifically urge the adoption of a formula for reform: the consociational formula. The details should obviously be filled in by negotiations among the South Africans themselves. But there is no good reason for sympathetic democrats elsewhere not to point out clearly that the consociational formula provides the only fair and viable option.

Chapter 2

NON-CONSOCIATIONAL REFORM PROPOSALS

As noted in Chapter 1, there are four broad alternatives for constitutional reform: majoritarian, non-democratic, partitionist, and consociational. The first three will be the subject of this chapter, while the reform plans that are or claim to be consociational will be discussed in Chapter 3.

The fourfold classification of alternatives is exhaustive, but the categories are not mutually exclusive either logically or empirically. For instance, a hypothetical proposal of dividing the country into a majoritarian, a consociational, and a non-democratic state would combine all four possibilities. The proposals that I shall review have the tendency of overlapping two or more categories. The 1983 constitution ostensibly combines consociation for whites, Coloureds, and Asians with partition for the African homelands, and it also has clearly undemocratic features, especially regarding the Africans who do not live in the homelands. Edgar H. Brookes, a member of the SPROCAS political commission, issued a now well-known dissent from the consociationally oriented report of the commission, combining a strong endorsement of majoritarianism with an argument for a temporarily restricted franchise (Brookes 1973). Most of the advocates of majority rule are willing to consider substantial modifications that entail at least a partial acceptance of consociational elements.

MAJORITARIAN PROPOSALS

Majority-rule democracy in an undivided South Africa is the first preference of an overwhelming majority of black South Africans, both leaders and rank and file (Hanf, Weiland, and Vierdag 1981:346-48; Buthelezi Commission 1982, 1:259-62; Mabude 1983: 567-70; Adam 1980b:621-25). This is particularly true for the African majority, but by and large it applies to the Coloured and

Asian minorities as well. With a few exceptions—notably Alan Paton's multiracial Liberal Party, which disbanded in 1968 (see Paton 1959, 1968; Paton and Mathews 1972)—majoritarianism receives virtually no support in the white community.

There are three main reasons why majoritarian democracy has appeared to be an especially desirable goal in South Africa. The first is the very strong influence of the Westminster model in all former British colonies—Lewis compares it to "brainwashing" (1965:55). With its emphasis on individual instead of group rights, majoritarianism is also clearly in line with traditional British and American liberalism (Van Dyke 1975, 1982). It was the SPROCAS report's accent on the group basis of society that made Brookes issue his vigorous dissent: "Those of us who have intimate African, Coloured, and Indian friends know well that there are no group differences which divide us as much as friendship and our common humanity unite us. This turning from the individual to the group gives its direction to the whole Report" (1973:242). It is after all only very recently that American liberals have started accepting the legitimacy of group affiliation as a criterion in public policy and that they have begun to support affirmative action programs.

Second, the traditionally liberal sentiments are reinforced by a widely felt abhorrence of the apartheid system of racial discrimination and white minority rule. The revulsion is often so strong that, as Schlemmer states, it leads to demands for the "total elimination of the meaning of colour in our society" without much thought of what the consequences for the different groups might be (1970:47). Very little sympathy is felt for the whites, and "any support for change which even partially accommodates the self-interest of a White elite [is regarded as] uninspired compromise at best, and may even be rank conservatism merely disguised with trappings of tender-mindedness" (ibid.). Majority rule is certainly superior to minority rule, and few people feel much concern that after so many years of white minority domination, the roles of oppressor and oppressed might be reversed under majority rule. As I shall discuss below, however, majority rule may well be just as harmful to blacks as it is to whites.

The third reason for the appeal of majoritarianism in South Africa is that it has an almost perfect fit with the political traditions of the white-dominated regime since South African independence in 1910. Until the adoption of the 1983 constitution, South Africa was governed largely according to the Westminster model.

The basic principles were those of majority rule, limited of course to the members of the white minority community: British-style parliamentarism with a sharp distinction between government and opposition, plurality elections in single-member districts, and a unitary and centralized government (Boulle 1980b:2-8, and 1984: 73-78; Cadoux 1980:190-94; Lewsen 1982; G.C. Olivier 1978c; N.J.J. Olivier and van Wyk 1978; Vosloo and Schrire 1978; van Wyk 1983). The non-federal and highly centralized nature of the South African political system deserves special emphasis because the republic was misleadingly called the Union of South Africa— implying a federal structure—from 1910 until its departure from the British Commonwealth in 1961.

The potentially majoritarian character of the South African constitutions between 1910 and 1983 can be demonstrated by the fact that majority rule could have been introduced in South Africa by shifting from a racially restricted to a universal franchise without changing any other constitutional rule. This made it possible for Nthato Motlana, chairman of the Soweto Committee of Ten, to advocate majority rule by means of taking the pre-1983 constitution and simply deleting all reference to race from it: "Basically we have a beautiful constitution. I have no objections to this constitution, except where it refers to race. . . . Without any racial provisions, universal suffrage would apply, and general elections could be held in the normal way" (quoted in Barratt 1980:38). Similarly, the Liberal Party simply accepted the existing constitutional principles and concentrated on the extension of the suffrage to blacks. In a recent interview Paton stated the following: "We really did not discuss the structure of the constitution—we never did that" (Bhengu 1984:11). In particular, the possibility of federalism was never considered because "we were brought up in a unitary state" (ibid.).

The above three reasons are explanations of the strong appeal of majoritarian reform proposals, but they cannot be regarded as arguments in favor of majority rule. And they certainly do not negate the proposition stated in Chapter 1 that majoritarianism is both undemocratic and likely to be unworkable in plural societies. Because the interests of the different segments in a plural society diverge widely and are hard to reconcile and because voters' loyalties tend to be rigidly tied to their own segment and to "float" very little, a democratic alternation in office is unlikely. Minorities that are excluded from power will probably remain excluded and will almost inevitably lose their allegiance to the regime. Hence majority rule in plural societies spells majority dictatorship and civil strife rather than democracy. If this is true for plural societies in general, it definitely applies to South Africa, which is among the more extreme cases of a plural society. It is significant that with regard to South Africa the terms "majority rule" and "black majority rule" tend to be used interchangeably.

It is not surprising that South Africa's white minority is ill-disposed toward proposals for majoritarian democracy. Pik Botha argues that "for us a political system of one man one vote within one political entity means our destruction. It's a statistical fact, not a political one" (quoted in Starcke 1978:66). Botha makes the mistake of equating the "one man, one vote" ideal with majority rule — this ideal also underlies consociational democracy — but his fear of a majority versus minority situation is not unrealistic.

Even van den Berghe, who is not at all an apologist for South Africa's whites — on the contrary, he is an extreme partitionist who is in favor of solving the South African problem by the emigration of all whites — points out that majority rule can "easily become a liberal veneer for racial domination" (1979a: 7). His reasoning is squarely based on the fundamental incompatibility between majoritarian democracy and the nature of plural societies: "If your constituency has the good fortune to contain a demographic majority, racism can easily be disguised as democracy. The ideological sleight of hand, of course, is that an ascriptive, racially-defined majority is a far cry from a majority made up of shifting coalitions of individuals on the basis of commonality of beliefs and interests" *(ibid.)*

One crucial qualification must be attached to the prediction of inevitable black majority domination in South Africa, however. It is wrong to interpret the basic problem in terms of a dichotomous black-white conflict. Far from being homogeneous communities, the black and white groups are each deeply divided into a number of ethnic groups. White South Africa, composed of linguistically and culturally distinct Afrikaner and English-speaking segments, is just as much a plural society as ethnically divided Belgium, Canada, and Switzerland. Black South Africa is made up of Africans, Coloureds, and Asians, and the Africans are further divided into several ethnic groups, the largest of which are the Zulus and Xhosas. It is not easy to determine exactly which of these ought to be identified as the separate segments of a plural society, but there is no doubt that an exclusively black South Africa would be an ethnically plural society

on a par with most of the black states in Africa.* These ethnic
cleavages are currently muted by the feelings of black solidarity in
opposition to white minority rule, but they are bound to reassert
themselves in a situation of universal suffrage and free electoral
competition.

One conclusion that can be drawn from the above discussion
is that whites may have less to fear from majority rule since the
blacks do not form a homogeneous majority. But the much more
important conclusion is that majoritarianism is as inappropriate
and as dangerous for South Africa's black citizens as it is for South
Africa as a whole. All of the tensions and hostilities typical of plural
societies are likely to manifest themselves among the black ethnic
groups if South Africa becomes a majoritarian democracy.

The example of independence and democratization in Zimbabwe—largely along majoritarian lines—is highly instructive for
South Africa.† After Ian Smith's white minority regime was replaced
by predominantly black rule, inter-ethnic strife broke out between
the Shona majority, led by Prime Minister Robert Mugabe, and the
Ndebele minority with Joshua Nkomo as its principal leader. Nkomo
was driven from power, and temporarily into exile as well; the
Ndebeles became victims of organized persecution; and the last two
ministers belonging to the Ndebele-based party were expelled from
the cabinet in November 1984. An editorial in the *New York Times*
noted that in 1980 "Zimbabwe's long-delayed achievement of
majority rule was welcomed with optimism and good will," but that
four years later "Zimbabwe writhes in tribal hatred and communal
violence"—for much of which Mugabe must be blamed. The editorial concludes as follows: "It was certainly right for people and
governments in the West to condemn Ian Smith's campaigns against
Zimbabwe's black majority a decade ago. But for the same reasons, it
is important now to condemn Robert Mugabe's campaigns against

---

*The question of the number and relative sizes of the segments in the South
African society will be discussed further in Chapter 5 in the analysis of the
various factors that may help or hinder consociational democracy.

†Zimbabwe's electoral system has a few consociational features: guaranteed
overrepresentation of the white minority (20 percent of the seats in parliament
for about 3 percent of the population) and proportional representation for the
election of the black legislators (Lijphart 1985). However, when one ethnic
group comprises a majority of the population, PR can obviously not prevent
this majority from gaining a majority of the seats.

the Ndebele minority" (1984). It would be even more important — and more just — to condemn Zimbabwe's majoritarian system as the underlying cause of its civil strife.

A similar lesson can be learned from the South African black homeland of Bophuthatswana, nominally independent since 1977. It has a clear Tswana majority — about two thirds of the population — and this majority exercises virtually exclusive control of Bophuthatswana politics. In 1983 there were no non-Tswana blacks in the cabinet and only two non-Tswanas in the ninety-six-member legislative assembly. The antagonism between the Tswanas and the increasing number of other blacks is strikingly demonstrated by President Lucas Mangope's statement that "we might later on have to do what the Nigerians did to the Ghanaians" — referring to the mass expulsion of aliens from Nigeria in early 1983 (quoted in Lelyveld 1983).

The above examples show the tendency of majority rule to become majority dictatorship in plural societies. However, it may also lead to minority dictatorship if an ethnic minority is able to take preemptive action. A clear although admittedly extreme example is Burundi, where the small Tutsi minority has suppressed the Hutu majority by a variety of methods, including "selective genocide," in which about 100,000 Hutus were massacred in 1972 (Lemarchand and Martin 1974; Kuper 1977:87-107, 197-208, 238-43).

The introduction of majoritarian democracy in South Africa would undoubtedly be fraught with grave danger, but it is difficult to predict exactly what its consequences would be. One scenario has been suggested by Alvin Rabushka: "Black tribal leaders would form a temporary coalition and attain a majority in Parliament, which would, in turn, lead to the exclusion of Whites and perhaps Coloureds from the political process" (1978:185). The broad coalition of black leaders would be unstable and would "give way to extremist pressures arising within each tribal group and lead, sooner or later, to the collapse of democratic institutions and the establishment of authoritarian rule by the most powerful tribe over all other South Africans, a pattern typical of several new African nations" (ibid.). This forecast is of course highly speculative, but it cannot be regarded as unduly pessimistic. Majoritarian democracy would serve nobody's true interest in South Africa. It would obviously hurt not only the white minority, but also, contrary to what is routinely assumed, the black majority — or, more accurately, the various black minorities.

FLEXIBILITY IN MAJORITARIAN DEMANDS

In view of the serious disadvantages and risks inherent in majoritarian democracy for South Africa, it is very fortunate that virtually all of its advocates are *moderate* majoritarians. Hardly anyone is committed to pure and unconditional majority rule or is unwilling to consider compromise solutions.

The majoritarians stress several objectives. Their highest priority is the calling of a national convention where a democratic constitution will be negotiated by the representatives of all groups in South Africa. The willingness to negotiate implies a willingness to compromise on the question of majority rule, but it is perfectly understandable that black leaders are reluctant to indicate the exact extent to which they will be willing to deviate from the majoritarian principle before a national convention is actually held. And it does not make sense to make concessions before it is certain that there will be a national convention at all. Thus the pre-convention commitment to majority rule is a point of departure in the bargaining process instead of an unalterable final goal.

Moreover, the advocates of majority rule have made their readiness to compromise unmistakably clear. For instance, the African National Congress (ANC) has not even arrived yet "at any position regarding political institutions and procedures for the protection of minority rights"; hence its formal commitment to majority rule does not mean that it is wedded to a "winner take all" system (Karis 1984:402). M. Gatsha Buthelezi, Chief Minister of the KwaZulu homeland and leader of the Inkatha political movement, has stated that he personally believes in majority rule (Starcke 1978:76), but he has also repeatedly emphasized the need for compromise. In October 1984 he again stated that he was ready to deviate from his "cherished ideal" and called upon both blacks and whites "to recognize the necessity of moving away from government by racial domination" (Buthelezi 1984).

The largest party in the Coloured community, the Labour Party, officially adopted the 1979 report of the Du Preez Commission as its constitutional policy and hence also the commission's preference for a Westminster system of government. In effect, as Boulle states, the Labour Party opted for "a fully-democratized version of the South African constitution as it existed in 1980" (1984:113). On the other hand, the party endorsed a decidedly unmajoritarian electoral system for parliamentary elections: an extreme form of party-list proportional representation in a single, countrywide district, but subject to a 5 percent threshold. Even more important, in early 1983 the Labour Party decided to participate in the new constitutional arrangements proposed by the South African government. This decision was highly controversial within the party, but it indicates that some of the leaders of the Coloured community are not unalterably wedded to majoritarianism or unreceptive to genuine consociational democracy.

On the question of federalism, it should not be difficult to arrive at a compromise agreement. Novelist Nadine Gordimer is in error when she refers to "the nonnegotiable principle of the African National Congress, a unitary South Africa," and she is an excessive purist when she is unable to "support a federal South Africa" (1983:22). There is nothing in the basic ANC Freedom Charter of 1955 that can be construed as rejecting a federal constitution (Adam 1983b:16; Karis and Carter, eds. 1977, 3:205-8). A recent statement by Thabo Mbeki, ANC director of information and publicity, explicitly endorses federalism: "We have agitated and struggled for a South Africa governed according to the principles of the Constitution of the United States and the Universal Declaration of Human Rights" (1983). A somewhat more careful statement was issued by Buthelezi and C.M. Phatudi, Chief Minister of Lebowa: "We have decided to explore federalism, amongst other options, as a possible compromise solution if it is accepted by a majority of South Africans" (1984:14). Motlana does not go as far: he prefers a unitary government, but "if the whites can convince us that a federal form of state is better, we will not fight over that" (quoted in Barratt 1980:42).

Motlana's pronouncements on a few other specific points are also revealing. He is in favor of "a constitution that will protect human rights, the rights of individuals," but he objects to the idea of minority rights because these are group rights. He even compares minority rights to "dodges, subterfuges, fraudulent schemes, manoeuvres" (Starcke 1978:118). But he is willing to recognize the rights of linguistic minorities—that, for example, the Zulu and Afrikaans languages "will be officially protected" in areas where there are many Zulus and Afrikaners (quoted in Barratt 1980:44). He rejects consociationalism mainly because he fears that the minority veto will be used by the whites as a "blocking mechanism . . . to hold up the changes that are necessary." But he endorses a kind of qualified veto which he describes as a "procedure whereby certain legislation would require the votes of, say, 80 percent of the states in the federation," necessitating at least "a certain proportion of white support" (quoted in Barratt 1980:42-43).

Finally, there is a great deal of terminological confusion that makes the majoritarian position appear to be much more absolute and adamant than it really is. This confusion has to do with three key concepts which political scientists use to distinguish between majoritarian and consociational democracy and to which I have already made frequent reference in the foregoing discussion: unitary government, majority rule, and one-man, one-vote.

The technical meaning of the term "unitary" in political science is "non-federal." In the debate about South African political and constitutional change, however, it merely means united, unified, or undivided. This is its more common and widely accepted meaning; *Webster's Unabridged Dictionary* and the *Oxford English Dictionary* do not even list "non-federal" among the meanings of "unitary." The demand for a unitary South Africa is therefore synonymous with ANC spokesman Johnny Makatini's call for "an unfragmented South Africa" (1983:1) and Tutu's call for "an undivided South Africa" (1982:56). Another good example of the synonymous nature of the terms "unitary" and "undivided" is provided by two of Allan Boesak's statements of his basic political goals. He writes of his commitment to "a nonracist, open, democratic South Africa, a unitary state, one nation in which all citizens will have the rights accorded them by ordinance of almighty God" (1984:118), and he describes these aims as "one, undivided South Africa that shall belong to all its people: an open democracy from which no South African shall be excluded" (p. 155). There can be no doubt that the import of these statements is identical, and a desire for a non-federal structure is not even implied. Demands for a unitary South Africa entail a rejection of partition, especially the establishment of independent ethnic homelands; they definitely do not entail a rejection of federalism.*

---

*Yet another sense of the term "unitary" is "uniform," as when Tutu alternately calls for "a uniform educational system" and "a unitary educational system" (1982:57, 101). Political scientists are not always precise in their use of this set of terms either. For instance, Robert I. Rotberg writes that "a unified or federated South Africa provides so many advantages for all" (1980a:9). Here the correct contrast is between unitary and federated, not between unified and federated. What Rotberg intends to say is "an undivided South Africa, under a unitary or a federal government, provides so many advantages for all."

In this book (and elsewhere) I have used the term "majority rule" strictly as a synonym of majoritarianism and as the fundamental principle that underlies majoritarian democracy, but I admit that this is not its generally accepted usage in political science. It usually does not carry a precise technical meaning and tends to be used loosely to mean democracy—as is the case in the South African constitutional debate. For example, Inkatha spokesman Gibson Thula writes that blacks want both majority rule and power-sharing, obviously not recognizing anything contradictory between these two goals: "The blacks want to share in the central decision-making processes of our country and they desire majority rule" (1978:7). Similarly, Tutu believes "in majority rule, not *black* majority rule" (1982:40). But he also calls for "political power-sharing" (p. 44). Clearly therefore the frequently stated commitment to majority rule is not an exclusive commitment to majoritarian democracy and does not imply a rejection of consociationalism.*

The most serious confusion concerns the third key term: one-person, one-vote. Almost everyone—including both politicians and social scientists—takes this concept to mean majoritarian democracy. Buthelezi states that the whites in South Africa "will not be able to accept a one-man, one-vote system" (1984). Heribert Adam and Hermann Giliomee judge that "hardly a single prominent white South African" supports a one-person, one-vote system (1979:264)— although they are obviously aware of the fact that the PFP is formally committed to consociationalism. Rabushka argues that the establishment of "one-man, one-vote democracy would ensure the collapse of democratic institutions" (1978:185). The mistake in all three instances is not to recognize that one-person, one-vote is a basic democratic principle which consociational and majoritarian democracy have in common. It is a serious injustice to consociational democracy to imply that it entails something less than one-person, one-vote.† As I have argued in Chapter 1 and as I shall develop

---

*I must also admit of course that the term "power-sharing" sometimes merely means "democracy" and that it does not necessarily imply a preference for consociational democracy.

†Murray Forsyth is only barely right when he claims that "one man, one vote on a common roll is ... not a principle of consociational democracy" (1984:15). The crucial term which he adds is "on a common roll." When the segments of a plural society can be identified without ambiguity or controversy, the use of separate segmental voter rolls is indeed perfectly compatible with consociational principles as long as the one-person, one-vote rule is respected.

further in Chapter 4, consociational democracy embodies the one-person, one-vote ideal at least as much as majoritarian democracy, and in some respects even more—especially in plural societies.

In sum, when the views of the majority-rule advocates are carefully examined, it becomes clear that they are not ideological and rigid majoritarians. It is not an exaggeration to say that many if not most of them are already semi-consociationalists; they are decidedly not anti-consociational. Hence the difference between the majoritarian and consociational approaches to democracy in South Africa is not an unbridgeable gap.

NON-DEMOCRATIC PROPOSALS

There are several reform plans which are not or not completely democratic. These include proposals that envisage the establishment of new democratic institutions as the eventual goal but only after a long period of transition under the old non-democratic authorities.* They also include all of the schemes for the establishment of sovereign ethnic homelands that are completely independent of the remainder of South Africa—in particular the official grand apartheid policy of the government. These schemes, which I shall refer to as homeland partition, will be discussed later in this chapter, but it should be pointed out here that they are fundamentally undemocratic for two reasons: (1) They were developed unilaterally by the central white government and presented to the homeland leaders on a take-it-or-leave-it basis instead of being negotiated or jointly decided; (2) While the homeland governments have the option to refuse independence, this option leaves them in an undemocratic constitutional limbo—part of South Africa, but not part of the South African political system.

Consociational Cyprus in the 1960-63 period is a good example (Lijphart 1977a: 159; 1985). However, separate rolls are not required by consociational theory, and they are very rare in consociational practice. In the South African case (as I shall argue in Chapter 3), one-person, one-vote on a common roll—in conjunction with proportional representation—is the optimal consociational method since the segments of the South African plural society cannot be predetermined.

*One example is Wolfgang H. Thomas's (1977, 1979) proposal along consociational lines; it involves a gradual, evolutionary, stepwise process, the last step of which would be an undivided South Africa governed by a multiracial legislature and executive.

The main non-democratic proposals rely directly or indirectly on the principle of a qualified franchise based on educational or economic criteria—initially restricted but gradually expanding and eventually including all adult citizens. I deliberately use the neutral term "non-democratic" instead of "undemocratic" because I do not want to impugn the democratic motives of the reformers in question. For instance, Brookes is a spokesman for the traditionally liberal — and majoritarian—democratic position. He regards universal suffrage as an absolute moral value and describes it as "the logical political application of the Christian belief that every human being is of infinite (and therefore equal) value in the sight of God" (1973:244). Yet he adds that the immediate establishment of the universal franchise in South Africa "would mean black rule over the whites," and that he therefore prefers an extension of the suffrage "by agreed stages, to get us used to the idea of really working together, provided that the direction is uniform and aimed at a satisfactory end" (ibid.). Similarly, Leo Marquard proposes a federal system assuming that its government will be "on a broad democratic basis" (1971:13), but he still finds that a qualified franchise is acceptable provided that "the qualifications are common and not based on race or sex or religion [and] not subject to alteration at the discretion of a racial minority" (p. 126).

Most of the specific plans for a qualified franchise conform at least superficially with the one-person, one-vote principle. Instead of completely excluding the citizens who do not qualify, they give them votes too, but votes that do not carry the same weight as those of the fully qualified voters. This was the policy of the Progressive Party. According to Helen Suzman, who for many years was the lone Progressive Party representative in the South African parliament, there should be an "ordinary voters roll, which will list the fully qualified voters of all races," based on a combination of educational and economic criteria, but "unqualified people should also have a voice in Parliament" (1972:228). For this purpose the Progressive Party proposed that 10 percent of the parliamentary seats be reserved "for the representatives of South Africans who cannot qualify for the ordinary vote, but who are 18 years old and literate. Once their number diminishes below 20 per cent of the total of those entitled to vote, the number of seats will be reduced proportionally" (ibid.). Ultimately, when all voters qualified for the "ordinary voters roll," the "special voters roll" would disappear. A proposal along the same lines and with a comparable ratio for the two classes of parliamentary seats was recently put forward by the outspoken industrialist A. D. Wassenaar: 85 percent of the representatives would be elected by qualified voters and 7 percent by unqualified voters; in addition, special interests like agriculture and commerce would fill 8 percent of the seats (Hill 1983:161; Ranchod 1983:452-53).

Giving special weight to educational and economic criteria does not even require the device of separate qualified and unqualified voters' registers. For instance, it has been suggested that electoral districts could be drawn up "on the basis of socio-economic characteristics rather than population size" (Schlemmer 1983a:500). This would mean a deliberate malapportionment in favor of the wealthier areas and hence in practice in favor of the white and to some extent Coloured and Asian voters. Another method would be the direct and fully democratic election of the representative bodies at the lower levels but indirect election at the higher levels. In such indirect elections the "number of representatives . . . in the tier of government above would be calculated principally on its relative financial contribution" (Hirsch 1978:10-11).

Although all of the above schemes favor the white minority, they can be defended on the ground that they are not overtly discriminatory since they are not based on explicit racial criteria. This is an important consideration in South Africa because the official classification into four racial groups has become so objectionable to most blacks, and to many whites as well, that any system of election based on it is doomed to failure. Even as a purely temporary and transitional arrangement Walter Dean Burnham's idea of adding about 30 or 40 black representatives to the 165-member parliament "proportionalized so far as possible among the discrete nonwhite communal groups" (1980:101) would be hard to accept because it preserves the old racial distinctions.

The objection that the various schemes of qualified and weighted voting clearly violate the one-person, one-vote, one-value criterion (although narrowly adhering to the one-person, one-vote principle) may be countered by pointing out that several impeccably democratic proposals do not conform to this criterion either. Consociationalism accepts and approves of the notion of minority overrepresentation, and the overrepresentation of the smaller component units in a federal system is an entirely uncontroversial precept of federal theory.*

*Another argument for a qualified franchise is that it would temper the tendency toward ethnic voting in a plural society (van der Ross 1981:51, and

These counterarguments must be rejected for four important reasons. First, while the qualified or weighted franchise avoids explicit racial criteria, race—especially the black-white distinction—is the real issue. The probable ratio of white to black voters has always been everybody's main concern and, as Paul N. Malherbe puts it, the "bugbear for anxious speculation" (1974:11). Second, a qualified franchise does not lead to minority overrepresentation in general, but to the overrepresentation of one particular minority: the whites. Burnham (1980:96) has calculated that even the modest educational qualification of completing six years of schooling would give whites about 74 percent of the qualified electorate, Africans 13 percent, Coloureds 9 percent, and Asians 4 percent. Reserving 10 percent of the parliamentary seats for the non-qualified voters would reduce the white proportion to about 67 percent and would increase the African to about 20 percent; the Coloured and Asian percentages would remain approximately the same. Both of these calculations show that the Coloured and Asian minorities would be represented on a roughly proportional basis in the electorate and that only the white minority would be overrepresented.

Third, the degree of white overrepresentation would far exceed the normal and reasonable standards. In consociational theory, for instance, the maximum extent of overrepresentation envisaged is parity of representation with the other segments in a plural society—that is, 50 percent in a dichotomously divided society, 33 percent when there are three segments, and so on. This maximum is clearly violated by giving a minority of less than one sixth of the population two thirds or more of the voting power, thereby translating a relatively small popular minority into a huge electoral majority.

Finally, while a qualified franchise would gradually admit more blacks to full voting rights—as long as the threshold could not be raised by the white minority—and would concomitantly reduce white overrepresentation, it would obviously take a very long time before substantially equal voting rights would be achieved. Hence

1983:529). However, comparative empirical evidence shows that ethnic voting is strong in ethnically divided societies among all socioeconomic classes and even in highly industrialized democracies (Lijphart 1979a, 1980c). In plural societies ethnic voting or, more generally, segmental voting is entirely normal and inevitable—and, it should be emphasized, not necessarily harmful, especially if the democratic system is consociational. For further discussions of the franchise question, see Ranchod (1983:452-53), Schlemmer (1978b:259-62), and Wiechers (1981:184-87).

white minority overrepresentation by means of a qualified franchise essentially means the continuation of white minority domination with only token concessions to blacks into the foreseeable future.

The time factor is crucial in this respect. A restricted but gradually expanding franchise in the 1980s can no longer be reconciled with the rising expectations and increasing impatience of black South Africans. This impatience and frustration are clearly stated in Boesak's "three little words that express eloquently our seriousness in this struggle": all, here, and now:

> We want *all* our rights; not just some, not just those that the government sees fit to give. . . . We want all our rights right *here*— in South Africa, in a united South Africa. . . . We want our rights *now*. We have been waiting so long; we have been struggling so long. We have pleaded, petitioned, cried, marched, been jailed, exiled, killed for too long. *Now* is the time (1984:121).

Motlana couched the time demands of the Soweto Committee of Ten in comparable terms: "Right away, not after ten steps or twenty steps. Right away" (quoted in J. Johnson and Magubane 1979:87).

Non-democratic transitional arrangements can be considered seriously only for transitions of short duration—measured in years instead of in decades. Thus a qualified franchise can be a solution, or part of a solution, not by establishing a fixed threshold which can gradually be crossed by more and more citizens in the long run, but by a relatively rapid lowering of the threshold. For instance, assuming four-year parliamentary terms of office, a third or a fourth of the initially non-qualified citizens could be admitted to the franchise in each of three or four successive elections, and universal suffrage would apply in the last of these. This is the maximum delay that would be acceptable. It seems highly doubtful that such a short delay would serve anybody's interests.

A temporarily restricted franchise should be considered alongside the two alternatives of majoritarian and consociational democracy. None of the problems that are necessarily associated with majority rule in a plural society (discussed earlier) will disappear by a clever manipulation of the franchise. These problems will plague a majoritarian South Africa regardless of whether there is a short or a long delay in achieving full democracy—and obviously even during the transition if it takes place under a Westminster-style regime. On the other hand, consociational democracy maintains civil peace and safeguards the rights of minorities by such means as assured participation in the government, guaranteed group autonomy, and a minority veto on vital issues. A qualified franchise would add nothing significant to this.

In essence, the qualified franchise is either insufficient or unnecessary: it cannot help to pave the way for a successful majoritarian democracy, and it is not needed as a pathway to consociational democracy. It is not regrettable, therefore, that opinion surveys have found so little support for this "solution" at the leadership and mass levels (Hanf, Weiland, and Vierdag 1981:223, 287, 346-47; Buthelezi Commission 1982, 1:261-63, 302-3) or that after the demise of the Progressive Party in the 1970s no South African political party or movement, black or white, has advocated it.

PARTITIONIST PROPOSALS

There are five logical solutions to the problems of violence and democratic weakness in plural societies: assimilation, consociation, partition, mass emigration, and genocide (see Duchacek 1977; du Plessis 1978:2-8). I mention the last possibility merely in order to make the list exhaustive. Assimilation involves changing a society from a plural to a homogeneous one by erasing the differences between the segments, thus preparing it for a successful majoritarian regime. Assimilation is not a practical solution, however, because it is extremely slow. On the basis of historical evidence Karl W. Deutsch (1984:135) estimates that the full assimilation of different linguistic or cultural groups requires between three and seven hundred years. In the case of deeply plural South Africa it is not realistic to expect that full assimilation would require less time than Deutsch's estimates. Consociational democracy, described in Chapter 1, will be analyzed further in the context of South African politics in Chapter 3.

In contrast with assimilation, which tries to change the people, and with consociation, which tries to change a governmental system, partition attempts to solve the problems of a plural society by changing the boundaries. It tries to separate the societal groups from each other and to make each segment as far as possible into a homogeneous society. Hence unlike consociational democracy, which accepts the plural nature of a society, but like assimilation, partition aims at making the plural society less plural. The mass emigration of a segment from a plural society can have the same effect. In Deutsch's words, "Spatial separation, though not likely to directly reduce incompatibilities of outlook among different groups, should reduce opportunities for collision and conflicts" (1984:134). He cites the example of Cyprus: the spatial proximity of the Greek and Turkish communities produced bloody conflicts, but these conflicts "declined after [the groups'] forced separation through the Turkish invasion of Cyprus in 1974 which resulted in the concentration of most of the ethnic Turks in one part of the island and most of the ethnic Greeks in another" *(ibid.)*.

A positive view of partition is challenged by some critics who have pointed out that (1) The process of partitioning a state is often attended by violence, and (2) Once a partition has been completed, hostilities do not always cease. The answer to the first objection is that most of the violence in the partitioning process is caused not by partition itself but by efforts to prevent it (see Nasir 1978). With regard to the second objection, Newell M. Stultz correctly argues as follows: "The case for partition must be that it avoids higher levels of violence, not that it ends inter-communal violence altogether" (1979:12). Most authors agree that for deeply divided societies partition has "theoretical merits" (Schrire 1978a:9), that it "rests on a firm theoretical footing" (Rabushka 1978:189), or even that it is "theoretically the most appropriate solution" (Schlemmer 1978a: 393; see also Dahl, ed. 1966:358).

The above discussion suggests an important criterion by which proposals for partition should be judged: will a proposed partition create homogeneous societies out of an originally plural society, or at the very least will the separate societies resulting from partition be substantially more homogeneous than the original plural society? Because partition is a drastic method, merely small reductions in the plural character of a deeply divided society cannot be justified.

Two additional criteria follow not just from an empirical perspective, but also on moral grounds: does partition entail a fair division into viable independent states, and is it voluntary? Vernon Van Dyke puts it like this: "Where independence can be granted . . . on a fair basis [and where the people involved] want it, the case for granting it is strong" (1983:15). As early as 1939, the long-time president of the liberal South African Institute of Race Relations, R. F. Alfred Hoernlé, carefully considered the question of partition in the South African context. While he rejected it on practical grounds, he concluded that "a policy of complete territorial segregation was as compatible [with basic Christian, democratic, and liberal principles] as a policy of complete assimilation" (Whyte 1952:6; Hoernlé 1939:168-78).

The fairness criterion prescribes that there be an equitable division of land and resources and that the new states be economically and politically viable. The criterion of voluntary choice means that a segment ought to be free to secede from a plural society but should not be forced to do so. It also implies that partition should be the result of multilateral negotiation instead of a unilateral decision. A difficulty arises in situations where one or more segments desire partition but others are opposed to it. Here the issue becomes more problematic from a moral point of view, but as long as the other criteria are satisfied, the case for partition must still be considered sufficiently strong (Beran 1984). When we apply these moral criteria to the two options that go beyond partition—mass emigration and genocide—it is obvious that the latter cannot meet them, but emigration can at least in principle be both fair and voluntary.

Two kinds of partition are important in the case of South Africa. I shall refer to these as homeland partition and radical partition. Homeland partition is officially called "separate development," and it may also be called "grand apartheid" or "macro-segregation"—in contrast with the micro-segregation of public and private facilities and the meso-segregation of residential areas (van den Berghe 1978). It entails the partition of South Africa into eleven separate sovereign states: ten ethnic African homelands and a residual state for whites, Coloureds, and Asians. Homeland partition has long been official government and National Party policy, although President Botha has thrown doubts on some of its basic tenets in a series of pronouncements in 1985. By and large the New Republic Party has also supported homeland partition. The Conservative Party and the Reconstituted National Party (Herstigte Nasionale Party—HNP) have been even more strongly committed to it than the National Party, and they advocate the addition of a twelfth independent state: a Coloured homeland to be located somewhere in the western part of Cape Province. As I shall show in the next section, homeland partition must be rejected because it fails all three criteria of acceptable partition.

Proposals for radical partition exist in several different versions, but they typically envisage a dichotomous division of the country roughly along a north-south boundary. The eastern state would be predominantly African and would control at least half (or somewhat more) of the present territory of South Africa; the western state would be predominantly non-African. Radical partition does not perform much better than homeland partition on the three criteria stated above. It may be superior in allocating a fair division of land and resources to the partitioned populations, but it would require massive resettlement and concomitant pain and costs. At best, it would be a solution of last resort.

The two types of partition will be evaluated in greater detail in the next two sections, but I should like to list the major differences between them here. First, homeland partition entails the creation of many more sovereign entities than radical partition. In this sense, the homeland policy is actually more "radical" than radical partition. Indeed it could be argued that the two differ in degree only and shade into each other. For instance, P. Roelf Botha (1978:213-19) proposes a thorough consolidation and expansion of the homelands which would reduce their number from ten to seven. If the process of merging, consolidating, and expanding the homelands were continued to its logical limits, the result would be a single homeland in the eastern half of the country—roughly coterminous with the predominantly African eastern state in the radical partition plans. Conversely, some radical partitionists delineate more than two states. In practice, however, the intermediate forms of partition are not serious contenders, and the two basic types can be treated as distinct proposals.

A closely connected second difference concerns the apportionment of territory. About 13 percent would be allocated to the African states in the homelands plan and 50 percent or more in the radical proposals. These first two differences are the main reason why radical partition is much more equitable than homeland partition.

Third, homeland partition has been the government's policy, and, at least until recently, was actually being implemented. Four homelands have become nominally independent and sovereign states: Transkei, Bophuthatswana, Ciskei, and Venda. The radical proposals exist on paper only and are purely speculative.

Fourth, homeland partition has been supported by all of the white political parties except the PFP, and it is rejected by all black parties and groups; radical partition is rejected by black and white parties alike. The same patterns of support and rejection show up in public opinion surveys (Hanf, Weiland, and Vierdag 1981:221-22, 235-36, 344-46; Buthelezi Commission 1982, 1:258-64, 294-96).

Fifth, homeland partition was designed and developed by South Africans, whereas most of the radical partitionists have been foreign observers of the South African political scene.

Finally, under homeland partition a confederation is proposed to which the new independent states could all belong; sometimes it is proposed that neighboring black states like Zimbabwe, Botswana, Swaziland, and Lesotho could join too. Plans for radical partition usually do not include such a confederal arrangement as an essential ingredient. Upon closer examination, however, this difference turns out to be more imaginary than real. Most experts agree that a confederation is merely a cooperative arrangement or association of separate sovereign states. In a confederation, unlike in a federation, sovereignty resides at the level of the member states, not at the level of whatever joint institutions may be set up (Duchacek 1982: 145-49; Kriek 1983a, 1983b; T.D. Venter 1975; Wiechers 1978: 109-10). A few authors do not draw such a sharp distinction between federalism and confederalism (e.g., C.J. Hughes 1983), but it is absolutely clear that when confederation is advocated as an element of homeland partition in South Africa, it does not imply unification under a central sovereign authority. The government itself has made this perfectly clear by its preference for the even vaguer and less consequential term "constellation of states" (Geldenhuys 1979; Geldenhuys and Venter 1979; Holland 1983; Rhoodie 1980a).

In an analysis that is largely favorable to the homelands policy, Edwin S. Munger (1978:269) predicts that it will eventually lead to a federal United States of South Africa. Not only is such a development highly unlikely in the foreseeable future, but it has never been even a long-term goal of homeland partition policy. Chester A. Crocker is much closer to the truth when he writes that "the constellation concept is a thinly disguised rubric under which finally to admit the essential unity of South Africa" (1981:339). Somewhat less kindly, it can also be described as a convenient excuse to ignore South Africa's unity. Realistically constellation and confederation add nothing of significance to partition.

HOMELAND PARTITION

If homeland partition—or separate development—can ideally be described as "a way of trying to disentangle" a plural society (Pakendorf 1980:145), to what extent has it achieved this goal so far, and how much can it achieve in the future? Table 2.1 provides some summary measures. It uses Douglas W. Rae and Michael Taylor's "index of fragmentation" (1970:22-23). This index defines fragmentation as the probability that a randomly selected pair of individuals in a plural society will belong to different segments. It can vary between 0 and 1. The value is 0 for a completely homogeneous society because the probability of belonging to different segments is obviously nil. A hypothetical plural society where each individual belongs to a different segment yields an index of 1. Between the extremes there are intermediate situations; for example, a plural society with two segments of equal size has an index of fragmentation of .50; a society with three equal segments is obviously more fragmented and has an index of .67; and a plural society with a two-thirds majority segment and a one-third minority segment has a lower index of fragmentation—.44—because it is closer to the completely homogeneous end of the continuum.

Although there is universal agreement that South Africa should be regarded as a plural society, there is very little agreement about what the segments of this plural society are. For this reason, Table 2.1 presents indices of fragmentation under four alternative assumptions. Two of these entail dichotomous—and undoubtedly oversimplified— divisions. The first, a division between the African and non-African populations, reflects the philosophy behind the 1983 constitution, which includes whites, Coloureds, and Asians in the South African political system but excludes the Africans (Constitutional Committee of the President's Council 1982a:38-40). The second is between whites and all blacks (Africans, Coloureds, and Asians); this division can be said to reflect current black radical opinion. The third alternative is the government's official fourfold racial classification. The fourth alternative—which in my opinion is the most accurate view of the South African plural society—entails a multiple division by ethnic groups: the Africans can be divided into ten ethnic segments and the whites into Afrikaners and English-speakers. It is more doubtful that the Coloureds and Asians can each be considered an ethnic segment, but I make this assumption here for the sake of brevity and convenience. (I shall discuss the structure of the South African plural society at greater length in Chapter 5.) Table 2.1 is based on the demographic statistics of the 1970 census, the last census before several of the homelands became formally independent.

Separate development has clearly succeeded in creating home-lands that are homogeneously African to a high degree. According to the first three classifications of the segments in Table 2.1, the fragmentation in the homelands is .01, indicating virtually perfect homogeneity. When the African population is divided into ethnic groups (the fourth classification), the index of fragmentation rises to a high .78—but this is an artifact of the simplifying assumption

Table 2.1

INDICES OF FRAGMENTATION FOR SOUTH AFRICA
(UNPARTITIONED), THE HOMELANDS (TREATED AS ONE UNIT),
AND RESIDUAL NON-HOMELAND AREA
(BASED ON 1970 CENSUS)[a]

	Index of Fragmentation[b]		
Segments	South Africa	Home-lands	Residual Area
Africans and non-Africans	.42	.01	.49
Blacks and whites	.29	.01	.38
Four racial groups[c]	.47	.01	.60
Fourteen ethnic groups[d]	.89	.78[e]	.90

Sources: Calculated from data in Horrell 1973:37-38 and Butler, Rotberg, and Adams 1977:4. See also Rae and Taylor 1970.

[a]The 1970 census was the last one before several of the homelands became formally independent.

[b]For a detailed explanation of the index, see pp. 35-36.

[c]Africans, whites, Coloureds, Asians.

[d]Ten major African ethnic groups, Afrikaners, English-speaking whites, Coloureds, and Asians. For the purpose of calculation, "other Africans" and "other whites" were counted as additional groups.

[e]The index would be much lower for each of the homelands considered separately.

that the ten homelands can be treated as a single entity. When we look at the homelands individually, we find that they are quite homogeneous in ethnic terms too. The main exceptions are Lebowa, which serves as the homeland of two ethnic groups, the Pedis and the North Ndebeles, and Bophuthatswana, which has a population that is about one-third non-Tswana. In contrast, in the most populous homeland, KwaZulu, about 98 percent of the people are Zulus, and in all of the homelands taken together only about 10 percent of the Africans live in a homeland other than their own (Butler, Rotberg, and Adams 1977:4-5, 121).

Compared with the homogeneity of the homelands, fragmentation in the residual area remains high. The indices of .60 and .90

partly reflect the fact that the non-African population consists of at least four different segments. If there were a separate Coloured homeland, these indices would be lower, but this has never been the government's policy (Brown 1980:116; A. du Toit 1975:39). A more important reason for the high degree of fragmentation in the residual area is the very large number of Africans who do *not* live in the homelands. According to the 1970 census, 46.5 percent of the Africans lived in the homelands and 53.5 percent in the residual area. Moreover, Africans formed a clear majority—almost 56 percent—of the total population in the residual area (Butler, Rotberg, and Adams 1977:4-5). This is why in the first row of Table 2.1, in which the non-Africans are counted as one segment, the index of fragmentation in the residual area is still a high .49.

It is also worth noting not only that the indices of fragmentation for the residual area are all high,but also that they are even higher than those for South Africa as a whole. The indices reflect the relatively high degree of "homogeneity" in unpartitioned South Africa provided by the large African majority. In the residual area the size of the African majority is reduced, thus raising the indices. These results should not be dismissed as merely statistical oddities. The substantively important conclusion to be drawn is that home-land partition has failed to create a homogeneous non-homeland area, regardless of how one counts the segments of South Africa's plural society, and that its main effect has been to reduce—not to eliminate—the majority status of the African population.

This conclusion remains valid when we examine the homelands policy over time. From the very beginning it was highly unlikely that separate development would ever mean genuine partition. The government-appointed Tomlinson Commission of the early 1950s, which favored the "ultimate, complete separation between Europeans and Bantu [Africans]" (McDonald 1979:28-29), nonetheless pre-dicted that the homelands would be able to accommodate only 60 percent of the Africans by 1981 and 70 percent by 2000. In the latter year there would still be an African majority in the area outside of the homelands, even according to the commission's own much too optimistic estimates *(ibid.)*. Recent figures indicate that the African population in the residual area is increasing instead of decreasing. Two factors are responsible for this trend: an increasing proportion of Africans in the total South African population, and enormously strong economic incentives that draw Africans away from the homelands and to the cities, legally or illegally. It has even been estimated that by 2000 as many as 75 percent of the Africans would be urbanized (H.W. van der Merwe 1983:110; see also Kriek 1976: 73-76).

The government has tried to solve the inconsistency between the principle of partition and the practice of homeland partition by claiming that the Africans in the non-homeland area are citizens of their respective homelands and not of the residual area (called the Republic of South Africa). They can therefore be regarded as temporary "guest workers" in the republic, and do not have to be counted as members of the plural society in the non-homeland area. This sleight of hand would artificially reduce the non-homeland indices of fragmentation for Africans and non-Africans from .49 to 0, for the racial groups from .60 to .55, and for the ethnic groups from .90 to .73.* However, such an explanation is obviously an evasion rather than a solution of the problem—a resort to "international-law fictions as a substitute for constitutional-law solutions" (Dugard 1980: 26). Harry Oppenheimer, former chairman of the Anglo American Corporation of South Africa, criticizes the concept of homeland citizenship for non-homeland Africans as follows: "What is wrong with the homelands policy is not that independence is given to people in the Transkei and Bophuthatswana, but the fact that the independence given to these people is used as an excuse to withhold civil rights from Xhosa and Tswana people who live in Johannesburg" (quoted in Starcke 1978:153).

Recent statements by President Botha appear to signal a basic shift in the government's homeland partition policy. In January 1985 Botha declared that his government now accepted "the permanence in the Republic of South Africa in large numbers of black population communities who find themselves outside national states [homelands]" (quoted in Cowell 1985b). They should be treated as "entities in their own right [that] must be given political participation and a say at higher levels" (ibid.)—presumably within the political system of the republic instead of the homelands. He went even further in September 1985 when he stressed his commitment to the principle of a united South Africa, one citizenship and a universal franchise" (quoted in Cowell 1985c). It is not yet clear how much of this rhetoric will carry over into substantive policy changes, but at the

---

*The index of fragmentation for the black-white dichotomy would go up from .38 to .48 because the large black majority (74:26) would change to a smaller (59:41) white majority.

very least it appears that the international-law fiction of homeland citizenship has been discarded.

The fact that homeland partition has created a high degree of homogeneity in the homelands but not in the non-homeland area should not be read to mean that it has "succeeded" in the homelands. On the contrary, especially when the other two criteria (fairness and voluntary choice) are applied, it becomes clear that homeland partition is also a failure for the homelands themselves. Above all, it does not entail an equitable division of South Africa's wealth. While three of the homelands—Transkei, Bophuthatswana, and KwaZulu—are larger than the internationally accepted sovereign state of Lesotho (which is also enclosed within South African territory), most of the others are considerably smaller; in Stultz's words, they are "ministates among ministates" (1980:201). The 13 percent of the total South African land area reserved for the homelands contrasts sharply with the proportion of Africans in the total population and even with half of this proportion if we assume that only about half of the Africans will live in the homelands: approximately 73 and 37 percent respectively.

The homelands are not entirely devoid of fertile land and mineral resources (Rabushka 1978:187-88; Starcke 1978:208), and in economic terms they do not compare unfavorably with some of the independent black states in Africa, but they compare very unfavorably with the rest of South Africa. In particular, South Africa is a highly industrialized country, but the homelands have virtually no industry. Another problem is a lack of territorial contiguity of most homelands. Munger argues that this is not necessarily bad:

> Many nations have much further-flung noncontiguous land units. Indonesia is spread out across thousands of miles. West Berlin is as much an outlier of the Federal Republic as the Thaba Nchu area is of Bophuthatswana. KwaZulu is now in five pieces [sic], but so is the United States if you consider Alaska, Puerto Rico, Hawaii, and the Virgin Islands (1978:260).

While noncontiguity may not be unprecedented, it afflicts the homelands to an extreme degree. The most fragmented homeland is KwaZulu, which had 48 separate territorial components in 1973 and will still have 10 separate areas—not 5, as Munger states— when all of the proposed consolidations have been completed. The 10 homelands together included 112 territorial components in

1973, and these will eventually be reduced to no less than 35 (Schrire 1978b:xv).

There have been a few countervailing advantages to homeland partition. For instance, the macro-segregation of separate develop-ment has often ended segregation at the meso and micro levels for the inhabitants of the homelands (Seiler 1979:13). More important, the homelands policy has given African leaders an offi-cially sanctioned power base and a political platform which they can use to promote the interests of the African masses and to work for major and minor reforms in the system. In particular, Buthelezi has used his leadership of KwaZulu to speak out against homeland partition, to refuse independence for KwaZulu, and to organize Inkatha, which reaches across homeland and ethnic boundaries and appeals to Zulus and other Africans in the homelands as well as in the large cities (Butler, Rotberg, and Adams 1977:224-30; Vigne 1978:85-87).

Even the leaders who unlike Buthelezi have accepted indepen-dence for their homelands argue that it can be a pragmatic weapon *against* homeland partition. For instance, Mangope claims that he did not accept "full sovereign independence" for Bophuthatswana but merely a "greater independence" (1979:4), and that he wants "to use apartheid to abolish apartheid" (quoted in Lelyveld 1983). Kaiser Matanzima, leader of the first homeland to opt for indepen-dence, Transkei, interprets this step as a temporary solution between the "present unsatisfactory form" of the Republic of South Africa and an eventual multiracial "mighty industrial state," not just a confederation or constellation of states (1976:3).

Because of the asymmetrical power relationship between the South African government and the homeland governments, the acceptance of formal independence by four homelands cannot be interpreted as the voluntary choice required by the third criterion of acceptable partition. As noted, the only groups who have favored homeland partition are the whites—especially the Afrikaners.* Beran, who argues the general philosophical case for partition and secession,

---

*Black rejection of partition involves a paradox when we compare South Africa with the rest of Africa, as Adam points out: "It is probably safe to say that the majority of people in independent Africa would welcome greater self-determination at the periphery, including secession from existing states, while the black majority of South Africans clearly favors preserving the unitary [i.e., unified] state" (1983a:132).

points out that "If the part of the state which challenges its unity includes the central government and lays claim to the legal identity of the existing state, we have a case of expulsion rather than secession" (1984:21). According to Beran's terminology, homeland partition is not partition but expulsion. If the white population should want to secede against the wishes of the black majority, it should be free to do so on equitable terms—which would have to be very different from the terms of homeland partition.

Homeland partition therefore violates all three criteria of acceptable partition. Mlahleni Njisane, a former Transkeian ambassador to South Africa, concludes that "Separate development has failed dismally to live up to its ideals" (1980:105) if homogeneity, fairness, and voluntarism were ever its intentions. The Constitutional Committee of the President's Council (1982a:32) cites my discussion of partition (in Lijphart 1977a:44-45) in support of its recommendation to maintain homeland partition and to exclude Africans from the proposed consociational arrangement in the new South African constitution.* I must admit that in that work I made the mistake of not spelling out the criteria for partition in sufficiently clear terms. I certainly never meant to give or even to imply approval of separate development as a proper use of partition. This book gives me a welcome opportunity to present an explicit statement of the basic criteria and to set the record straight.

RADICAL PARTITION

The most striking contrast between radical and homeland partition, when they are judged by the three basic criteria of acceptable partition, is that the radical proposals perform much better on the criterion of fairness. Of the many plans for radical partition, I shall focus on the two most recent, which are also the most specific and detailed as well as the most persuasive—i.e., those of Blenck and von der Ropp (1976) and of the South African economist Gavin Maasdorp (1980).[†]

*The committee states that it "followed Lijphart's reasoning closely" (1982a: 32, 41). To its credit, it also stresses that it assumed a fair and negotiated partition.

[†]Other proposals and discussions of radical partition can be found in Cowen 1961:71), Giniewski (1961:219-26), Mander (1963), Legum and Legum (1964: 221-26), G. Carter (1966:14-16), Tiryakian (1967), and de St. Jorre (1977:25-

The radical partition plans entail a fair division of land and resources because fairness is their primary objective. In addition, they try to maximize the homogeneity of the populations of the separate states. Austin T. Turk is clearly too pessimistic when he argues that "the absence of acceptable criteria for the negotiated division of territory and the absence of clues suggesting 'natural' dividing lines" are major stumbling blocks (1967:409). In fact, the application of the homogeneity and fairness criteria produces strikingly similar proposals—i.e., the dichotomous division of South Africa into an eastern state and a western state by a boundary that roughly passes through Sishen, Kimberley, Bloemfontein, and Port Elizabeth. This is indeed a natural dividing line suggested by the geographical concentration of the African majority east of it. Maasdorp calls the eastern state Capricornia and the western one Capeland; in order to facilitate the discussion, I shall also use these names. Maasdorp's Capeland is somewhat smaller than his Capricornia: about 47 and 53 percent of South African territory respectively. Blenck and von der Ropp propose two states of roughly the same size. The explanation of this slight difference between the two proposals is that Maasdorp allocates the Bloemfontein area to Capricornia, whereas Blenck and von der Ropp give it to Capeland.*

Capricornia and Capeland would be relatively large countries with strong economies. As Stultz states, "It can scarcely be doubted that the richest country in Africa which is more than twice the size of France could be divided to create two viable national economies" (1979:11). Capricornia would account for about 75 percent of South Africa's gross domestic product, a percentage that corresponds closely with the size of Capricornia's mainly or purely African population. The roughly equal division of the total land area seems to discriminate in favor of Capeland's projected smaller population, but when factors such as rainfall, fertility, and types of agriculture are taken into consideration, this apparent unfairness disappears.

The sectoral structure of the two economies would be broadly similar, although mining would be relatively more important in

27). In addition, Stultz (1977:11-17), Geldenhuys (1981:200-203, and 1985: 90-93), and du Pisani (1983:245-56) provide useful summaries. The Blenck-von der Ropp proposal has been defended and elaborated in subsequent articles by von der Ropp)1978, 1979, 1981, 1985).

*Tiryakian's (1967:220) suggested partition map is considerably more generous to Capeland, giving it almost the entire Orange Free State as well as the southern part of the Transvaal.

Capricornia and agriculture in Capeland. Capricornia would include the industrial area around Johannesburg—South Africa's industrial heart—as well as the Durban metropolitan and industrial region, but Capeland would have the Cape Peninsula and Port Elizabeth-Uitenhage areas of industrial concentration. The gold mines in the Transvaal and the Orange Free State would belong to Capricornia, but the Kimberley diamond mines to Capeland. Both states would have three major ports (Blenck and von der Ropp 1976:323-26; Maasdorp 1980:125-32).

Compared with its considerable success in ensuring a fair economic division, radical partition is an almost complete failure in disentangling South Africa's plural society. Table 2.2 presents the

Table 2.2

INDICES OF FRAGMENTATION FOR SOUTH AFRICA
(UNPARTITIONED), CAPRICORNIA, AND CAPELAND
(BASED ON 1970 CENSUS)

Segments	Index of Fragmentation		
	South Africa	Capricornia	Capeland
Without resettlement			
Africans and non-Africans	.42	.33	.36(.40)
Blacks and whites	.29	.26	.40
Four racial groups[a]	.47	.35(.34)[c]	.63(.65)
After resettlement			
Africans and non-Africans	.42	.00	.00
Blacks and whites	.29	.00	.48
Four racial groups[a]	.47	.00	.55
Fourteen ethnic groups[b]	.89	.78	.73

Sources: Calculated from data in Maasdorp 1980:130; Blenck and von der Ropp 1976:322; and Butler, Rotberg, and Adams 1977:4. See also Rae and Taylor 1970.

[a]Africans, whites, Coloureds, Asians.

[b]The ten major African ethnic groups, Afrikaners, English-speaking whites, Coloureds, and Asians. For the purpose of calculation, "other Africans" and "other whites" were counted as additional groups.

[c]Where the boundaries proposed by Maasdorp and by Blenck and von der Ropp do not yield identical indices of fragmentation, the Blenck-von der Ropp values are in parentheses.

relevant indices of fragmentation, Without large-scale population transfers between Capeland and Capricornia, the two new states would not be much more homogeneous than South Africa unpartitioned. Capricornia would be slightly less fragmented, but Capeland would become more fragmented according to two of the three classifications of segmentation. It is especially worth noting that the indices of fragmentation for Africans versus non-Africans are only slightly lower in Capricornia (.33) and in Capeland (.36 according to Maasdorp's figures and .40 according to Blenck and von der Ropp's) than the .42 for unpartitioned South Africa because this dichotomy provides the main rationale for the "natural dividing line" between the two states. It is also important to note that without population resettlements, Capricornia would have a four-fifths African majority and Capeland a three-fourths non-African majority, but that the whites would not have a majority in Capeland. Instead the Coloured population would be a near-majority, and white and African populations would be roughly equal in size, each numbering about one fourth of Capeland's population.

Large-scale population transfers could obviously lead to higher levels of homogeneity, and they are advocated by Blenck and von der Ropp (1976:326) for this reason. On the basis of the 1970 census figures, about 2.7 million whites, 1 million Africans, 0.6 million Asians, and 0.3 million Coloureds would have to relocate in order to achieve a complete unscrambling of the African and non-African populations. Proportionally the burden of resettlement would fall most heavily on the Asian and white populations, of whom 97 and 72 percent respectively would have to move. The Coloureds and Africans would be relatively less affected (15 and 7 percent respectively would have to move). Such drastic resettlement would by definition produce a homogeneously African Capricornia and a homogeneously non-African Capeland. However, as Table 2.2 shows, when we use the black-white or the fourfold racial classification, the indices of fragmentation are higher in Capeland than in South Africa unpartitioned even *after* these large-scale resettlements. The most damaging evidence against radical partition is evident from the last row of figures in the table: the fragmentation of South Africa's plural society in terms of its ethnic segments would decrease only slightly. Even radical partition in conjunction with drastic population transfers would merely divide one plural society into two plural societies.

In view of its heavy economic and psychological costs and

its limited benefits, it is almost inconceivable that radical partition will ever be freely negotiated and agreed upon. Virtually nobody in South Africa currently favors it. For the whites, who have shown the greatest interest in separatism, who have the greatest fear of being dominated by other groups, and who would have to move in large numbers in order to settle in a still multiracial Capeland, it might make more sense to opt for an even more radical partition: a completely white "homeland" (G.C. Olivier 1980:185; van den Berghe 1983:151; R.W. Howe 1978:253). This would be in line with homeland partitionist thinking, but it would entail even more resettlement and in a much smaller area than Capeland—probably restricted to the Western Cape if, as Jordan K. Ngubane suggests (1979:316), a "proportional partition" were applied.

Faced with such choices, many whites may well prefer to emigrate from South Africa instead of moving within South Africa (Maasdorp 1980:116). Van den Berghe even recommends massive emigration of South African whites as "the most desirable and humane solution to the Southern African problem" (1979b:62). However, the vast majority of the whites—and the Afrikaners in particular—would reject voluntary emigration. As Adam states, the Afrikaners "justly claim indigenous status as a white African tribe. . . . To conceive of massive emigration of South African whites as a solution is as unrealistic as the proposal that the American Blacks should resettle in Africa" (1977:428).

Radical partition in any form, including mass emigration and withdrawal into a white homeland, is so unattractive that it is much more likely to be the outcome of a civil war than a solution that will prevent a civil war. However, radical partition may serve one useful purpose, and it should therefore not be rejected completely. If negotiations were begun for a consociational democracy, it would be a good idea to formulate not only a consociational constitution, but also a radical partition scheme as a fallback solution. If, contrary to all good intentions and reasonable expectations, a consociation were to fail, the availability of an agreed upon fallback plan for partition may help to avoid or minimize violence. It should therefore decrease the negotiators' reluctance to attempt a consociational solution. More important, such a fallback plan would increase the likelihood that a consociational democracy could be negotiated and that it would work well because the participants in the negotiations and in the actual operation of a consociational government would have the sobering knowledge of exactly what the partitionist alternative would entail.

Chapter 3

CONSOCIATIONAL, SEMI-CONSOCIATIONAL, AND QUASI-CONSOCIATIONAL PROPOSALS

Since the late 1970s the debate about constitutional reform in South Africa has been dominated by the concept of South Africa as a plural society and by the consociational model of democratization (G. C. Olivier 1980:187). All of the recent detailed proposals for democratic reform contain important consociational elements—without necessarily being fully consociational or even genuinely consociational. In this chapter I shall review these plans and evaluate them in terms of the four basic criteria of consociationalism: executive power-sharing, segmental autonomy, proportionality, and minority veto. I shall ask two basic questions concerning each of the proposals: (1) To what extent is it consociational? (2) If the proposal or part of it can be regarded as consociational, does it implement the consociational principles optimally in the light of the South African circumstances?

The earliest proposal that can be considered at least partly consociational is contained in the final report of SPROCAS, published in 1973. Although it was not favorably received in white political circles and initially was not even given much attention, it laid the groundwork for much of the reformist thinking in the National Party as well as in the white opposition parties in the late 1970s (Seiler 1979:10-11; Hill 1983:156). After discussing the SPROCAS plan, I shall turn to the proposals of the white political parties: the National Party, whose proposals became the 1983 constitution; the New Republic Party (NRP), whose ideas are amendments instead of alternatives to those of the National Party; and the PFP, which has formulated an entirely different design for a democratic constitution. Finally, I shall discuss the proposals aimed at parts of South Africa but with significant implications for South Africa as a whole: the Quail Report on the Ciskei and the reports of the Buthelezi Commission and the Lombard Commission for the KwaZulu-Natal area.

SPROCAS PROPOSAL

SPROCAS was launched in 1969 as an initiative of the Christian Institute and the South African Council of Churches. It was a follow-up to the 1968 "Message to the People of South Africa," in which the Council of Churches had condemned apartheid as anti-Christian, and it was designed to supplement the negative critique of the "Message" with practical and constructive suggestions and "some vision of what South African society could be if Christianity was taken seriously" (quoted in Walshe 1983:102). SPROCAS established six study commissions for different fields and published a large number of papers and reports, culminating in an extensive report of the political commission and a final, coordinated report on the entire project (Randall 1973b:103-34; Stadler 1975; Walshe 1983:102-48; Woldring 1977).

The final SPROCAS report summarizes the recommendations for the political system in extremely brief terms—less than one page—but it nevertheless indicates a clear and close affinity with consociational thinking. It proclaims democratic representation at all levels of government, decentralization of power, freedom of association, and freedom for all kinds of voluntary associations and groups "to manage their own affairs within bounds fixed by law" (Randall 1973b:99). In the South African plural society, the report concludes, "these ideals may best be furthered through a federal structure, proportional representation, and large measures of regional or communal autonomy, which will help to separate and distribute the power of government" (ibid.).

The SPROCAS political commission's report is much more specific. After a survey of the possible alternatives to the Westminster model—including a favorable review of the literature on consociational democracy—the commission formulates a two-stage model for reform (Randall 1973a:144-242). The first stage entails the rapid extension of democratic rights to all non-white citizens by using or adapting existing institutions as much as possible. For the Africans, Coloureds, and Asians living in the "common area"—that is, outside of the homelands—representative councils on a communal basis will be created at both the national and local levels. The Africans in the homelands will have democratically elected regional authorities; the regions will coincide with the homelands to a large extent, but they will not be defined on a strict ethnic basis. The regional and communal authorities will have full powers in their own local governments and over their own cultural and educational affairs. They will also serve as the representatives of the African, Coloured, and Asian populations in the negotiations with the central government that is still under white control (pp. 230-33). At the end of the first stage

> [there will be a] round of negotiations and/or a series of confer-ences involving all the major regional and communal authorities as well as the central government and Parliament in order to prepare the way for a basic constitutional transition and [to] determine the political structure of a new political system (Randall 1973a:237).

The second stage entails the new constitutional setup. Because a new constitution should be decided by a national convention, the political commission merely provides the main outlines of what it considers to be desirable rules and institutions. It recommends a multiracial federal system of government with a federal legislature "elected on an indirect basis (the various regional and communal authorities to act as electoral colleges) or by a combination of indirect and direct election, where the latter may be based on some form of proportional representation, or embody a combination of constituen-cy and proportional representation as in the German Federal Repub-lic" (Randall 1973a:239).

One possible criticism of these SPROCAS proposals is that they rely heavily on the official fourfold racial classification and on the ethnically defined homeland governments. The use of these racial and ethnic categories has two serious drawbacks: they are arbitrary, and they have been unilaterally imposed by the white regime instead of being voluntarily agreed on. However, SPROCAS states clearly that it does not want to perpetuate these distinctions under the new constitution. The racially based communal councils and the largely ethnically based regional authorities are merely temporary expedients in the first stage of reform. In the second stage, communal authorities and group representation will still be allowed and recognized but on a strictly voluntary basis: "It is clear that the political enforcement of social or cultural differences can never be acceptable, and that membership cannot unilaterally be decreed on arbitrary grounds but should be on the basis of voluntary affiliation" (Randall 1973a:216). Thus the SPROCAS approach is to *allow* group formation along ethnic or racial lines instead of either *imposing* or *outlawing* it:

> If cultural diversity is valued and tolerated, and groups are allowed a measure of cultural and educational autonomy, the ideal of a non-discriminatory society must require the desegregation of all

areas of public life and the removal of discriminatory norms and practices in all spheres of government. On a voluntary basis groups may be formed along ethnic or even racial lines and may as such claim recognition by, and protection of, the law (Randall 1973a: 217-18).

The old racial and ethnic criteria will still be relevant in the first stage of reform, but in the second stage they will give way to "a system of local, regional, communal and federal rights, all accepting the principle of voluntary individual affiliation" (Randall 1973a: 241).

The arbitrariness of the official racial and ethnic classification manifests itself particularly with regard to the white and Coloured categories. Because South Africa has not had a system of free group formation, it is difficult to determine what the relevant groups for a consociational type of government would be. To put it slightly differently, although South Africa is undoubtedly a plural society, the constituent segments of this plural society can be finally determined only by a process of free and voluntary affiliation and free competition. Nevertheless, in some cases it is already quite clear that the officially decreed groups do not coincide with the segments in the South African plural society. For example, the Coloureds are a residual category of citizens who are not African, white, or Asian, and they lack the cohesiveness and communal identification that normally characterizes a segment in a plural society (P. du Toit and Theron 1984). The whites do not constitute a single segment either. They are divided into Afrikaans and English-speaking segments; the Afrikaners could even be regarded as a self-conscious nation with strong and genuine nationalistic feelings.

SPROCAS is well aware of these problems. It argues that the African, Coloured, and Asian communal councils operating in the first stage of reform "should be replaced at the earliest opportunity by a system of voluntary affiliation," which could result in communal councils organized along completely different lines. The whites could opt for white communal authorities or for "an Afrikaans National Cultural Council, an English National Cultural Council, etc." (Randall 1973a:232, 240). The overall conclusion must be that SPROCAS uses the official racial and ethnic classification only as a starting point and a short-term expedient. It cannot be accused of perpetuating the categories or trying to reify them into the true segments of the South African plural society.

A second possible criticism of the SPROCAS recommendations (already mentioned in Chapter 2) is what Brookes has referred to as SPROCAS's tendency of "turning from the individual to the group" (1973:243). Similarly, Hill states that the commission's "pluralist assumption that people should be seen first and foremost as members of groups [constitutes a] demolition of liberalism" (1983:155). These accusations are not well-founded for several reasons. First, groups are an empirical reality in plural societies; they have to be taken into account and cannot simply be wished away. This fact also explains the commission's acceptance, albeit with evident reluctance and some distaste, of a certain degree of optional self-segregation (Randall 1973a:218, 241-42). Second, the SPROCAS commission emphasizes group rights not instead of or at the expense of individual rights, but in addition to them (Randall 1973a:217). Third, it is only a narrow and old-fashioned liberalism that ignores groups as empirical and moral entities (Van Dyke 1975, 1982).

From the consociational point of view the SPROCAS proposals cannot be faulted for what they say but only for what they fail to say. On the one hand, segmental autonomy is a prominent feature, both in the plan's territorial federalism and especially in its corporate-federal provision for communal councils; the latter are important in view of the geographical intermixture of the ethnic segments. SPROCAS also expresses a clear preference for PR, citing the West German example. On the other hand, there is no explicit provision for a minority veto, although such a veto would be a logical extension of SPROCAS's concern with the protection of group rights. SPROCAS recommends a federal executive which will be "responsible to a legislative assembly representative of all the citizens of the Republic" (Randall 1973a:239), and it discusses the composition of this legislature, but it is silent on the crucial question of what the executive should look like. Executive power-sharing is not prescribed or even implied, although it fits the general spirit of the SPROCAS plan and could be added without difficulty.

In spite of these omissions, the SPROCAS proposals must be regarded as a milestone in the development of consociational thinking in South Africa. However, because of these omissions, they are only semi-consociational rather than fully consociational.

NATIONAL PARTY PROPOSALS, 1977-83

The proposals for constitutional reform by the National Party and the government—the terms "government" and "National Party" can be used interchangeably in this context because the National Party has controlled the government since 1948—have assumed different forms from their original formulation in 1977 to their incorporation in the constitution approved by the white parliament and a white voters' referendum in 1983. Their genesis can be traced to the report of the Theron Commission, a government-appointed advisory body composed of twelve white and six Coloured persons, which met from 1973 to 1976 (Cloete 1977). With regard to constitutional reform the commission's 1976 report urged "a direct say for Coloureds at the various levels of government and on the various decision-making bodies," and it argued that "the existing Westminster-founded system of government will have to be changed to adapt it to the specific requirements of the South African plural population structure" (quoted in Boulle 1984:130). It recommended the appointment of a committee of experts, including Coloured members, to make more detailed proposals. Instead the government named an all-white cabinet committee under the chairmanship of P. W. Botha—who later became prime minister and, after the adoption of the 1983 constitution, the first incumbent of the powerful presidency provided for in the new constitution.

The intellectual origins of the government's constitutional designs can be traced back even farther—to 1969-73 and the SPROCAS study commissions. Similar ideas were also developed outside of SPROCAS. For instance, W. B. Vosloo, professor of political science at the Afrikaans University of Stellenbosch and not a member of SPROCAS, suggested in an October 1971 seminar presentation that separate representative and executive bodies could be adapted or created for the Coloured, Asian, and urban African populations and that their leaders as well as the white government should be linked at the top "more or less after the pattern of the so-called 'consociational' model of plural societies" (1974:13-14).*

*Vosloo presented these ideas only a few months after my first series of guest lectures on consociational democracy at Stellenbosch and several other South African universities. In revised form, his arguments were prominently published as the very first article of the new South African journal of political science, *Politikon*, launched in 1974.

From 1977 to 1983 the government's proposals went through several forms and phases. They were first publicly announced in 1977, but they were not formulated in a draft bill until 1979. This bill was referred to a joint select committee of both houses which was subsequently converted into a commission of inquiry, the Schlebusch Commission. It in turn recommended establishing an advisory President's Council with white, Coloured, and Asian members on a permanent basis; the council was given constitutional recognition in 1980 and started operating in 1981. The Constitutional Committee of the President's Council, the most prominent of its five standing committees, issued two reports in 1982, and the government itself formulated a set of constitutional guidelines which were contained in the prime minister's address to the National Party's 1982 congress in Bloemfontein. The government submitted its draft constitution bill to parliament in May 1983. With several minor amendments, it received parliamentary approval in September and the white voters' consent in November 1983.

All of the twists and turns in this process do not need to detain us in this study. They are thoroughly and ably analyzed by Boulle (1984).* I shall focus on the first and last versions: the 1977 proposals and the 1983 constitution. There was a great deal of continuity in the various versions produced during this period, but there was also a general trend toward greater complexity and less consociationalism.

*In addition, analyses and commentaries may be found in the following: Adam (1984a, 1984b); Austin (1985); Boesak (1984:111-22); Boulle (1980a, 1980b, 1983); Dean (1983); de Crespigny (1981); de Crespigny and Collins (1983); Degenaar (1982); W. J. de Klerk (1977); Devenish (1982); Dugard (1980); du Plessis (1978); A. du Toit (1980a, 1980b, 1983); Frankel (1980); Geldenhuys (1981); Giliomee (1980, 1982); Gutteridge (1981); Hanf and Weiland (1980); Hanf, Weiland, and Vierdag (1981:408-19); Heard (1978); Heunis (1981); Huntington (1981); Irvine (1978, 1984); Jooste (1983); Koornhof (1979); Legum (1982); Mabude (1983); Maré (1983); Nattrass (1978); Nieuwoudt (1977), G. C. Olivier (1978a, 1980, 1981); N. J. J. Olivier (1985); Oppenheimer (1982); Pakendorf (1980); Potgieter (1977); Price (1980); Rajah, Curry, and Ngcobe (1978); Ranchod (1983); Rauche (1983a, 1983b); Rhoodie (1978a, 1978b, 1980a, 1980b, 1983b); Saul and Gelb (1981:58-62); Schlemmer (1980b, 1983a); Schrire (1978a); Slabbert (1983); Stultz (1984); Terreblanche (1978); Vandenbosch (1979); H. W. van der Merwe (1983); van der Ross (1981, 1983); van der Vyver (1978); van der Werff (1985); van Jaarsveld (1980); A. J. Venter (1981, 1983); von der Ropp (1984); Vosloo (1980); Weaver (1983); Welsh (1980, 1983); Woodward (1981); Worrall (1978, 1981); and Zimmermann (1978).

Throughout the constitution-making process, consociational theory and terminology were frequently invoked by both insiders and outside commentators. The 1977 proposals were called an embryonic form of "consociational engineering" (G. C. Olivier 1978a: 346), "a system of power-sharing" (van der Vyver 1978:253), and "the basis for a consociational democracy" (du Plessis 1978:10). Denis Worrall, the first chairman of the Constitutional Committee of the President's Council, stressed the pervasive influence of consociational thinking on constitutional reform plans: "Consociational democratic theory rules the theoretical roost in political science in this country, [and] its domination of constitutional theory is almost as complete" (1981:33). In its *First Report*, the Constitutional Committee under Worrall's chairmanship stated that it "followed Lijphart's reasoning closely" (1982a:32), and it made no fewer than twenty-six references to my writings.

In the final phase, however, government spokesmen retreated from this stance. In a parliamentary debate on 17 May 1983, Minister C. V. van der Merwe argued that the new constitution did not entail power-sharing but only a "sharing of responsibility" (South Africa 1983a: col. 7191). J. C. Heunis, Minister of Constitutional Development and Planning, stated the following on 18 August 1983:

> We often argue incorrectly that what we are trying to do is break away completely from the Westminster dispensation. Surely we do not want to break away completely from it. . . . We have never said that we are exchanging this particular system for another academic model. . . . The President's Council recommended a consociational democracy [but] we did not accept that. We accepted elements of a new system, and retained elements of the old" (South Africa 1983a: col. 11579).

At first blush, the 1977 proposals appear to have many consociational elements (Boulle 1984:149-70; van der Vyver 1978:252-56; Vosloo 1980:204-14; Worrall 1978:126-32). Segmental autonomy is introduced by giving decision-making authority in all matters of exclusive group concern to three separate parliaments (white, Coloured, and Asian), elected by separate electorates, and to three separate cabinets and three prime ministers responsible to these parliaments.*

*According to the 1977 proposals, each parliament would also have some members—about 11 percent of the total membership—either indirectly elected by the other, popularly elected members or appointed by the president. In the final 1983 version this figure was reduced to approximately 7 percent.

Separate regional-provincial and local authorities would operate under their respective parliaments and cabinets. Executive power-sharing takes the form of a council of cabinets, in which the three prime ministers and several other ministers from the three cabinets would be represented. This council would be chaired by the state president, elected by an electoral college, which in turn would be elected by the three parliaments. A minority veto is implied by a rule that the council of cabinets must make its decisions by consensus and that legislation applicable to all three groups has to be approved by all three parliaments.

The proportionality principle is evident in a 4:2:1 ratio used for the relative sizes of the white, Coloured, and Asian parliaments and, more important, for their relative shares of seats on the presidential electoral college and advisory presidential council. This ratio slightly underrepresents the Coloured community and overrepresents the Asians (Boulle 1984:167). A 5:3:1 ratio would have been a closer approximation, but it would have meant a minor overrepresentation for both Coloureds and Asians. Nevertheless, the 4:2:1 formula can be regarded as roughly proportional. On the council of cabinets there would be seven white, four Coloured, and three Asian ministers, plus a presumably white president. This is also an approximately proportional ratio, although again at a slight disadvantage to the Coloureds and an advantage to the Asians.

Most of these features can also be found in the 1983 constitution. Several apparent changes are terminological rather than substantive. For one thing, instead of three parliaments, there is a single tricameral parliament consisting of a white House of Assembly, a Coloured House of Representatives, and an Asian House of Delegates. The term "tricameralism" is somewhat deceptive because the new South African parliament differs from the bicameral legislatures of many other countries in a way other than in the number of its chambers: the two chambers of bicameral parliaments are usually elected according to different procedures but by the *same* electorate, whereas the three South African chambers are elected by strictly separate sets of voters. For another thing, the council of cabinets has simply become the "cabinet," and the three separate cabinets have become mere "ministers' councils." And the presidential council is now the "president's council."

The major substantive difference between the initial and final versions of the National Party plan is a sharply increased power for the state president. He or she now has the authority to decide whether a matter is of common concern or of exclusive concern to the separate groups—"general affairs" versus "own affairs" in the new constitution. This is a very important power which was left ambiguous in the 1977 formulation. In addition, instead of the members of the national cabinet being named by the three ministers' councils, the president now has the power of appointment. Moreover, he is not bound by any proportional or other ratio when he appoints the cabinet. Similarly, he can appoint one fourth of the members of the president's council—the others are elected by the majority and opposition parties in the three houses according to the 4:2:1 formula— without having to adhere to any group ratio.

THE 1983 CONSTITUTION: A CRITIQUE

In spite of its apparently consociational features and the consociational rhetoric used to justify it until the final stage of deliberations, the 1983 constitution does not measure up to the basic requirements of consociationalism for several reasons. Its gravest weakness is that there is no provision at all for the representation and participation of the African population. The exclusion of the Africans is not only unconsociational but also undemocratic.

From the first National Party constitutional formulations in 1977, it was clear of course that the African population would not be a candidate for inclusion in the new setup. The *First Report* of the Constitutional Committee of the President's Council was therefore rather adventurous in even considering the option of "the continuation of the direction of official constitutional policy with respect to Blacks [Africans] in the Black national states [homelands], but the accommodation of Blacks outside the Black states with Whites, Coloureds and Indians in a consociational democracy" (1982a:36)— but not the option of including both non-homeland and homeland Africans. The committee described the option of including the non-homeland Africans as "the most serious rival" to the alternative of an exclusive white-Coloured-Asian system (p. 38), but it argued that the differences between the Africans on the one hand and whites, Coloureds, and Asians on the other were too big an obstacle: "The obviously sensible course is to start by applying the consociational model where it can reasonably be expected to secure a more democratic political system—that is, in the context of the White, Coloured and Indian communities. If the model were to operate successfully, . . . other possibilities might present themselves" (p. 40).

Following this assumption of a fundamental distinction between Africans and non-Africans, the committee recommended a "consociational" approach for the latter and a homeland-partitionist solution for the former. Regardless of whether there really are such great and perhaps even irreconcilable differences between Africans and non-Africans—a question that I shall explore in Chapter 5—homeland partition is an entirely inadequate solution. The committttee's own group-oriented logic and the basic requirements of democracy should have mandated the addition of one African chamber of parliament, or perhaps several African ethnic chambers, as well as African participation in the cabinet, the presidential electoral college, etc. to the 1983 constitution. Without these additions, this is simply not "a democratic constitution," contrary to the committee chairman's claims (Worrall 1981:31).

A second weakness of the 1983 constitution is that the Coloured and Asian minorities lack an effective veto power. In the 1977 version of the constitution, the council of cabinets was supposed to operate by consensus instead of majority vote, but this consensus would be determined by the president—probably a white president since he would be elected by an electoral college with a white majority. No consensus and consensus-determination rules were written into the final version, but the president still has dominant power in the cabinet because he can appoint its members at will and in fact (as noted) does not even have to include any Coloured or Asian ministers. With regard to disputes on "general affairs," the 1977 proposal stipulated that the Coloured and Asian parliaments could be bypassed because the president would be given the power to break a legislative deadlock with the aid of one of the parliaments—presumably the white one. According to the 1983 constitution, the president can accomplish the same end with the aid of the President's Council—which has a white majority.

In strict constitutional terms, therefore, the minority veto is at best only suspensive: it gives the minority chambers the power to delay but not to stop legislation to which they are opposed. In terms of practical politics, the veto will probably be somewhat stronger. W. Vause Raw, the leader of the NRP, asserted in the parliamentary debate that the "ultimate safeguard" against abusing the power to override Coloured and Indian wishes would be the fact that "the withdrawal of Coloureds and Indians would destroy the credibility of the whole system. I believe that that knowledge alone will lead to the greatest effort to reach consensus, because no Government wants to see a mockery made of its whole constitutional development" (South Africa 1983a: col. 7113; see also Stultz 1984:368). The term "safe-guard" is far too strong, but it is indeed not very likely that the president will easily decide to provoke such a possible walkout.

A third major problem from a consociational perspective is that the new constitution is based on the official racial classification—for the purpose of including the whites, Coloureds, and Asians as separate components in the political system and excluding the Africans. It is not intrinsically wrong to mention the segments of a plural society in the society's constitution. For instance, the Belgian constitution officially recognizes Dutch-speaking and French-speaking segments, and the 1960 constitution of Cyprus distinguishes between Greek and Turkish Cypriots; these official designations of segments are generally accepted and uncontroversial. However, the official fourfold classification in South Africa is both highly controversial and does not coincide with the division into ethnic segments.

As discussed above, the SPROCAS proposal also relied on the predetermined fourfold racial classification, but two important differences make the SPROCAS plan acceptable and the 1983 constitution unacceptable by consociational standards: (1) SPROCAS uses the classification as a temporary measure prior to the writing of a constitution instead of enshrining it in the constitution; and (2) SPROCAS uses the African population category for the purpose of inclusion instead of exclusion.

A fourth, closely related problem is that the 1983 constitution does not merely preserve white dominance but the domination of the National Party, at least as long as the Nationalists retain the voting support of the bulk of the Afrikaners. The privileged position of the National Party in the new constitutional arrangements is assured by five factors: (1) The white group is defined as a single constituent unit (as discussed above); (2) The whites have a numerical majority over the Coloureds and Asians combined; (3) Within the white community there is a clear Afrikaner majority; (4) A high degree of ethnic voting among whites gives the Afrikaner-supported National Party a virtually permanent electoral majority; and (5) The new constitution does not provide for proportional representation in elections.

The application of the proportionality rule is limited to the 4:2:1 ratio for the sizes of the three parliamentary chambers and the delegations they elect to the presidential electoral college and the President's Council. The elections themselves are on a purely majoritarian basis. The three houses are elected by plurality in single-member districts, and they elect their representatives in the electoral college and the president's council by majority vote. This makes it possible for the National Party majority in the white House of Assembly to elect an exclusively National Party delegation to the presidential electoral college, where the delegation has a majority of fifty out of eighty-eight seats—more than sufficient to guarantee the election of a National Party president. In the sixty-member President's Council, which has the important task of resolving parliamentary deadlocks, twenty members are elected by the National Party majority in the white chamber, and fifteen are appointed by the National Party president—again a clear majority of thirty-five of the seats.

Of the above five factors, the second, third, and fourth are empirical facts of South African political life, and the first and fifth factors engineer them into National Party predominance. Both the creation of a single white chamber and the majoritarian electoral system are crucial ingredients in this scheme. If all other principal provisions of the 1983 constitution remained the same but either the white chamber were split into separate Afrikaans and English-speaking chambers or PR were introduced for all elections, there would be a potential majority coalition of Coloured, Asian, and white Anglophone representatives. These three groups account for about two thirds of the total white-Coloured-Asian population. In the presidential electoral college their representatives could have a clear majority of roughly fifty-five of the seats, and they would therefore be able to elect a non-Nationalist president. But what Dugard calls the "fraudulent" device of mandating a single white chamber and conducting majoritarian elections ensures that "so long as the National Party retains its majority support in the white community, it will rule South Africa" (1980:27).

The constitution's provision for National Party dominance occasioned vigorous debate in the parliamentary discussions prior to its adoption. The leader of the mainly English-supported PFP, F. van Zyl Slabbert, argued that the proposed constitution was "nothing but a political tool [for the National Party] to run the country as it deems fit" (South Africa 1983a: cols. 7069-70). Furthermore, he stated that "in some respects this proposed constitution is moving away from the good aspects of the Westminster system and has carried over some of its worst aspects, of which majority domination by a single party is one" (*ibid.*). National Party predominance has simply been perpetuated from the old to the new constitution, but whereas the party used to rule as the representative of a majority within a minority--that is, the Afrikaner majority within the white minority-- it now rules as the representative of a minority within a minority-- the Afrikaner minority within the enfranchised non-African minority of the total population.

These four weaknesses of the 1983 constitution must be regarded as very serious flaws and fundamental deviations from the consociational model of democracy. In addition, the new constitution has four other less serious weaknesses—features that are not violations of consociational principles but that are not optimal applications of consociationalism either. First, although a strong presidency is not necessarily incompatible with the principle of executive power-sharing—for instance, consociational democracy in Lebanon operated for many decades under a grand coalition of a president and other top officeholders—it nonetheless makes power-sharing more difficult. In presidential systems the president is inevitably the single most important political leader, and he or she is bound to represent one particular segment to the exclusion of other segments. Andries P. Treurnicht, the leader of the Conservative Party (formed in 1982 by breakaway right-wing Nationalists), criticized the government's 1983 proposals on the ground that they meant the "mixing" of races: "We are going to get this in a mixed Parliament, in a mixed Government and in a mixed President's Council. The only thing that they cannot also mix is the President" (South Africa 1983a: col. 7087). His last point is well-taken: one person cannot be a "mixed" or grand coalition. Cabinets offer better settings for collegial and coequal power-sharing. The new South African constitution has created not just a preeminent president but one with almost autocratic powers.*

Second, the original government proposal was discussed exclusively within the National Party before it was made public in 1977.

---

*The Constitutional Committee of the President's Council cites my earlier argument against presidential government in a consociational system (Lijphart 1980a:64-65), but states that it has to be concerned not only with the accommodation of heterogeneity, best served by a collegial executive, but also with political reform in a highly dynamic society, which calls for "strong leadership" (1982a:56-57). This is in line with Huntington's assertion that "social and economic reform is normally facilitated by a relatively high concentration of power in the political system, [and the] route from a limited uni-racial democracy to a broader multi-racial democracy could run through some form of autocracy" (1981:19-20). But is it realistic to assume that a president elected by—and hence especially representative of—one segment can transcend this segment's self-interests and particularistic outlook? (See also Stultz 1984.)

Neither the white opposition nor the leaders of the Coloured and Asian communities, which were to be incorporated in the plan, were consulted beforehand. While it is not impossible that a consociational constitution could be produced unilaterally, negotiations among the leaders of all segments are much more likely to lead to a genuine consociation, to its widespread acceptance, and to its subsequent satisfactory operation. Outsiders were invited to participate in only one phase of the constitution-making process: deliberations on the newly created President's Council from 1981 to 1982. But the council was merely a government-appointed advisory body and a far cry from a constitutional convention. Moreover, Boulle points out the following:

> The government nominated a majority of whites to the council as a whole, as well as to each individual committee, and most of the white nominees, and all the committee chairmen, were in addition government supporters. These factors ensured that the preponderant views on the council would be compatible with, and supportive of, government policy (1984:173).

Third, instead of applying a strict proportionality rule, it is especially suitable if consociational democracies give minorities a certain degree of overrepresentation when a plural society contains a majority segment and one or more minority segments. Thus it would have been appropriate to overrepresent the Coloured and Asian populations, perhaps to the extent of giving them jointly a numerical weight equal to that of the whites. For instance, instead of the 4:2:1 ratio, a 4:3:1 or 3:2:1 ratio could have been used. But of course these alternatives would have interfered with the retention of decisive power by the white chamber and the National Party.

Fourth, the 4:2:1 ratio is fixed permanently in the constitution. It was roughly proportional in 1976 and can still be regarded as such today, but it may well become disproportional in the future, especially because of the relatively high rate of growth of the Coloured population. A rigidly fixed ratio of representation caused serious tensions in Lebanon in the 1960s and 1970s and weakened its consociational democracy. As a general rule, such fixed ratios are inadvisable.

In view of all these defects, the 1983 constitution can obviously not be regarded as even semi-consociational; it is at best quasi-consociational. But could it be argued that it is at least a step in the direction of consociationalism? Even though it allows only a limited degree of Coloured and Asian participation, could the next step be full power-sharing with Coloureds and Asians, followed by inclusive power-sharing with the Africans too? Two utterly contradictory interpretations are possible.

On the one hand, if Coloured and Asians are included now, "the next logical step" is the inclusion of the urban Africans, according to Piet Cillié, one of the most influential people in the Afrikaans press (quoted in H. W. van der Merwe 1983:117). On the basis of this interpretation, Raw justified the NRP's vote in favor of the 1983 constitution: "Whilst the Bill does not satisfy our desire for the accommodation of *all* races, it is a step forward. . . . We believe it can be extended to what we envisage as the ideal" (South Africa 1983a: col. 7089). For the same reason, the Conservative Party condemned the new constitution; Treurnicht stated, "If one shares power, one loses it" (South Africa 1983a: col. 7114). Another right-wing critic put it this way: "If consociation is adopted in respect of Whites, Coloureds and Indians, are there any moral grounds for excluding the Blacks who are permanently settled in the country?" (Jooste 1983: 429). Marxist writers Saul and Gelb argue that "even the contemplation of some kind of multiracial decision-making and eventual representation—contrasting as it does with the N.P.'s self-confident driving of the Coloureds out of national political institutions in the 1950s— is an index of the pressure the regime feels" (1981:59). This may well lead to African involvement too since "the philosophy of cooptation is strongly afoot within Afrikaner intellectual circles" (*ibid.*).

The opposite interpretation is that the inclusion of Coloureds and Asians merely represents the correction of a flaw in the government's homeland policy. Because these two groups do not have homelands, some other solution had to be found. If the 1983 constitution is viewed as this solution and if the homelands are the solution for the Africans, the new constitution is obviously not a first step, but the final step. This argument is presented in a recent official government publication: Because of the homeland policy,

> it is . . . untrue to maintain that Blacks are excluded from the constitutional process in South Africa. What is true is that the Coloureds and Indians have to date been left out, and will now be brought into the constitutional process. . . . If the Coloureds and Indians had had regions traditionally their own, . . . then it would have been possible to grant them full political rights in their own territories" (Groenewald 1984:17).

The *New York Times* accepted this view when it editorialized that the new constitution simply eliminated a "doctrinal flaw" and was not "a step away from apartheid. . . . More likely, apartheid for blacks has gained a longer lease" (1983). Similarly, de St. Jorre comments that the constitution is "a way of coopting Indians and coloreds, . . . and shutting out blacks more decisively than ever" (1983).

In government circles, both of these conflicting views can be encountered. Publicly the "first step" interpretation is downplayed, but "some members say behind closed doors . . . that the new constitution is only a beginning, that it may eventually lead to giving political participation to urban blacks" (Starcke 1978:53). As could be expected, there are also differences between different wings of the National Party. For instance, P. G. J. Koornhof, a former cabinet member who belongs to the more liberal wing of the party, calls the government's constitutional policy "open-ended" (1979:95). And President Botha's September 1985 statement that he and his party were "committed to the principle of a united South Africa, one citizenship and a universal franchise" (quoted in Cowell 1985c) is a clear indication that Africans can somehow be included in the new constitutional arrangements. However, the most obvious "next step"— setting up a fourth chamber of parliament, similar to the solution proposed by the NRP (which I shall discuss in the next section)—was flatly rejected in an official policy statement of the National Party in April 1985 (C. J. van der Merwe 1985:7).

In spite of the 1983 constitution's many flaws, the fact that it represents a break with the Westminster tradition and that it has introduced some elements of consociational thinking—albeit in unsatisfactory form—may be considered a favorable development. But as Hanf, Weiland, and Vierdag point out, the new constitution may have the effect of giving consociationalism a bad name: "We can assume that the majority of blacks will simply regard 'consociation' or 'plural democracy' as more new labels for apartheid, and that sham consociation will thereby destroy the prospect of a genuine and acceptable regulation of conflict in the future" (1981:419). Slabbert has also argued that "if you appropriate the logic of consociationalism and paste it on like some sort of political Band-Aid in order to keep the status quo, you actually aggravate the problem" (quoted in Lelyveld 1982; see also Degenaar 1983:95). Nevertheless, Slabbert points out that there are some hopeful signs too: "Fundamental aspects of Government policy seem to have come into the debate which, up to now, have never been conceded, [and within the

National Party there is] far more enthusiasm and support for the idea of reform as such" than for the new constitution as a specific manifestation of reform (1983:47).

If the 1983 constitution can be judged to be a step in the right direction, it is, as the *Economist* concludes, "a paltry step" (1983: 18). It is not a sufficient response to the urgent need for democratization along consociational lines.

NEW REPUBLIC PARTY PROPOSALS

The NRP and PFP are white opposition parties that are mainly supported by English-speakers and are both to the left of the National Party on constitutional policy. Although the NRP is the smaller of the two, its program will be discussed first because it has a close affinity with National Party thinking.* The NRP gave its qualified support to the 1983 constitution; as one of its main reasons it cited the constitution's acceptance of "the philosophy for which we stand, namely of group control over intimate group affairs and of joint responsibility and decision-making in matters of joint concern" (South Africa 1983a: col. 7113). But Raw also described the constitution as merely "a starting point for reform in South Africa" (col. 7110), and he indicated that his party's approval was far from whole-hearted: "We shall not vote against the Bill" (col. 7115).

The NRP program can be seen as an elaboration and improvement of the 1983 constitution (New Republic Party 1980; Boulle 1984:111-12; Geldenhuys 1981:205-7; Hill 1983:162-64; Mabude 1983:565-67; Sutton 1978; A.J. Venter 1981:135-39). The party favors a corporate, non-territorial federation on the basis of four population groups: non-homeland Africans, whites, Coloureds, and Asians; the homelands and the Africans living in the homelands will not become part of the federation but may join it via a confederal arrangement.

The four constituent units of the federal state will each have a group parliament and a group executive, as well as local and intermediate governments with responsibility for each group's internal affairs. At the federal level there will be an indirectly elected

---

*The NRP program is also reminiscent of the "race federation" concept of the defunct United Party (Jacobs 1971:52-61), of which the NRP is ideologically the most direct successor.

bicameral parliament: "As commonly accepted in general federal practice, the Lower House must represent the public and the Upper House the constituent parts of the federation" (New Republic Party 1980:4). The lower house will be elected by the group parliaments, presumably in proportion to the sizes of the four population groups, although the NRP states that the exact numbers "shall be agreed upon after negotiation" (ibid.). In each group's delegation to the lower house the political parties will be represented proportionally on the basis of the votes cast in the election to the group parliament. In the upper house the four groups will have equal numbers of representatives, appointed by each of the four group executives. The federal executive will be a Swiss-style collegial body elected in a joint session of the two houses by means of PR "to ensure that each of the four groups can choose at least one of the members" (p. 5). As in Switzerland, the chairmanship of the federal executive will rotate annually, and the chair will act as ceremonial head of state.

These proposals resemble the main features of the 1983 constitution, but where they differ, the NRP plan represents a distinct improvement in every instance. In the parliamentary debate on the 1983 constitution, Raw criticized the government's complete exclusion of the African population and stated that "We believe that there can be no final solution to South Africa's constitutional development without an agreed accommodation for the Black people" (South Africa 1983a: col. 7111). Another NRP spokesman, William M. Sutton, had already reacted to the original version of the National Party plan in a similar vein: "The one element vital for success is omitted. The only guarantee of success is the satisfaction of Black aspirations, something which the rigid orthodoxy of N.P. thinking cannot conceive of outside the homeland set-up" (1977). However, the NRP plan is itself only a halfway solution because it includes only the Africans outside the homelands. For the homeland Africans the NRP solution is identical with that of the National Party: homeland partition.

The NRP's constitutional policy suffers at least partly from one other weakness that also afflicts the 1983 constitution: it is based on the official fourfold racial classification. The NRP wants to make group affiliation voluntary instead of compulsory, but this would not solve the problem that the four groups do not coincide with the segments of the South African plural society.

The NRP proposals do not provide for a minority veto. Two groups acting together can stop legislation in the federal upper house

because they will control half of its seats. Thus, for instance, the two
smallest minority groups, Coloureds and Asians, have a joint veto—
unlike in the 1983 constitution—but they do not each have a veto.
And the ethnic segments within the African and white groups obviously do not have minority veto power either.

For the rest, however, the NRP proposals are free from the
defects for which I have criticized the 1983 constitution. The NRP
does not try to preserve white domination or the predominance of
one particular party. In the federal parliament the National Party
could never have more than one fourth of the upper house seats and
probably not more than one fifth or one sixth of the seats in the
lower house. Instead of a presidential executive, the NRP recommends an optimally consociational collegial power-sharing executive
with a rotating chair. In contrast with the National Party's unilateral
approach, it argues that "all population groups should be involved in
the drafting of a new constitutional framework by means of mutual
consultation and negotiation" (New Republic Party 1980:ii). The
NRP does not try to fix ratios of representation on an inflexible basis,
with the exception of the equal representation of all four groups in
the federal upper house—which is of course perfectly proper from a
consociational point of view and represents the principle of minority
overrepresentation. Otherwise PR is used consistently and exten-
sively.

On account of the defects noted and in spite of its many good
points, the NRP constitutional plan does not qualify as a consociational design. However, representation and participation for the
homeland Africans as well as a minority veto provision could be
added easily to the NRP proposals without requiring their complete
overhaul, so they come close to being semi-consociational.

PROGRESSIVE FEDERAL PARTY PROPOSALS

In November 1978 the federal congress of the PFP approved
constitutional proposals which were a radical innovation compared
with the political reform plans of the two parties from which the
PFP traces its descent: the Progressive Party and the United Party
(especially the latter's more liberal wing). The PFP abandoned both
the Progressive Party's idea of a qualified but gradually expanding
franchise in the existing Westminster-style regime and the United
Party's proposal of a race federation. Instead it advocates a thoroughly

consociational system based on the assumption that South Africa is a plural society but that its segments cannot be predetermined. This consociation will be fully democratic with universal suffrage and will cover the entire territory of South Africa.

The PFP's proposals are guidelines and do not constitute a detailed constitutional blueprint. Like the NRP but unlike the National Party, the PFP believes that a new constitution should emerge from negotiations among representatives from all significant parties and groups. For this purpose it proposes that a broadly representative national convention or constitutional conference be held: "If a Constitution is to bring about co-operation between groups then groups should co-operate in bringing about the Constitution" (Progressive Federal Party 1978:8). At this constitutional convention, the PFP will advocate a federal and decentralized system of government, a bicameral federal parliament with a proportionally elected lower house and a senate representing the states, a power-sharing federal cabinet, and a strong minority veto (Boulle 1981:248-50, and 1984:109-11; Frankel 1980:483-84; Geldenhuys 1981:219-24; Hanf and Weiland 1980:102-4; Hill 1983:159-61; Seiler 1979:11-12; Slabbert 1985; A. J. Venter 1981:134, 136-39). Let us examine these proposals in greater detail in terms of the four principles of consociational democracy.

The grand coalition principle is incorporated in the PFP's method of selecting the executive. The PFP opts for a basically parliamentary system of government with a cabinet (Federal Executive Council) responsible to the lower house (Federal Assembly). The lower house will be elected by PR, and it will in turn elect the prime minister by majority vote. Then a power-sharing Cabinet will be formed: "The Prime Minister will appoint members to the Executive Council proportional to the strength of the various political parties in the Federal Assembly. In doing so the Prime Minister will have to negotiate with the leaders of the relevant parties" (Progressive Federal Party 1978: 34). Slabbert and Welsh (1979:148) further suggest that all parties with a minimum of 10 or 15 percent of the seats should be entitled to representation in the cabinet.

The PFP approach to power-sharing has two advantages: it is a very simple and straightforward arrangement, and—especially important—it is formulated in terms of proportional participation by political parties instead of predetermined population segments. The second point is crucial because there is so little agreement about what the exact segments of the South African plural society are. The fourfold racial classification is clearly unacceptable to most South Africans. It is much more plausible to think of the ethnic groups as the segments of the plural society, but not everybody agrees with this. Moreover, even if there were sufficient agreement on ethnicity as the main criterion, it would not be easy to identify all of the ethnic segments unequivocally.

An example of the problems in specifying segments is Slabbert and Welsh's (1979:36) argument that the English-speaking whites and the Coloureds are merely residual groups rather than real ethnic groups because neither has developed a sense of ethnic identity. Moreover, the white government's insistence on African ethnic differences in connection with its homelands policy has had the ironic effect of making ethnicity highly suspect among many Africans. As Tutu states, "We Blacks (most of us) execrate ethnicity with all our being" (1984:121). P.W. Botha describes the Africans as "separate peoples, proud peoples, with their own cultures, their own ways of living, own traditions, own ideals. Why must we always try to force a Zulu to become something other than a Zulu?" (quoted in Starcke 1978: p. 59). Of course an equally pertinent question would be, Why should a Zulu be forced to remain a Zulu instead of being allowed to identify with some other group? Instead of the four racial groups or the dozen or so ethnic groups, Adam argues that three "cultural heritage groups" may emerge once free affiliation and group competition are allowed (1983a:141): (1) An African heritage stream, consisting mainly of Africans but also joined by some Coloureds and even some whites, with probably some subdivisions along linguistic lines; (2) An Afrikaans heritage group, consisting of the Afrikaners and many Afrikaans-speaking Coloureds; and (3) An English heritage line, composed of the white English-speakers, most Indians, and some Coloureds and Africans.

These conflicting viewpoints do not pose a problem for consociational engineering because it is not necessary to predetermine the segments. One of the tests of whether a society is genuinely plural is whether or not its political parties are organized along segmental lines (Lijphart 1981a:356). We can turn this logic around: if we know that a society is plural but cannot identify the segments with complete confidence, we can take our cue from the political parties that form under conditions of free association and competition. PR is the optimal electoral system for allowing the segments to manifest themselves in the form of political parties (Luyt 1978:23). The beauty of PR is not just that it yields proportional results and permits

minority representation—two important advantages from a consociational perspective—but also that *it permits the segments to define
themselves.* Hence the adoption of PR obviates the need for any
prior sorting of divergent claims about the segmental composition of
a plural society. The proof of segmental identity is electoral success.

While the PFP's proposal for executive power-sharing and proportional participation in the cabinet is generally satisfactory, there
is room for two minor improvements. One concerns the preeminent
position of the prime minister. Because the prime minister is the only
member of the cabinet to be elected by parliament and because he or
she appoints the other ministers, the prime ministership has some of
the same disadvantages as the office of an elected president in a
presidential system, albeit not to the same degree. The cabinet is still
a collegial but not a coequal power-sharing body. A multimember
executive elected in its entirety by parliament by means of PR and
with a rotating chairmanship—as proposed by the NRP—comes closer
to the consociational ideal (Benyon 1978:7).

Second, the minimum level of 10 or 15 percent of the seats that
will qualify a party for participation in the cabinet appears to be a
relatively low percentage; however, if the parties are organized along
ethnic lines, only a few of them will be able to meet this requirement,
given South Africa's large number of ethnic groups. Only the Zulus
and Xhosas, each numbering close to 20 percent of the total population, exceed the 15 percent level. At the 10 percent level only one
other ethnic group, the Afrikaners, barely qualifies. The advantage of
a 10 or 15 percent minimum cited by Slabbert and Welsh is that it
would help "those parties that sought to build as wide . . . an electoral base as possible" (1979:148). This argument conflicts with the
spirit of PR, which is a permissive electoral system. It allows ethnic,
interethnic, and interracial parties equally without favoring any one
particular type. The logic of trying to constrain the party system in
the direction of only a few large parties points to the abandonment
of PR and the adoption of a majoritarian electoral system—which is
of course completely contrary to the consociational idea. Hence it is
preferable to have a considerably lower minimum than 10 or 15
percent or not to set any formal minimum level at all. Because for
practical reasons the cabinet will probably not be larger than about
twenty members, no party with less than 4 or 5 percent of the parliamentary seats can realistically expect to enter the cabinet anyway.

The segmental autonomy proposed by the PFP takes the form
of territorial federalism supplemented by corporate federalism. The

PFP favors a high degree of decentralization of powers and functions to "strong self-governing states," each of which will have an equal representation in the federal senate (Progressive Federal Party 1978: 26). The party's constitutional proposal does not include a specification of these states or their boundaries but asserts that this decision should be made by the national convention on the advice of an impartial commission. This commission should use criteria like economic viability, administrative effectiveness, and homogeneity, and in general it should try to form states that are "smaller rather than larger" (pp. 34-35).

These guidelines appear to imply merely that the number of states should be greater than the current four provinces, but the exact number likely to be recommended by an impartial commission can actually be predicted with considerable accuracy. Maasdorp (1980: 133-42) has drawn two detailed maps, one based on a regional economic planning approach and the other on the basis of drastically consolidated homelands. These two approaches yield very similar results: ten and twelve states respectively, with largely coinciding boundaries. There is one major difference: the northern part of the Transvaal becomes one state in the former plan but is divided into three states in the latter. Slabbert and Welsh mention "perhaps ten" states that could be formed as "reasonably coherent entities" (1979: 140). Among the authors who have given some thought to this question, there is a remarkable degree of consensus about a delimitation of the kind suggested by Maasdorp, although a few of them suggest that the large cities could become separate city-states, raising the total number of states slightly (Buthelezi 1978:52-58; Marquard 1971:71; Ngubane 1963:225; Parsons 1978: 465-66; Ranchod 1978a:379, and 1978b:49; Thula 1980a:165).

Because of the ethnic diversity and geographical intermixture of South Africa's population, these ten or twelve states would not be ethnically homogeneous. However, most of the population groups except the whites have certain areas of geographical concentration, and the ten or twelve states would therefore be less heterogeneous than the country as a whole. The major exception would be the state encompassing the extremely multi-ethnic industrial area in and around Johannesburg. Thus although the ethnic differences in each of the states would be less complicated and more manageable, each state would still be a plural society. Hence it will be necessary that at the state level too the consociational principles of executive power-sharing, veto, and proportionality be applied. The PFP recognizes this and recommends that the states "be entitled to decide on their own form of government," but that they must adhere to the principles of consensus and proportional representation (Progressive Federal Party 1978:35).

Because territorial federalism can make only a limited contribution to segmental autonomy, the PFP also proposes a system of corporate federalism: "A cultural group may establish a Cultural Council to assist in maintaining and promoting its cultural interests and apply to have that Council registered with the Federal Constitutional Court" (Progressive Federal Party 1978:34). These cultural councils will be publicly recognized bodies almost on a par with the states of the federation. In the federal senate, where the states will be represented by equal numbers of senators, each cultural council will also be able to name one senator.

Presumably Afrikaans, Zulu, and other cultural councils will be established, and one of their main responsibilities will be the administration of schools for those who wish to receive an education according to a group's linguistic and cultural traditions. The voluntary self-segregation that such schools may entail is acceptable as long as the option of multicultural and multi-ethnic education is also made available and provided that all schools are treated equally. For instance, Gibson Thula, a member of Inkatha's central committee, argues in favor of eliminating all vestiges of discrimination in education and establishing a common core curriculum, but he acknowledges that different cultures may have different ways of looking at events; consequently different groups must "enjoy the right to be schooled in terms of their own approach to culture" (1980b:42-43). This right must be recognized by the state, and it must even be "enshrined and protected in the constitution" (p. 43; see also Hanf 1980 and 1984).

There may be a danger in the PFP's recommendation that cultural councils be officially registered by the Federal Constitutional Court. It will undoubtedly be necessary to test applicants for cultural council status in order to make sure that they are bona fide cultural groups and that they are not too small, especially because the cultural councils will have a guaranteed representation in the senate. It is imperative, however, that the system of registration be permissive rather than restrictive. The cultural councils are an excellent method of providing segmental autonomy without having to predetermine the segments. Like PR, they allow the segments to define themselves, and, again as with PR, this process of self-definition can work best if it is as free as possible from unnecessary restrictions and constraints.

The proportionality principle is in evidence throughout the PFP constitutional proposals: for the election of the legislature and the selection of the executive, and at both the federal and state levels— although the proposals are silent on proportionality with regard to public service appointments and the allocation of public funds. However, Slabbert and Welsh discuss the need for a redistribution of income and resources and for desegregating the civil service, police, and armed forces, and they argue that proportionality is the most equitable principle: "As far as possible members of each politically salient group should be employed at each level proportionately to the size of the group in relation to the others" (1979:160).

The PFP proposes three types of minority veto. The most important is a veto in the lower house of the federal parliament: "Except in the case of money bills, matters of administrative detail and the election of a Prime Minister, all decisions of the Federal Assembly will be based on consensus, i.e. a minority veto of 10% to 15% will apply" (Progressive Federal Party 1978:33). Second, "no legislation affecting the interests of a particular State or cultural group represented in the Senate may be passed by the Senate unless it has first been referred to and approved by the State Legislature or Cultural Council concerned" (p. 34). Third, constitutional amendments will require the support of both federal chambers, presumably subject to the 10 to 15 percent veto in the lower house, and the legislatures of two thirds of the states (p. 38). The two-thirds majority for constitutional amendments is a normal provision in democratic constitutions, but the other two types of veto are both strong and unusual. In particular, the 10 to 15 percent minority veto in the Federal Assembly has occasioned unfavorable reactions.

A minority veto in the range of 10 to 15 percent does seem very strong. It means that an extraordinary majority of 85 or 90 percent is needed to pass legislation. But it must be emphasized that money bills and prime ministerial elections are exempted from the veto, so the veto cannot be used to prevent the formation of a government or to disrupt its day-to-day operation.* Moreover, for South Africa a 10 to 15 percent veto may be considered too high instead of too low

*It is worth pointing out, however, that a minority veto even on financial legislation does not necessarily present big problems. For instance, in California (where I live) the state budget has to be passed by two-thirds majorities in both houses of the state legislature. The minority veto of about 34 percent has occasionally caused delays and temporary deadlocks but never a permanent paralysis or a breakdown of the government.

because (as noted) only three minorities exceed the 10 percent level. The others would have to form an inter-ethnic coalition in order to avail themselves of the veto. Also, as Slabbert and Welsh point out, while a minority veto may be abused "as a permanent blocking device or as a means of creating deadlocks," its main and normal purpose is "to force negotiation and consensus between parties. . . . Horse-trading, give-and-take, bargaining and tradeoffs are common features of all democratic governments, and it is often the threat of deadlocks or vetos that induces a consensus" (1979:152). An abuse of the veto is discouraged too by the knowledge that it may be a weapon not only for but also against a minority, and that permanent deadlock and the resulting breakdown of a government is not in anybody's interest.

These arguments do not mean that the PFP's veto proposals are necessarily optimal and not susceptible to improvement. For instance, it may be worth considering a suspensive instead of an absolute veto on certain issues. It may also be advisable to institute variable veto percentages for different types of questions. Since only three ethnic minorities reach the 10 percent level, a veto on specifically cultural and linguistic matters could be reduced to, say, 5 percent; on all other questions it might be raised to 20 or 25 percent. But these are details that can be refined in further negotiations. Some form of minority veto is clearly necessary, and the PFP's proposal is by no means unreasonable. Tutu's argument that the PFP veto provision should not be made into the critical element for judging the PFP proposals as a whole is clearly right. He expresses his reservation about the minority veto but concludes the following: "I don't want to split hairs, because on the whole I find these proposals largely acceptable" (1984:122).

Hanf and Weiland call the PFP constitutional proposals "a text-book case of consociational democracy" (1980:102). I concur with this overall judgment. Although I believe that the proposals can be strengthened in some respects—such as by introducing a more co-equal collegial executive, easier access to the power-sharing executive for small ethnic parties, and a variable minority veto—they are without any doubt fully consociational.

CISKEI COMMISSION PROPOSALS

The constitutional reform plans discussed thus far are comprehensive designs that cover the entire country and are meant as long-term, if not permanent, solutions. We must now examine three more limited proposals which also have significant consociational features: a report by the Ciskei Commission (1980)—officially known as the Quail Report—and reports on KwaZulu-Natal by Lombard et al. (1980) and the Buthelezi Commission (1982). These proposals are limited in the sense that they concern only certain areas within South Africa and are designed as interim or temporary measures pending an overall settlement of the South African problem.

In spite of their geographically and temporally limited scope, these plans are important for three reasons. First, by combining closely connected homeland and non-homeland areas into a single autonomous region under democratic multiracial government, they offer a constructive and evolutionary way out of the conundrum of homeland partition. Second, the reforms are potentially applicable to the country as a whole. For instance, after the publication of the 1982 reports of the Buthelezi Commission and the Constitutional Committee of the President's Council—both at least ostensibly based on consociational premises—Slabbert suggested that a joint meeting of the two bodies could be fruitful (see Oppenheimer 1982:4). Third, probably the most important aspect of these proposals is that they can be seen as complementary to the kind of federal design envisaged by the PFP. In a consociational-federal system, both the federal and state governments have to be ruled by consociational methods. KwaZulu-Natal and a geographically expanded Ciskei would be obvious candidates for statehood in such a federation. On the federal maps proposed by Maasdorp (1980:133-42), one state coincides closely with KwaZulu-Natal and another roughly combines the Ciskei with the Transkei and the non-homeland area between them. Therefore, these reports provide suggestions on how the states can be governed consociationally within an overall federal and consociational system.

The eight-member Ciskei Commission was created to advise the government of the Ciskei homeland on whether to become the fourth nominally independent homeland after the Transkei, Bophuthatswana, and Venda. The commission recommended strongly against independence (which the Ciskei government, supported by a referendum, proceeded to accept anyway). As the best alternative to independence, the commission proposed a "multiracial condominium" in an autonomous region within South Africa for an experimental period of about ten years (Ciskei Commission 1980:123-25; see also Boulle 1984:134-36; Geldenhuys 1981:208-10; Hill 1983:15-18). The condominium would include the Ciskei homeland, the non-homeland areas already earmarked for incorporation in it, the non-homeland corridor between the Ciskei and the Transkei, and the city of East London. The government of the condominium appears to be consociational, although the commission itself does not use this term, stating only that an essential element of its proposed constitution would be that "power should be effectively shared between the blacks and whites in a manner acceptable to both of them" (Ciskei Commission 1980:124).*

As an illustration of how an acceptable power-sharing system could be arranged, the commission suggests the establishment of a bicameral legislature with "one black and one white house of equal size, one or the other including representation of the coloured community" (Ciskei Commission 1980:124); virtually no Asians live in the area. The passage of legislation would require "a two-thirds majority in both houses, thus necessitating cooperation between them. By this means neither blacks nor whites could be dominated or swamped by the other community" (ibid.). The premier and a cabinet chosen by him would be responsible to both legislative houses.† Hence the cabinet would have to be a power-sharing executive including both Africans and whites and perhaps one or more Coloureds as well.

In addition to the power-sharing cabinet, the plan's consociational features include a veto for the white minority and, instead of proportionality, equal representation for the African majority and the white minority by means of the two houses with equal sizes and

---

*In a different section of the report the commission discusses the possibility of a consociational government for South Africa as a whole (Ciskei Commission 1980:110-11).

†A cabinet responsible to two houses in a parliamentary system requires majority support in each house. However, the Ciskei Commission states that in practice a majority in one house and merely "a good deal of support in the other" would be needed (1980:124), without explaining this anomaly. The franchise proposed by the commission "could be universal or with a property or educational qualification" (ibid.). The latter option would make the proposal non-democratic as defined in Chapter 2.

powers. The commission calls its proposal a "sketch" rather than a "blueprint," and it does not make any provision for segmental autonomy. However, it would not be difficult to add such a feature: the two houses could be made jointly responsible for general legislation but separately responsible for each group's internal affairs—following the example of the 1983 constitution and the proposals of the NRP.

A major drawback of the Ciskei plan is that it relies on the official racial categories. This problem is alleviated to some extent by the fact that the proposed system of elections requires the racial classification of the legislative candidates but not of the voters. All voters can be registered on a common roll, and each voter will have "two votes to be cast for one black and one white candidate in each constituency" (Ciskei Commission 1980:124). This appears to be a clever solution, but it is in fact a most unsatisfactory one. It violates the basic principle of representation: being the representative of a certain group does not mean merely belonging to that group, but being chosen by the group. Such representation is especially vital in a consociational democracy, where segments' leaders have to negotiate with each other in order to reach mutually acceptable compromises. The Ciskei Commission's method makes it possible for the African (mainly Xhosa) majority to elect majorities—and probably even two-thirds majorities—in both houses, although their representatives in one house will be white. On account of this serious flaw, the commission's suggestions must be rejected as fundamentally unconsociational.

LOMBARD COMMISSION PROPOSALS FOR KWAZULU-NATAL

The two proposals for the province of Natal and the homeland of KwaZulu—consisting of a patchwork of noncontiguous pieces of land within the province—grew out of a realization that their high degree of economic and territorial interdependence made complete independence for KwaZulu a most undesirable option and that in fact a change in the opposite direction was clearly preferable: KwaZulu and Natal should be politically and administratively integrated. The Lombard Commission was a small group appointed by the South African Sugar Association and the Durban Chamber of Commerce, and it consisted entirely of social scientists. The Buthelezi Commission was a broadly representative forty-four member body consisting of political party and interest group representatives, as well as academic experts, appointed by the KwaZulu legislature; only the National Party and the ANC declined to participate.

The Lombard Commission avoids detailed institutional proposals because it argues that a constitution for an autonomous, unified Natal-KwaZulu "can emerge only from consultation and negotiation among the political powers involved" (Lombard et al. 1980:48). Therefore it restricts itself to a "brief, tentative and incomplete" presentation of "some possible political configurations which might be considered by the responsible political powers" in KwaZulu and Natal (*ibid.*; see also Boulle 1984:136-37; Geldenhuys 1981:210-12; Hill 1983:170-74; N.J.J. Olivier 1981:69-73; Riekert 1981:41-51; Schlemmer 1981:206-11; Vorster 1981:166-81).

The commission suggests that the "key building blocks" for the new constitution could be the three geopolitical areas of KwaZulu, the white-owned rural area along the main transport corridors in Natal, and the Durban metropolitan area. There could be three levels of government: local, sub-provincial governments serving each of the three geopolitical areas, and a KwaZulu-Natal regional government. At the regional level there could be a KwaZulu-Natal legislature elected by the three sub-provincial authorities: "The principle governing the distribution of the seats would have to be further investigated and negotiated" (Lombard et al. 1980:49-50), but initially the legislature might consist of equal numbers of representatives of the three sub-provincial areas. The regional executive could be "elected by popular vote throughout the region" (p. 50)—presumably like a president in a presidential system of government—or it could be a council of about four members elected by the regional legislature.

An advantage of the Lombard plan over the Ciskei Commission proposals is that it is not based on any racial or ethnic classification. In fact it emphasizes that "in view of the fact that people have become extremely sensitive about any exercise in population classification, [the delineation of the three sub-provincial areas] does not in any way refer to individuals. . . . No statutory barriers should be imposed upon *individuals* that wish to and are able to migrate" from one area to another (Lombard et al. 1980:49).

Boulle (1984:148) reports that the South African government rejected the Lombard plan because it envisaged power-sharing between whites and Africans. However, although the plan appears to have several consociational implications, it is far from explicitly consociational. No power-sharing executive is specified, and the proposed small executive council of only four members cannot easily be a grand coalition since the population of KwaZulu-Natal is overwhelmingly Zulu, and Asians and whites are minorities of only about 11 and 10 percent respectively. A popularly elected regional president is even less desirable from a consociational point of view. Segmental autonomy is provided in the sub-provincial KwaZulu and rural corridor areas for Zulus and whites respectively, but it requires the preservation of the labyrinthine boundaries between the two areas. PR is not specified as the electoral method, although it would be especially important in the ethnically heterogeneous Durban area. No minority veto is suggested for the regional legislature, and the four-member regional executive is explicitly permitted to "operate on the basis of majority voting" (Lombard et al. 1980:50).

These proposals can be made more consociational by relatively minor adjustments, such as increasing the size of the regional executive council and filling in some of the gaps—for instance, specifying PR for all direct and indirect elections. As it stands, however, the Lombard plan can at most be regarded as semi-consociational.

BUTHELEZI COMMISSION PROPOSALS FOR KWAZULU-NATAL

In contrast with the above two proposals, the report of the Buthelezi Commission is not only much more specific and detailed, but also much more consociational. The report reviews the entire range of institutional alternatives, and it finds "great merit" in the following characteristic of consociational democracy:

It acknowledges the right of every group to be involved in the governmental process, and it allows the introduction of a universal franchise while still ensuring minority groups not only that their rights will be protected as they might be in any other constitutional system, but that they will be represented in the executive of government (Buthelezi Commission 1982, 1:111-12; see also Boulle 1984:137-39; Hill 1983: 203-5; Kriek 1982; Schreiner 1982; Sklar 1982:11-12; Southall 1983).

The Buthelezi Commission's commitment to a democratic universal franchise includes the premise that all elections will be free and competitive. Southall's accusation that "radical political parties or groups would be excluded from the ballot" (1983:97) is therefore completely unfounded.

In accordance with this consociational philosophy, the Buthelezi Commission recommends a proportionally elected unicameral legislature, which in turn elects the chief minister. The chief minister then chooses a "consociational executive" (Buthelezi Commission 1982, 1:114) from among the members of the legislature "in such a way as to give proportional representation to cultural, regional and political groups" (vol. 2:131). This power-sharing arrangement is complemented by segmental autonomy on a non-territorial basis: there will be a bill of cultural group rights with regard to language, religion, and education, and responsibility for these functions will be delegated to "private associations, supported by public funds on a proportional basis" (ibid.).

The electoral system for the KwaZulu-Natal legislature will be PR in relatively large districts. Moreover, a special provision could be made for very small parties which might not be able to win seats in the PR districts; such a "minimum group representation" could give one or more seats to a group "if it received, say, more than one percent of the total votes cast in the region as a whole" (Buthelezi Commission 1982, 1:114). Contrary to Southall's (1983:98) charge that there is a "deliberate" omission of any reference to proportionality in the composition of the bureaucracy, the commission states explicitly that the principle of proportionality should apply not only to the legislature and to the executive but also to the civil service: "Civil service training colleges [should be established] in order to make the civil service more representative within a reasonable period of time" (Buthelezi Commission 1982, 2:131). Also, two types of minority veto are proposed: an absolute veto on matters concerning linguistic, religious, and educational group rights, and a suspensive veto on other, less fundamental issues. The latter would be available to minorities of a specified minimum size in the legislature; the commission's political and constitutional subcommittee suggests a minimum of 5-10 percent, and the full commission's final report specifies "a minimum support of, say, ten percent" (vol. 1:114).

Like the Lombard Commission but unlike the Ciskei Commission, the Buthelezi Commission eschews any predetermined racial classification. It relies on PR to allow the segments to manifest themselves and to participate in the legislature and the executive. In order to establish this non-racially defined consociational government, however, the existing racially based institutions have to be used. The commission therefore recommends a transitional consociational executive which "for historic reasons only" should consist of equal representations of the white Natal provincial executive and the black KwaZulu government, as well as a few Asian and Coloured representatives. Southall's allegation that the executive will be "racially structured for an unspecified period of time" (1983:99) is incorrect: three intermediate stages of a maximum of one year each are proposed, and the total transitional period would therefore not last longer than three years (Buthelezi Commission 1982, 1:113, and 2:132).

There are many obvious parallels between the recommendations of the Buthelezi Commission for KwaZulu-Natal and the proposals of the PFP for a federal South Africa—including the election of the prime minister by the legislature and the appointment of the other ministers by the prime minister. Above I criticized this method of composing a power-sharing executive because it gives undue prominence to the representative of one segment. However, this is much less of a problem at the state than at the federal level. For South Africa as a whole, with its many minority segments, a coequal cabinet with a rotating chairmanship is the most suitable consociational executive. In contrast, in most of the dozen or so states in the proposed South African federation, one ethnic group has a numerical preponderance which is appropriately expressed by means of a chief executive who is more than just *primus inter pares*. In KwaZulu-Natal, for instance, there will normally be a Zulu premier. In states with two or three large and approximately equal population segments, an informal arrangement may be worked out to take turns in the premiership.

Boulle writes that the proposals of the Buthelezi Commission "show the pervasive influence of consociational thinking" (1984: 138). Kriek's critical review of the commission's report notes "a high degree of bias in favor of consociational democracy among the members of the commission" (1982:98). Both are right at least in the sense that the Buthelezi Commission's political and constitutional recommendations are unexceptionally consociational. Hence they can serve as a model for state government in a consociational-federal South Africa—not only for the state of KwaZulu-Natal but also, with the necessary adaptations, for the other states in the federation.

OPTIMAL CONSOCIATIONAL GUIDELINES FOR SOUTH AFRICA

From my critical comments on the seven consociational, semi-consociational, and quasi-consociational proposals for political reform in this chapter, several general conclusions about the optimal form of a South African consociational constitution can be distilled:

1. The segments should be allowed to emerge spontaneously by means of PR elections and corporate federalism instead of being predetermined—thus avoiding the entire controversial and vexatious issue of whether the segments should be defined in racial, ethnic, cultural, or some other terms. This guideline presupposes complete freedom of association, individual freedom of affiliation, and free competition among groups and parties.

2. Proportional representation should be used for legislative elections at all levels—federal, state, and local.

3. The executives at all levels should be proportionally constituted—elected or appointed—collegial bodies. At the federal level proportional election by the legislature and a rotating chairmanship appear to be optimal.

4. Proportionality should be the normative target for appointments to the civil service (including the police, the armed forces, and the judiciary).

5. Group autonomy should be introduced by means of a combination of territorial and corporate federalism.

6. The state boundaries in the territorial federation should be drawn in such a way as to yield economically viable and administratively effective states with relatively homogeneous populations. Because complete homogeneity cannot be attained, the states should also have consociational constitutions.

7. Corporate federalism should be the principal method for organizing cultural and educational autonomy. It can take the institutional form of private associations that are publicly funded on a proportional basis or of formal, publicly recognized "cultural councils."

8. A minority veto should be available to even relatively small groups, and it should consist of an absolute veto on the most fundamental issues, such as cultural autonomy, and a suspensive veto on non-fundamental questions.

I should like to state as emphatically as possible that I regard the above eight guidelines as *optimal—not as the only feasible ones*. For instance, as far as the first guideline is concerned, it is not impossible that a constitutional convention would agree on an explicit definition of segments and elections by means of separate segmental voting registers; if such an agreement can be reached, there is no reason to expect that it would not work well. Somewhat more likely, perhaps, is an agreement to permit one or a few groups to officially designate themselves as separate segments, to be registered on separate voters' rolls, to have a specified number of representatives in parliament, to run their own schools, and so on, while all other citizens participate together in free PR elections and can form associations for cultural autonomy as needed without any predetermination of these other segments.

For all of the reasons discussed at length in this chapter, however, it will be much less difficult for a national convention in South Africa to reach agreement on a constitution that follows these eight guidelines. These can obviously be satisfied by a variety of specific rules and institutions. A constitution based on these guidelines is also likely to operate with the greatest flexibility and effectiveness. Hence such a constitution offers the best chance for democracy and peace in South Africa.

Chapter 4

CONSOCIATIONAL THEORY AND ITS CRITICS

My recommendation of a consociational form of government for South Africa is based on the argument that it is by far the best solution for the problems of this country (as discussed in Chapters 2 and 3) and on two further firm convictions: (1) The theory of consociational democracy is a basically valid empirical theory; and (2) South Africa satisfies the criteria for its application as a normative theory. I shall treat the second point in Chapter 5. In this chapter I shall discuss the host of criticisms raised against consociational theory in the very extensive literature that has developed on consociationalism since its initial formulation in the late 1960s.

Most of the critiques of consociational theory can be shown to be based on faulty arguments or interpretations, and none of them can do any damage to consociationalism as a normative model. This does not mean that the critics have not performed a valuable service. On the contrary, their critical analyses have resulted in the strengthening of numerous details and nuances in the theory. Even those that are completely wrong have constituted a challenge to restate and elaborate the theory in a clearer and more explicit way in order to minimize misunderstandings. I should add that a few ambiguous and exaggerated statements in my own earlier writings have been responsible for some of the erroneous objections to consociational theory. This chapter gives me the opportunity to correct these shortcomings. For reasons of space—and in order not to strain the reader's patience—it will be impossible to do justice to each and every critical remark that has ever been uttered with regard to consociational theory. I shall therefore focus on the most important and the potentially most damaging criticisms.

Because this chapter will be a dialogue with my critics, it may give the impression that the consociational literature consists largely of negative commentaries. This is certainly not the case. It is worth emphasizing that a large number of scholars have constructively used consociationalism as an analytical tool or as a normative model in their studies not only of the clearest examples of consociational democracy—Austria, Belgium, Cyprus, Lebanon, Malaysia, the Netherlands, and Switzerland*—but also of more than twenty other countries in various parts of the world: Canada, Chile, Colombia, Fiji, Gabon, Gambia, Guyana, Indonesia, Israel, Italy, Ivory Coast, Kenya, Liechtenstein, Nigeria, Portugal, the Soviet Union, Spain, Sri Lanka, Sudan, Suriname, Tanzania, Uruguay, Venezuela, and Yugoslavia.[†] In addition, the consociational model has been applied to the supranational European Community (Lindberg 1974) and to the subnational political systems of Manitoba (Staples 1974), New Brunswick (Aunger 1981), and Northern Ireland (Aunger 1981; Birrell 1981; Schmitt 1977).

I shall organize my discussion in terms of the major propositions of consociational theory and six categories of criticism. A schematic diagram is presented in Figure 4.1. The arrows indicate probable causal relationships. For instance, a consociational democracy under favorable conditions is likely to maintain civil peace and to remain

*The most important analyses of these countries from a consociational perspective are the following: Austria—Bluhm (1973); Lehmbruch (1967, 1974); Powell (1970); K. Steiner (1972); Stiefbold (1974); Belgium—Billiet (1984); Claeys and Loeb-Mayer (1984); Covell (1981); Dierickx (1978, 1984); J. A. Dunn (1972); Frognier (1978); Heisler (1974, 1977); Huyse (1970, 1980, 1981, 1982, 1984); Pijnenburg (1984); Zolberg (1977); Lebanon—Dekmejian (1978); Hudson (1976); Koury (1976); Lehmbruch (1974); Messarra (1977, 1983, 1984); Malyasia—Milne (1981); Milne and Mauzy (1978); von Vorys (1975); the Netherlands—Bank (1984); Daalder (1971, 1974b, 1981); van den Berg and Molleman (1974); van Schendelen (1978); and Switzerland—Daalder (1971); J. A. Dunn (1972); Germann and Steiner (1985); Henderson (1981); Katz (1984); Kerr (1974, 1978); Lehmbruch (1967, 1968, 1974); Lehner (1984); McRae (1983); Schmid (1981); J. Steiner (1974, 1983); J. Steiner and Obler (1977).

[†]See the following: Canada—Cannon (1982); McRae (1974); Noel (1971, 1977a, 1977b); Ormsby (1974); Presthus (1973); Smiley (1977); Chile—van Klaveren (1983, 1984); Colombia—Dix (1980); Hartlyn (1981); Lanning (1974); Fiji—Milne (1975, 1981); Gabon— Doey and Bayart (1983); Gambia—A. Hughes (1982); Guyana—Milne (1981); Indonesia—McVey (1969); Israel—Gitelman and Naveh (1976); Smooha (1978); Italy—Graziano (1980); Ivory Coast—Sylla (1982); Kenya—Berg-Schlosser (1985); Liechtenstein—Batliner (1981); Nigeria— Chinwuba (1980); Portugal— Bruneau (1976); Soviet Union—van den Berghe (1981a); Spain—Gunther and Blough (1981); Gunther, Sani, and Shabad (1985); Huneeus (1981); Sri Lanka—Chehabi (1980); Sudan—Hanf (1979); Sklar (1982); Suriname—Bagley (1973); Dew (1972, 1974, 1975, 1978); Hoppe (1976); Sedoc-Dahlberg (1983); Tanzania—Sylla (1982); Uruguay—Lanning (1974); Venezuela—Levine (1973); and Yugoslavia—Bridge (1977); Cohen (1982); W. Dunn (1975); Goldman (1981a, 1981b, 1982, 1985).

Figure 4.1

SCHEMATIC PRESENTATION OF PRINCIPAL PROPOSITIONS OF CONSOCIATIONAL THEORY
AND SIX CATEGORIES OF CRITICISM (A – F)[a]

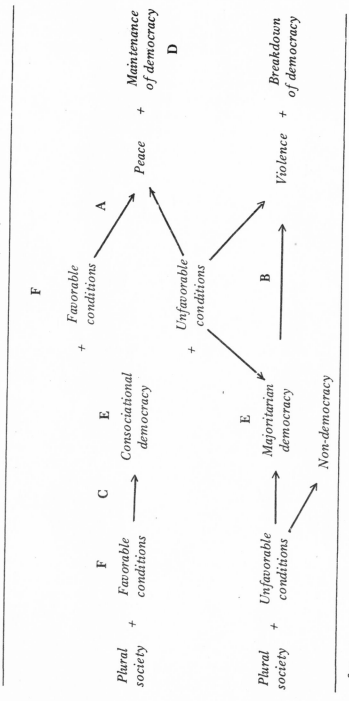

[a]The six categories of criticism are identified in the text on p. 86.

democratic. These favorable conditions will be examined in greater detail later in this chapter and in Chapter 5, but examples include the following situations: all segments are minorities; external threats unify the country; a high degree of socioeconomic equality exists among the segments; and there is a strong tradition of elite accommodation. If conditions are unfavorable, the consociational system may still succeed in maintaining peace and democracy, but it may also have the opposite effects of inter-segmental violence and a collapse of the democratic regime, either directly or after a period of majority rule. A majoritarian democracy in a plural society is likely to result in violence and democratic collapse. From the left-hand side of the figure, we see that under favorable circumstances a plural society is likely to develop into a consociational democracy. If conditions are unfavorable, however, a majoritarian democracy or a non-democratic system are more probable outcomes.

Of the six categories of criticism of consociational theory (A-F in Figure 4.1), the most fundamental criticisms belong to group A; they challenge the proposition that consociational democracy will yield peace and durable democracy. Conversely the criticisms in category B cast doubt on the postulated relationship between majoritarianism on the one hand and violence and democratic collapse on the other. Group C objections generally claim that the causal relationship indicated by the arrow—i.e., that consociational democracy is a response to the problems of pluralism—should be reversed. The critics in category D argue that the democratic system maintained by consociationalism is either not democratic at all or not sufficiently democratic; these charges are as serious as those in category A. Criticism E is that the twofold division into consociational and majoritarian democracy is inadequate and that additional decision modes must be considered. Group F takes issue with the conditions that are favorable or unfavorable to the development and maintenance of consociational democracy.

CONSOCIATIONAL THEORY AND THE SCIENTIFIC METHOD

Before turning to the six categories of substantive criticisms outlined above, let me first deal with one additional criticism—i.e., that consociational theory violates commonly accepted canons of scientific research. The main critic in this respect is van Schendelen (1983, 1984), who argues that my definitions of crucial concepts in consociational theory like democracy and plural society are too vague and not precisely measurable. He complains that my method is "impressionistic" (1984:42, citing J. Steiner 1981a:346). In my writings on consociationalism between 1968 and 1977, I did indeed experiment with different, not wholly satisfactory definitions of democracy, but in Lijphart 1977a and subsequent studies I have used it as a synonym of Dahl's (1971) concept of "polyarchy," which is still the clearest and most widely accepted definition available.

The concept of plural society is just about as difficult to define precisely as the concept of democracy. However, in Lijphart 1981a, I proposed that societal pluralism should be seen as a matter of degree—ranging in principle from 0 percent in a completely homogeneous society to 100 percent in the most extreme case of a plural society—and I suggested four criteria to determine whether a society is completely plural or deviates greatly or mildly from perfect pluralism: (1) Can the segments into which the society is divided be clearly identified? (2) Can the size of each segment be exactly determined? (3) Do the segmental boundaries and the boundaries between the different political, social, and economic organizations coincide? (4) Do the segmental parties receive the stable electoral support of their respective segments? These criteria define the concept of plural society more clearly but of course are not completely precise. The degrees of pluralism are still not exactly measurable, and a judgment of the extent to which a given society satisfies each of the criteria is necessarily "impressionistic"—but unfortunately no better method is available in the current stage of development of the social sciences.*

The basic trouble with van Schendelen's critique is that it takes a much too narrow view of the scientific enterprise. Especially in comparative macro-analysis, precise quantitative measurement is usually very difficult if not impossible to achieve. Researchers who insist on the exact measurement of their variables are likely to get bogged

*In addition to his dissatisfaction with the definitions of democracy and plural society, van Schendelen criticizes the vagueness associated with the terms democratic stability, accommodation, and favorable conditions. Like most other authors who have tried to define the concept of stability, I have had difficulty. The best solution, I have concluded, is to define it in terms of the maintenance of civil peace and a democratic system of government. This definition, which I use in this book, is straightforward and easy to apply, and it captures the essence of democratic stability. I used the term "politics of accommodation" in Lijphart 1968a as a synonym of what I have consistently called consociational democracy in my later writings. I believe that the latter term has been amply defined and that nothing needs to be added to it. I shall try to clarify what I mean by favorable conditions later in this chapter.

down in measurement problems, and hence they may never engage in the more important scientific task of establishing empirical relationships among the variables. It is much better to use a simple, rough, and indeed "impressionistic" twofold or threefold classification of the variables—for instance, a homogeneous versus a plural society, consociational versus majoritarian democracy, and civil peace versus violence—and to relate these variables to each other than to spend all of one's time in a probably futile effort to find exact measurements. Van Schendelen's unrealistically high standards of empirical research would have made the development of consociational theory as well as the formulation of consociationalism as a normative model impossible. Methodological perfectionism is extremely debilitating for political theory and practice.*

Van Schendelen (1984:42) also approvingly cites Lee E. Dutter's criticism that my method is "largely inductive" (Dutter 1978:566). I plead guilty to this charge, but at the same time I have to point out that the inductive approach is by far the most common in political science and the social sciences generally. Only a small minority of political scientists is committed to deductive or axiomatic reasoning. This may well be superior according to ideal scientific standards, but it has not yielded impressive results so far. The crucial question is not whether propositions that specify relationships among variables are arrived at inductively or deductively, but whether they are empirically valid or not. In the remainder of this chapter, I shall try to show—in response to a series of substantive criticisms—that the propositions of consociational theory are perfectly valid.

Parenthetically it is worth mentioning that the most important consociational proposition—linking consociational democracy to inter-segmental peace—has been arrived at deductively in Ronald Rogowski's (1974) axiomatic-rational study, although Rogowski uses slightly different terminology from mine. By deductive reasoning he expects plural societies "which have succeeded at coexistence to have superseded pure majoritarianism with 'neutral' or proportionately weighted procedures for adjudication and legislation" (p. 106). Conversely he expects societies "that have lacked or discarded such devices to have failed at coexistence" (ibid.).

---

*Van Schendelen's narrow conception of the social sciences is also reflected in his curious claim that most of my studies of consociational democracy are not based on "empirical research" (1984:34-35). Comparative research at the macro level apparently fails to satisfy his limited view of what constitutes legitimate empirical research in the social sciences.

CRITIQUE A

The criticisms in category A of Figure 4.1, which challenge the proposition that consociationalism is likely to lead to durable peace and democracy in plural societies, take a variety of forms. The most important type focuses on the seven clearest examples of consociational democracy and argues that one or more of these cases are either not genuinely consociational or not successful in maintaining peace and democracy. Two closely related criticisms are that in cases where both consociationalism and peace and democracy are evident, the relationship is spurious or the direction of causality should be reversed. The remaining criticisms emphasize the problems that consociations are likely to encounter and that allegedly tend to render them unsuccessful.

CAN CONSOCIATIONALISM YIELD CIVIL PEACE AND MAINTAIN DEMOCRACY?

Of the seven prime examples of consociational democracy, there is general agreement that the Cypriot attempt to operate a consociational system in 1960-63 quickly ended in civil war and must therefore be regarded as a failure (Lijphart 1977a:158-61). One consociational failure is obviously sufficient to disprove the hypothesis that consociationalism will necessarily guarantee peace and democracy in a plural society, but I have never made such a claim. My only claim is that consociational democracy has a good chance to succeed in a plural society and certainly a much better chance than majoritarian democracy. The other six cases can be counted as consociations that have maintained peace and democracy for long periods: Austria from 1945 to 1966, Belgium since the end of World War I and (as far as its linguistic-ethnic differences are concerned) especially since 1970, the Netherlands in 1917-67, Switzerland since 1943, Lebanon from 1943 to 1975, and Malaysia since 1955—in spite of a temporary democratic breakdown in 1969.*

---

*Because of a few troubling limitations on the freedom of expression, Malaysia may not qualify as fully democratic (Lijphart 1977a:155), but on the whole it is, in von Vorys's words, a successful "democracy without consensus" (1975:12; see also Milne and Mauzy 1978; Noble 1979). I shall leave out of consideration four additional, less clear-cut examples of consociationalism: the not fully independent Netherlands Antilles since 1950 and Suriname from 1958 to 1973, and

Switzerland and Lebanon have been favorite targets for the attacks of critics who have tried to show that one or more of these cases are either not consociational or not successful in preserving peace and democracy. The claim that Switzerland is not a consociational democracy is a direct challenge to my assertion that Switzerland is as "thoroughly consociational" as Austria and more so than Belgium and the Netherlands, especially with regard to executive power-sharing (Lijphart 1977a:104). How can Brian Barry maintain that the Swiss case "fails to fit" the consociational model "at every point" (1975a: 486)? For one thing, he argues that the seven-member executive Federal Council is not composed of "party oligarchs reaching concordats binding on their followers" (p. 482). It is indeed hard to find any party oligarchs in federal Switzerland because its party system is decentralized. The important point is that the Federal Council is a grand coalition of top representatives of all four major parties and that it is in addition meticulously representative of Switzerland's religious and linguistic segments.

Jürg Steiner and Jeffrey Obler are much more moderate than Barry in their overall judgment. They merely claim that "the Swiss decision-making process includes consociational as well as nonconsociational elements" (1977:328-29), and they argue that one of these non-consociational elements is the fact that "disagreement among Swiss political leaders is not uncommon" and quite visible to the public. But consociationalism does not require that there be no conflicts or that these be kept secret. Disagreements are inevitable in a plural society; the crucial characteristic of consociational decision-making is that conflicts are normally resolved by compromise. This is clearly the case in Switzerland.

Steiner and Obler also assert that the Swiss initiative and referendum procedure "undermines the consociational character of the

the semi-consociational cases of Israel and Canada (Lijphart 1977a: 119-34, 184-212). None of these can be used as evidence *against* consociational theory. Van Schendelen is completely wrong when he states the following: "In 1975 the Dutch Government left to their former colony Surinam a consociation-orientated constitution" (1983:20). This, he implies, led to mass emigration and democratic collapse: "A few years later approximately half the population had left the country and a military coup had taken place" (*ibid.*). In fact, by independence, consociational democracy had been replaced by majority rule, the Dutch government which granted independence to Suriname was hostile to consociationalism, the new constitution was not at all consociational, and both independence and the new constitution were imposed on Suriname against the strong objections of the large East Indian ethnic segment.

decision-making process [because] by its very character, the referendum is an institution that permits a majority to impose its solution on the minority [and because it is] a process of mass and not elite decision-making" (1977:328-29). However, they themselves immediately point out that the use of the referendum can serve as one kind of compromise if no substantive agreement can be found by the parties: "If no solution can be found in the Federal Council or in Parliament, the conflict is often settled through the referendum" (ibid.). Even more important, the initiative and referendum can be used by small minorities to try to upset parliamentary decisions; even if such an effort does not succeed, it forces the majority to pay the cost of a referendum campaign. Hence the initiative and referendum can serve as a minority veto. This potential veto in turn strengthens power-sharing as Lehner has forcefully pointed out: "Any coalition with a predictable and safe chance of winning has to include all parties and organizations that may be capable of calling for a successful referendum" (1984:30). In other words, Swiss direct democracy is an integral part of the consociational system (Mironesco 1982:82; Forsyth 1984:14). This example also reinforces the argument stated in previous chapters that a minority veto is not so much an immobilizing agent as a powerful stimulus for finding broadly acceptable compromises.

In spite of Barry's sweeping claim that Switzerland fails the consociational criteria "at every point," neither he nor other critics question the consociational functions of the division of Switzerland into cantons that are largely homogeneous (especially with regard to language) and of the extensive application of the proportionality principle. In fact, two non-consociational scholars who have taken a critical look at the Swiss case explicitly concede the importance of these consociational features. Harold E. Glass states that federalism and decentralized power have been "an integral part of the Swiss practice of minority accommodation" (1977:39). Christopher J. Hughes, who cautions against drawing general conclusions from the Swiss case, presents one lesson with an obviously wider relevance: proportional representation at both the national and cantonal levels has had "an extraordinary, sedative, effect on political strife" (1978: 303). Glass's overall judgment is that "compromise has been institutionalized in most areas of Swiss politics" (1978:362). Switzerland is clearly both consociational and spectacularly successful in maintaining peace and democracy.

Lebanon is a more difficult case. For more than three decades it was clearly consociational, but the civil war that began in 1975 and a subsequent breakdown of the consociational system *appear* to make it a spectacular consociational failure. However, this interpretation is utterly erroneous. Hanf puts the correct view in a nutshell: "What has happened since 1975 . . . was no breakdown of consociationalism because of internal tensions, but an ordinary international conflict due to the intervention first of the Palestinians, then of the Syrians"—and, of course, more recently of the Israelis. "It was no Lebanese civil war, but an inter-Arab [and Arab-Israeli] conflict on Lebanese territory" (1979). Lebanese diplomat Ghassan Tuéni, a member of the small Greek Orthodox minority, puts it even more strongly:

> Lebanon has been hostage to everybody else's wars and revolu-tions. . . . The major injustice done to the Lebanese—over and above the human, physical and political sacrifices—has been to describe these past wars with clichés such as Muslim-Christian, or Leftist-Rightist confrontations. What we were witnessing, in reality, were external conflicts projected upon internal divisions" (1982: 86; see also Burnham 1980:86; Dekmejian 1978; Harik 1984; Shaw 1978).

This does not mean that Lebanon's consociational democracy was blameless. It had a number of weak spots—especially a fixed 6:5 ratio for parliamentary elections which continued to give the Christian sects the majority of the seats in spite of the fact that the Moslems had gradually become the majority of the population (Lijphart 1977a: 149-50). But making a "clean break" with the consociational system (Ignatius 1983:1141; Hudson 1976) cannot be the answer. An exam-ination of the possible solutions of the Lebanese conflict leads to the irrefutable conclusion that there is simply no realistic alternative to consociationalism. Koury (1976:57-76) analyzes five concrete pro-posals and rejects two of them: majoritarian democracy because it is unsuitable for a divided country like Lebanon, and partition into a Christian and a Moslem state because it is an unnecessarily drastic solution. The remaining plans, which Koury regards as realistic possi-bilities, are variants of consociational democracy. The lesson of the Lebanese case is that its consociationalism needs to be repaired and improved—not replaced.

It is perhaps even more significant that a similar conclusion applies to Cyprus, which (as stated earlier) is admittedly a case of consociational failure. The consociational experiment begun in 1960 never worked well; terminated by the 1963 civil war, it appeared to be permanently doomed by a Turkish invasion in 1974 and the de facto partition of the island into a Greek Cypriot southern state and a Turkish Cypriot northern state. Nevertheless, 1985 proposals by UN Secretary General Javier Pérez de Cuéllar for a unified Cyprus under a single central government were again based on consociational principles. The unified state would be a "federal republic, with broad autonomy for the two ethnic-based communities" (M. Howe 1985). The federal executive would consist of a Greek Cypriot president, a Turkish Cypriot vice-president, and a ten-member cabinet including seven Greek and three Turkish Cypriot ministers. The legislature would be bicameral with "the two ethnic groups equally represented in the senate and a 7-to-3 ratio in favor of the Greek majority in the lower house" (*ibid.*). The rival Cypriot leaders were unable to reach an agreement on these proposals when they met at the United Nations in January 1985, although they were reported to be close to a compromise. Here again the essential conclusion is not that consociationalism is bound to be accepted or to work, but that it is the only solution that has any chance of being agreed upon and of working satisfactorily.*

THE QUESTION OF CAUSALITY

A different criticism of consociational theory admits that the principal supporting cases represent both consociationalism and the maintenance of peace and democracy, but argues that while the two factors may occur together in a plural society, the former may not be

*Van den Berghe lists the following as additional "ghastly" consociational failures: Pakistan-Bangladesh, Sri Lanka, Guyana, Canada, Zaire, and "numerous others"—which remain unnamed (1981a:82, 213). As noted, Canada is only semiconsociational and (so far at least) not a failure. The others may be failures, but they are certainly not consociational. Barry calls the Netherlands and Belgium "indubitably consociational" as well as "plausible supporting cases" for consociational theory (1975a:481, 501), but two critics disagree on the latter point. Dutter (1978) mistakenly cites the weakening of Dutch consociationalism after about 1967 as evidence of consociational failure. The opposite interpretation is correct: fifty years of successful consociational democracy paved the way for a pattern of government in which consociational methods had become much less essential. Kriek's characterization of Belgium as "one of the world's most unstable systems" (1982:99) is obviously a wild exaggeration. Even hypercritical van den Berghe grudgingly concedes that while Belgian consociational democracy "has more than its share of conflict, uneasy compromises, inefficiencies and inanities . . . , the alternatives are worse" (1981a:205; see also Obler, Steiner, and Dierickx 1977:33-40).

the cause of the latter. This argument has been put forward especially for the Swiss and Austrian cases. Steiner and Obler (1977:337) and Barry (1975a:493-95) state that the preservation of peace and democracy in Switzerland and Austria can plausibly be attributed to the high level of post-World War II prosperity. The problem with this assertion is that it is flatly contradicted by the examples of Belgium and Canada, where ethnic-linguistic tensions increased as economic well-being increased. Generally speaking, too, the postwar gains in West European standards of living have been accompanied by an intensification rather than a decline of ethnic conflict (Lijphart 1977b).

A second alternative by which Steiner and Obler explain the Swiss success is that Switzerland's "three major languages have about the same international prestige" (1977:337). The absence of such equality could possibly be a factor in Belgium's tense linguistic situation according to this line of thinking. But the same tension has prevailed in Canada between groups speaking two major world languages. Third, in Switzerland "the load on the central system is not very heavy. Because of the federal structure, many of the tricky problems faced by a subcultural country are dealt with primarily at the cantonal and even local level. Neutrality, too, removes many problems from the central political arena" (Steiner and Obler 1977: 337-38). These arguments are sound, but they do not conflict with consociational theory: autonomy and decentralization on a territorial or nonterritorial basis are integral features of consociations, and neutrality or an inactive foreign policy are generally recognized as favorable factors for consociational democracy.

In the final analysis, Steiner and Obler admit that these "other plausible explanations" do not "exclude consociational decision making as an explanatory factor" (1977:338). This conclusion can be stated much more strongly: since the alternative explanations either do not stand up to comparative scrutiny or do not contradict consociational theory, the only plausible explanation left is that consociational democracy is the cause and the preservation of peace and democracy the effect.

The logical remaining attack on this causal nexus is that the direction should be reversed: peace and democracy are the cause instead of the effect of consociational democracy. Although this is an extremely implausible hypothesis, it appears to have been proposed (in very cautious terms) by G. R. Boynton and W. H. Kwon (1978), and it has been repeated with much greater aplomb by other critics (van Schendelen 1983:19, and 1984:42-43; A. J. Venter 1980b:130-31, and 1983:281-82).

Boynton and Kwon present a three-step argument for their hypothesis. In their logical-deductive analysis, they distinguish among (1) The consociational structure of decision-making; (2) "Accommodation"—defined as the convergence of political viewpoints; and (3) Democratic stability. Their definition of the term "accommodation" poses a problem: in a successful consociation it is not at all necessary—and not even very likely—that policy preferences will converge to a marked degree; what is required is that the segmental representatives be willing to accept compromises, although they may retain their original preferences. On the basis of their terminology, however, Boynton and Kwon argue that consociational democracy does not "*guarantee* accommmodation and the resulting democratic stability" (1978:21; emphasis added). As I have pointed out above, I have never claimed such a guarantee but rather have always expressed this relationship in terms of probabilities.

Boynton and Kwon next argue that stability can in fact be guaranteed if the segmental leaders are "willing to discount their own views" (1978:24-25)—that is, if they are willing to compromise: consociational democracy plus an elite willingness to compromise will yield stability. Although this argument overlooks the problem of non-elite acceptance of elite decisions, it is not a startlingly new hypothesis, and it is close to my own point of view.* The structure of consociational democracy strongly encourages compromise but does not guarantee it. If the segmental representatives absolutely refuse to compromise, the consociation will almost certainly break down. However, the realization of this fact may well be a strong incentive for representatives to be more open to compromise.

Boynton and Kwon's last point—and here we finally get to the apparent claim that the causal nexus should be reversed—is that "a stable political system . . . is a necessary and sufficient condition for accommodation" (1978:21, 25). This claim is based on a definitional trick. A stable system is defined as "one able to solve its problems"; accommodation, as noted, is defined as the convergence of policy preferences—and is *not* synonymous with consociational democracy. Obviously if all problems are solved, there is nothing left to disagree about. The basic problem is that both terms—and particularly the

*It is also similar to Rogowski's (1974:106) logical-deductive hypothesis cited earlier.

concept of stability—are defined too narrowly. I admit that I have used the same definition of stability myself in some of my previous writings, but I have come to the conclusion that it is better to avoid this confusing concept altogether and to define the ultimate dependent variable in the consociational chain of propositions as the maintenance of peace and democracy.

UNNECESSARY EXPLANATIONS

The remaining type A criticisms emphasize the problems that consociational democracies may encounter and that are likely to make them fail. On the whole, the arguments are perfectly reasonable and plausible, but they are contradicted by at least equally plausible counterarguments as well as by the empirical evidence. They are explanations of why consociations are likely to be unsuccessful— something that does not need to be explained because it is not true.

The best-known and most frequently quoted argument of this kind is Barry's (1975a) claim that consociationalism may work in religiously or ideologically but not ethnically divided societies. He argues that "religious and class conflict is a conflict of organizations. Ethnic conflict is a conflict of solidary groups [which] do not need organization to work up a riot or a pogrom so long as they have some way of recognizing who belongs to which group" (pp. 502-3). Moreover, because religious and ideological segments are defined in terms of organizations, their leaders are more likely to control their followers. Barry also claims that religious and ideological issues are more susceptible to consociational solutions than ethnic issues because the question is "how the country is to be run" rather than "whether it should be a country at all" (ibid.).

One counterargument to Barry is that although ethnic segments do not need to be organized in order to be recognized as separate units, they tend to organize themselves just as consistently as other types of segments in plural societies. And segments of any sort are likely to question the unity of a country only if they are geographically concentrated. The principal weakness of Barry's criticism is that it focuses almost exclusively on the question of elite control of the segments and neglects the problem of reaching inter-segmental agreements: religious and ideological differences are likely to be logically and not just emotionallly incompatible, and hence less susceptible to compromise than ethnic differences. Giuseppe Di Palma states that in an ideologically divided society the segmental parties are likely to be "extreme and polarized" and will find it hard to cooperate in government, unlike ethnically based parties, which encounter "no ideological spread likely to interfere with any predisposition . . . to govern together" (1977:224). Hence, Di Palma concludes—in almost exact contrast to Barry—consociational democracy is suited for ethnically plural societies but not for ideologically divided societies. Marxist scholars present similar arguments, as we shall see below.

A final problem with Barry's criticism is that it is often difficult to distinguish between religious and ethnic cleavages. Lebanon's and Northern Ireland's segments are commonly described as religious or sectarian groups, but they can also legitimately be regarded as ethnic communities; Hanna E. Kassis (1985:216) applies the term "religious ethnicity" to the Lebanese case. Even when we leave aside these doubtful cases, it is still clear that "Barry's argument lacks empirical support" (Erkens 1983:33). Successful consociations include both ethnically plural societies—Belgium, Switzerland, and Malaysia—and countries in which the differences are purely religious and ideological— Austria and the Netherlands.

Because ethnically plural societies are more common in the Third World than in Western countries, Barry's erroneous argument can be used to advance the equally mistaken view that consociational democracy is a "Western" model that is foreign and unsuitable to non-Western societies. This view is implied by Sam C. Nolutshungu's statement that the consociational idea is advanced by "a group of Western scholars" (1982:26). Although Lewis did not use the term "consociational" in his 1965 work—I did not revive this old term, originally coined by Althusius, until 1968—his book is undoubtedly the first modern consociational treatise. Lewis is a black West Indian economist, and his 1965 work deals with the countries of West Africa. Another early contributor to the consociational literature was the Nigerian political scientist Claude Ake (1967a, 1967b). The main empirical cases of consociational democracy include Lebanon and Malaysia, non-Western countries in which consociationalism was developed by indigenous political leaders and was not imposed in any way by the West. Moreover, numerous non-Western leaders have emphasized that majority rule violates native traditions of trying to arrive at consensus through lengthy deliberations—traditions that closely fit the consociational idea (Lijphart 1977a:166-68; Smith 1969a). Lewis argues that the consociational form of democratic procedure "is at the heart of the original institutions" of the peoples of West Africa (1965:167).

As one of their two major attacks on consociational theory, Marxist scholars have made an argument very similar to Di Palma's assessment that consociational democracy is not suited for ideologically divided societies. (The second of these attacks will be discussed as a type C criticism below.) Consociational democracy may be able to bridge more or less "superficial" divisions like ethnic and cultural cleavages, but according to Graziano, "Deeper structural divisions . . . , especially class conflict," present a much greater challenge (1980: 349). Nolutshungu and Southall state in virtually identical words that consociational theory "is silent about class conflict and even about economic inequality in general" (Nolutshungu 1982:26-27; see also Southall 1983:99). This charge is only partly accurate. As we shall see, one of the important favorable conditions for consociational democracy is that the segments are roughly equal in socioeconomic terms—which is by no means always the case. In this sense consociational theory does take the question of economic inequality into consideration.

While consociational theory takes some account of class cleavages, it is true that it is mainly concerned with the relations among the segments of a plural society and that the segmental cleavages usually do not coincide with class divisions. Hence there is a certain logic to the hypothesis that when ethnic or religious segments are the most prominent collective actors in a plural society, class interests will have little chance to be articulated and promoted. Of course it does happen that segments are at least in part defined by socioeconomic divisions; the Socialist segments of Austria, Belgium, and the Netherlands are the clearest examples. Even more important, the leaders of segments which cut across class cleavages have to be responsive to all their followers and consequently cannot ignore socioeconomic problems.

The empirical evidence clearly shows that consociational Austria, Belgium, the Netherlands, and Switzerland have not performed any worse than their non-consociational European neighbors with regard to the solution of socioeconomic problems and the reduction of inequality and that unresolved class issues have never seriously threatened civil peace and democracy. It is therefore difficult to understand Zolberg's verdict that it is "not only misleading, from the point of view of social science, but cruel from the point of view of those affected, to propose [consociationalism] as a recipe for conflict management in societies where ethnic tensions are founded on injustice" (1977:142). With specific reference to South Africa, it is equally unjustified to claim, as Frankel does, that consociational plans "leave power and wealth where it [sic] has always been, i.e. in White hands" (1980:490). Consociational democracy in South Africa will mean the sharing of political power on an equal basis, accompanied by a substantial narrowing of the socioeconomic gap.

A different group of criticisms emphasizes the dangers of immobilism and paralysis to which consociational democracy is allegedly prone. All four of the basic principles of consociationalism appear to entail a degree of slowness and inefficiency, but these should not be exaggerated, as several critics have done (Hudson 1976: 113; Kriek 1976:85; van den Berghe 1981a:189; A. J. Venter 1983: 284-85). These critics overlook the necessity of a long-term perspective and the fact that consociationalism has a number of countervailing advantages that make for more instead of less decisiveness and efficiency (Lijphart 1977a:50-52).

If proportionality (in addition to individual merit) is a standard for appointment to the civil service, some administrative inefficiency may result. Segmental autonomy may require an increase in the number of governmental units and the duplication of facilities, such as schools, for the separate segments, both of which may involve additional costs.* But these slight increases in administrative inefficiency and expense are relatively minor problems; they are not a threat to the viability of the system. Potentially more serious is the danger that executive power-sharing and the minority veto will lead to paralysis in decision-making; majority rule appears to be much more decisive and effective. However, short-term efficiency under majoritarianism is bound to cause antagonism and frustration on the part of the losing segments and hence serious tensions and instability in the long run. Conversely, the relatively slow and ponderous operation of consociational democracy in the short run is more likely to

---

*Nordlinger rejects federalism as a consociational device for a different reason: "The combination of territorially distinctive segments and federalism's grant of partial autonomy sometimes provides additional impetus to demands for greater autonomy, [and when these demands are refused] secession and civil war may follow" (1972:32). However, it is hard to imagine that a centralized system could control strong separatist sentiment in the long run. Moreover, the secession of a segmentally homogeneous area from a plural society may not be a bad solution. As noted, the violence that may accompany such an effort at secession would not so much be caused by the secession itself as by efforts to oppose it.

be effective over time. Moreover, proportionality and autonomy contain significant aids to decisional effectiveness. The former is an extremely valuable time-saving formula for allocating resources and appointments.* The latter distributes the total decision-making load among several public and semi-public bodies, thus alleviating the burdens on each of them.

The strongest refutation of the charge of immobilism is the empirical evidence. Consociational Austria, Belgium, the Netherlands, and Switzerland have on the whole not been any less effective or more immobilist than majoritarian Britain or any other West European democracy. It is the abstract logic of majoritarian thinking that conjures up the threat of inevitable paralysis resulting from the veto and power-sharing; consociational practice shows that such fears are largely unfounded.

The final criticisms belonging to category A question the likelihood that leaders in a consociational democracy can maintain both inter-segmental cooperation and intra-segmental support. Adam claims that the consociational approach overlooks "situations in which ruling groups are not interested in conflict regulation but conflict perpetuation" (1983c:19), and Cynthia H. Enloe remarks that consociational democracy may break down as a result of "disaffection of the rank and file of each community with its own established elites" (1977:152). These observations are basically correct, but they do not contradict consociational theory. The theory does not claim that consociational solutions will always work; if they fail, it will be because segmental leaders are unable or unwilling to manage the inherently difficult inter- and intra-segmental balancing act. It may well be true as a general proposition that elite behavior is normally competitive and adversarial (Field and Higley 1980; Burton 1984:54-57).† In plural societies, an extra incentive for competition is that it is easier to retain mass support if no compromises with the opposition are attempted and if the opposition can be depicted as threatening.

*A. J. Venter states that a disadvantage of the proportionality rule is that "certain matters cannot be proportionally allocated—like the office of state president" (1983:284). This is a good argument—not against proportionality, but against having a strong state presidency in a consociation.

†This is also a more consistent and elegant explanation of why elite behavior tends to shift from coalescence to competition when a plural society becomes less plural and less inherently conflictual—as in the Netherlands after 1967—than was my earlier explanation based on the "dissatisfied voter" (Lijphart 1977a: 106-8), which Mogens N. Pedersen (1982:16-19) has rightly criticized.

From this perspective, cooperative consociational behavior by segmental leaders is the exception; it is stimulated by the realization that the general interest, including the long-term interest of the leaders themselves, requires it, and it is supported in favorable circumstances by consociational traditions and a formal consociational constitution.

CRITIQUE B: MAJORITARIANISM DOES NOT LEAD TO VIOLENCE AND DEMOCRATIC FAILURE

The second major category of criticisms (type B in Figure 4.1) challenges the proposition that majoritarian democracy in a plural society is likely to lead to violence and democratic collapse. It is important to emphasize that consociational theory does not claim that majority rule can *never* work in a plural society. Plural societies exhibit different degrees of pluralism, and majority rule may have a reasonable chance of success in a mildly plural country, while it is virtually doomed to failure in an extremely plural one. Regardless of the degree of pluralism, however, consociational theory asserts that the probability of successful majoritarianism is always much smaller than that of successful consociationalism. Hence it never makes sense to recommend majority rule instead of consociational democracy for a plural society.

One of the most important and constructive critiques of consociationalism—an aspect of which is a type B critique (to be discussed below)—is Ian Lustick's proposal of the "control" model as an alternative to the consociational model to assure political stability in plural societies. Lustick defines control as "a relationship in which the superior power of one segment is mobilized to enforce stability by constraining the political actions and opportunities of another segment or segments" (1979:328). Thus even in deeply plural societies consociationalism is not the only method available for maintaining civil peace. However, although control may be an alternative to consociational democracy, it is not an attractive alternative since it involves a relationship between superordinate and subordinate segments instead of the basically equal segments in consociational systems. Lustick himself is quite clear on this point. He argues that control is "substantially preferable to other conceivable solutions [like] civil war, extermination, or deportation," and he argues that it is worth considering in plural societies "where consociational techniques have not been, or cannot be, successfully employed" (1979:336).

In addition to the superordinate-subordinate segmental relationship, control is not an equal contender with consociationalism because it usually entails a political system that is not democratic. The only exception is the case of a majority segment which controls one or more minority segments in a majoritarian democracy. This is the case that makes control theory a type B critique of consociationalism. The classic example would be Northern Ireland, where Protestant majority control was relatively successful in preserving both peace and democratic institutions from the 1920s to the 1960s. The Northern Ireland case also shows that the "peace" and "democracy" achieved by majority control are highly questionable. Majority-control democracy spells majority dictatorship instead of genuine democracy. Moreover, while civil peace was maintained for four decades, it turned into civil war in the late 1960s. Even with the "advantage" of a strong majority segment, majoritarian democracy is neither an attractive nor an effective rival to consociational democracy.*

Some other critics have tried to strengthen the case of majoritarianism on the basis of the empirical evidence. Anthony Mughan criticizes my *Democracy in Plural Societies* on the ground that it "does not even provide any comparative evidence showing that in the Third World generally consociationalism has proved more successful in maintaining stable democracy in plural societies than any other type of democracy, for example, the adversarial type prevalent especially in Britain" (1979:516). In actual fact, I did canvass the political systems of the Third World, especially the former dependencies of Britain and France, for cases of successful majoritarian democracy in plural societies, and I found only one such case: India. Upon closer examination, however, I discovered that India was by no means purely majoritarian: the broadly aggregative Congress Party has served as an inter-ethnic coalition, and the Indian federal system was specifically designed to give autonomy to the linguistic segments (Lijphart 1977a: 180-81). This view is supported by Crawford Young: "Lijphart's theory of consociational democracy has application to the Indian

---

*Donald Rothchild (1984, 1985) has shown that many middle African states are governed by a mixture of consociational and control methods which he calls "hegemonial exchange." While such regimes are considerably more open than the pure control model, they are not completely democratic—and certainly much less so than consociational democracies.

pattern of integration. . . . At the summit is a national political elite who are committed to reconciling differences through bargaining amongst themselves" (1976:314). I do not want to argue that India should be regarded as a consociation, although it has a few striking consociational features, but it is not a clear case of majoritarian democracy either, and hence it does not contradict consociational theory.

Mughan does not mention India or any other specific empirical counterexamples to the consociational thesis. On the other hand, Powell points to four "plural societies with substantial, though not unbroken, records of democratic success [that might be regarded as counterexamples:] India, Ceylon, the Philippines, and Trinidad would seem to have done as well with conflict regulation as Lebanon and Malaysia" (1979:296). Two of these are examples of majority control in Lustick's sense of the term, and therefore more dictatorial than democratic in nature: there is Singhalese majority control in Sri Lanka and African majority control—albeit of a rather benevolent kind—in Trinidad (Vasil 1984:304-24; Young 1976:507-8). The Philippines should be regarded as an intermediate or doubtful case rather than as a counterexample—like India, but for different reasons. While Filipino society is culturally diverse, it is not deeply plural, with the exception of the Christian-Moslem split. Young writes that "ethnicity in the Philippines stands out by its diffuseness" (1976: 348). Also, the top layer of Filipino society is culturally integrated to a very high degree. Nonetheless, the Moslem minority was excluded and alienated, and Filipino democracy ended in 1972 after twenty-six years of democratic rule—comparable to Lebanon's thirty-three years, but without Lebanon's "excuse" of external destabilizing factors. In the Philippines democracy failed for purely internal reasons.

The final argument in category B, which is entirely speculative, rejects the necessity of power-sharing. Barry argues that executive power-sharing may be associated with successful democracy in plural societies but that it is not necessary. A majoritarian democracy can also work well as long as all parties simply behave with moderation and tolerance. He uses Austria as an example:

The willingness of the leaders of the Austrian People's Party in 1945 to offer a "grand coalition" and the willingness of the leaders of the Socialist party to accept the offer was deeply significant because it showed that they were prepared to act in an

accommodating way. But the same attitudes might well have served
to create a stable polity if the People's Party had formed a moderate government and the Socialist Party a moderate opposition"
(1975b:405).

The weak point in Barry's thinking is that he regards power-sharing
and political moderation as clearly different and separable factors.
This is not a realistic assumption. The best way to encourage moderation is to give a party the opportunity to participate in government.
Conversely, when there are widely divergent policy preferences
between a government and an opposition, there are few incentives
for the opposition to behave moderately. The faulty assumption
becomes even more obvious when Barry recommends "cooperation
without cooptation" for Northern Ireland (1975b:405-6). In this
plural society Barry's proposal would mean that the Protestant majority, however moderate, would be in power permanently, and that
the Roman Catholic minority would always be the "loyal" opposition. It is highly unrealistic to expect that a minority segment
condemned to permanent opposition will continue to be loyal and
constructive.

A recommendation of political moderation without the incentive
of power-sharing is insufficient. Neither Barry's proposal nor the
other type B criticisms succeed in making majoritarian democracy a
more attractive model for plural societies than consociational democracy.

CRITIQUE C: IS CONSOCIATIONAL DEMOCRACY CAUSE OR EFFECT IN "PLURAL" SOCIETIES?

The criticisms in category C of Figure 4.1 challenge the proposition that consociational democracy is a response to the problems of a
plural society and that it is designed to make such a society peaceful
and democratic in spite of its deep segmental divisions. These criticisms fall into three subcategories. The first questions whether the
plural societies which are successful consociations are really plural.
The second argues that the relationship should be reversed: consociationalism is a cause instead of a cure of segmental divisions. The third
category is a Marxist version of the second.

The argument that one or more of the six principal examples of
successful consociational democracy are not really plural societies is

potentially very damaging to consociational theory. If true, it would mean that consociationalism is unnecessary and irrelevant. Switzerland and the Netherlands are most frequently attacked with this argument. Several scholars have claimed that Switzerland is culturally heterogeneous but lacks the clear segmental cleavages of a true plural society (Bohn 1980, 1981; Germann 1975; Schmid 1981; J. Steiner 1974: 257-58). One answer to this criticism is that while it may be largely valid today, Switzerland was considerably more plural in the past; for instance, Katz (1984) found more evidence of pluralism in 1951 than in 1975. A more important answer is that Switzerland is indeed among the relatively less plural of the plural societies that have developed consociationalism, but it cannot be considered a homogeneous society by any stretch of the imagination. I myself have stated that "Switzerland is less clearly a plural society" than Austria, Belgium, and the Netherlands, because "its segments cannot be as easily defined" and because its various cleavages have not found organizational expression to the same extent as those of the other three countries (Lijphart 1977a:104; see also Henderson 1981).

It is worth noting that Steiner and Obler, while disagreeing with the view that Switzerland belongs to "the very segmented systems," do not urge the opposite view; they merely call Switzerland a "marginal case" (1977:335). It is even more significant that Schmid (1981), whose entire book is devoted to the thesis that Switzerland is not a plural society but rather is united by "a common civic culture" concludes that this common culture is not the sole explanation of Swiss peace and democracy; these must additionally be explained by "many institutional arrangements," such as "a grand coalition of the political leaders of all the major communities into which Switzerland is divided, . . . proportionality both for the election of parliaments and the allocation of civil-service appointments [and] a considerable degree of regional autonomy" (pp. 149, 156). This explanation in terms of consociational methods is obviously needed because Switzerland is not so very homogeneous after all.

The controversy in the Dutch case turns on the decades prior to the establishment of consociational democracy in 1917. There is general agreement that the Netherlands was a plural society at that time, but several authors argue that the inter-segmental tensions were not great enough to necessitate a consociational solution (Daalder 1974a:612-18; Bakvis 1981:66-69; Scholten 1980:343-46). Because serious civil strife did not develop or—depending on one's point of view—was averted, this controversy cannot be settled definitively.

However, the participants in the political process of that era spoke in terms of a grave threat. When the prime minister proposed the establishment of a special grand coalition of top party leaders to resolve the divisive conflict over state aid to religious schools, he described this conflict as "a wedge . . . driven into our national life and splitting our nation into two nations," and he urged that this dangerous wedge be "removed from our national life" (quoted in Lijphart 1977a:101). Daalder concludes that consociationalism offers "a better explanation of cases in which a viable state was reconstructed *after* an actual explosion (as in Austria after 1945) than of societies in which conflicts never reached such heights (as in Switzerland or the Netherlands)" (1974a:612). I agree only partly with this conclusion. Austria, with its experience of civil war and dictatorship in the 1930s, is a more convincing case solely because the Austrian evidence is incontrovertible and not because the Dutch and Swiss evidence clearly points to a different substantive conclusion.*

The second subcategory of type C criticisms—questioning the causal relationship—can be answered much more easily. Here again the Dutch case figures prominently. Daalder, for instance, points to the paradox that the Netherlands was a less deeply plural society before than after 1917, when consociational democracy was introduced: "Only after 1917 did the various Dutch groups develop their strong networks of subcultural interest organizations" (1974a:616; see also Ellemers 1984: 139-42; Scholten 1980:339). This pattern appears to indicate that consociationalism is not so much a response to pluralism as the cause of it. In Judith Nagata's words, "The depth of segmental cleavages frequently *follows* rather than precedes consociational arrangements, thus creating instead of resolving problems of pluralism" (1979:506). The critics are right in stating this paradox, but it can be resolved without difficulty. It is important to understand that consociationalism deals with the potential problems of a plural society not by trying to make the society less plural, but by making it more plural—at least initially. By explicitly recognizing the segments, by giving segmental organizations a vital formal function in the political system, by subsidizing them on a proportional basis,

---

*Even the Austrian case is sometimes questioned: "The existence of subcultural enmity in 1945 is assumed but never convincingly documented" (Obler, Steiner, and Dierickx 1977:25; A. J. Venter 1980b:135). Since a civil war had raged between the segments only about a decade earlier, it is extremely implausible to assume that hostility would have miraculously disappeared. In this case, the burden of proof must be on the side of the doubters.

and by encouraging segmental political parties through proportional representation, consociational democracy increases the organizational strength of the segments. But instead of creating conflict, the strengthened segments now play a constructive role in conflict resolution.*

A variant of the above criticism is the cynical view that segmental leaders promote both pluralism and consociationalism for their own selfish purposes. In the Netherlands, van Schendelen argues, "as trained politicians they did not only discern the dangers, but also the opportunities deriving from a divided society" (1984:45). The leaders followed a twofold recipe: "the institutionalization of the problems of society, thus creating a stable need for leadership, and the partial solution of these problems, thus creating a sense of effective leadership" (p. 46; see also van Schendelen 1978; Covell 1981: 199; Koch 1982a). Politicians obviously have selfish motives, but these do not necessarily conflict with the general interest. The goals of civil peace and a working democratic system are both a public good and an advantage for individual leaders. If these leaders were exclusively or mainly motivated by a desire to survive politically, it would be much more to their advantage to fan the flames of intersegmental antagonism than to engage in the risky enterprise of striking compromises with rival segmental leaders.

The third subcategory of type C criticisms, a further variant of the above argument, is the Marxist view that segmental cleavages are artificially created and maintained by political leaders in order to disguise class antagonism and suppress the class struggle. Such an interpretation of Dutch political and social developments from the late nineteenth century to the present has been proposed by M. Fennema (1976), Ronald A. Kieve (1981), and Siep Stuurman (1983). The basic problem of these analyses is that they cannot explain why it is so easy for conservative leaders to manipulate "superficial" cleavages in such a way as to obfuscate the really important and deep class division, while progressive leaders are unable to take advantage of objective class interests.

---

*The consociational encouragement of organization along segmental lines obviously does not entail, let alone require, any official ethnic classification "accompanied by the prohibition of mixed marriages and making criminal sexual relations between persons of different ethnic groups," as Amry Vandenbosch (1979:585) suggests. Equally absurd is Koen Koch's (1982b) suggestion that a consociational system in Belgium should entail the prohibition of Fleming-Walloon intermarriage.

In a thorough critique of Kieve's (1981) analysis, Bakvis correctly notes a "fundamental contradiction" that vitiates the entire structure of Kieve's argument: "It is argued on the one hand that the religious cleavage served to repress class conflict by mystifying class lines, while on the other it is baldly stated that the religious blocs were mere 'pillars of sand,' ready to be washed away" (1984:318). For instance, Kieve writes that "Catholic workers seemed to appreciate fully the fundamental conflict of interest," but almost immediately follows this statement with a comment on the church hierarchy's success in "blurring the class divisions—which might otherwise have caused the Catholic bloc to split into its constituent class parts" (1981:318-19). Bakvis concludes as follows:

> It may well be that the bourgeoisie successfully manipulated the religious cleavage to their own advantage, though . . . no evidence is brought to bear on this point. But logically Kieve cannot have it both ways: religious blocs cannot, first, both check class consciousness and not check it and, second, be mere "pillars of sand" yet at the same time play such an important role in repressing the formation of wide-scale, class-based organizations (1984:318; see also Erkens 1983:35-37).

Both the Marxist and non-Marxist critics seriously underestimate the strength and persistence of segmental divisions. These are social facts and not a mere fiction serving the political elite; they have to be accommodated and cannot simply be ignored or wished away.

CRITIQUE D: IS CONSOCIATIONAL DEMOCRACY SUFFICIENTLY DEMOCRATIC?

As serious as the charges in category A are the criticisms that consociational democracy is not sufficiently democratic or even not democratic at all. Part of the blame for these basically inaccurate and unjust accusations belongs to me because my own earlier writings have exaggerated the supposedly "undemocratic" features of consociational democracy. For instance, in *The Politics of Accommodation* I was very critical of the secrecy of Dutch politics, a lack of sharply defined alternatives in parliamentary elections and the overly deferential attitudes toward the political leadership, and in *Democracy in Plural Societies* I bent over backward presenting not only the great merits but also the disadvantages of consociationalism—including its democratic defects (Lijphart 1968a:131-34, 177-80; 1977a:47-50).

My main argument for advocating consociational democracy for plural societies in spite of the imperfectly democratic nature of consociationalism has been that plural societies do not have much choice. Majoritarian democracy may be preferable in terms of democratic quality, but because the probability that it will work in a plural society is very low or nil, it is not a realistic option. Practically speaking, the only choice is between consociational democracy and no democracy. Hanf expresses this idea in an outstandingly graphic way: Consociationalism may appear to be "mere water compared to the champagne of . . . majority-rule democracy, [but] this water is not so bad, and . . . the champagne of majority-rule democracy is simply not available in deeply divided societies" (1979). The basic justification for consociational democracy then is that while many people prefer champagne to water only a few "prefer to die of thirst if champagne is not available" (ibid.).

I still fully support the proposition that plural societies do not have two alternative democratic options and that consociationalism is their only democratic option. But I have come to the conclusion that it is necessary neither to defend consociational democracy solely on this basis, nor to be apologetic about it. There is nothing in consociationalism that true democrats have to be ashamed of. It is fully democratic—to the extent that any real-world democracy can approximate the democratic ideal—and it is just as democratic as majoritarianism. In order to prove this point, let us take a look at what the critics have to say.

The most extreme critics argue that consociational democracy is a contradiction in terms since consociationalism is not democratic at all. Van den Berghe calls the democracy of the consociational model a "façade," a "pretense," and "fiction" (1981a:82; 1981b:349). Nolutshungu argues that consociational democracy is "even further away from common notions of democracy than some elite theories" (1982:28). And Huntington states that consociational democracy should properly be called "consociational oligarchy": it entails an "elite conspiracy," which may be desirable in many societies, "but that does not make it democratic" (1981:14). The standard that Huntington uses to arrive at his negative judgment is Dahl's (1971) well-known and widely accepted definition of democracy—which Dahl prefers to call "polyarchy" in order to distinguish between operating democracies and democracy as an ideal. But what is Dahl's own judgment concerning the democratic nature of consociational democracy?

Dahl (1971:231-48) classifies 114 countries according to 31 scale types, from the highest degree of democracy to complete non-democracy, on the basis of ten operational indicators. He considers all countries in the highest eight scale types to be sufficiently democratic to deserve the label of democracy or polyarchy. The consociational democracies fare quite well in Dahl's ranking. The highest scale type includes eight countries: the four Nordic countries plus the Netherlands, Belgium, Luxembourg, and Switzerland. (I have not used Luxembourg in this study because it is a small and underanalyzed country, but it certainly qualifies as a consociational system [Lijphart 1977a:5; Lorwin 1971]).* Thus half of the democracies in Dahl's *highest* category are consociational democracies. The remaining four principal cases of consociationalism all fit among the top eight scale types: Cyprus is in scale type 4, together with (for instance) the United Kingdom and Italy; Austria is in type 5, in the company of several other democracies including Australia, Canada, Japan, and West Germany; Lebanon, together with France, fits type 6; and Malaysia is joined by Costa Rica in scale type 8.[†] Dahl's careful and objective rankings utterly refute the accusation that consociational democracy is not democratic.

Less extreme critics have called attention to specific democratic deficiencies that in their view tend to show up in consociational democracies. Rabushka and Shepsle raise the question of whether the high degree of secrecy in Dutch consociational politics may be a significant infringement "on what the common notion of democracy entails" (1972:216), and Dutter also comments on the undemocratic nature of making decisions "behind closed doors" (1978:565). There are two answers to this criticism. One is that the degree of secrecy in consociational democracy should not be exaggerated. Rabushka,

---

*How can van Schendelen claim that "in Dahl's own rank-order of poly-archies, the Netherlands . . . scores far from perfect and appears behind such countries as Jamaica, Costa Rica, and France" (1984:40)? This puzzle can be solved easily: the evidence to which van Schendelen refers is an *alphabetical* list of the countries that qualify as democracies, and hence the Netherlands is naturally listed below Costa Rica, France, and Jamaica—and above Sweden and the United Kingdom! (Dahl 1971:248).

[†]Dahl (1971:247-48) places Cyprus and Malaysia in the special category of "near-polyarchies" because of the incidence of violence in these countries, *not* because of defects in their democratic character.

Shepsle, and Dutter base their critical remarks on my description of Dutch politics, and I must certainly accept much of the blame for having created an overdrawn impression. The second answer is that secrecy is not a unique feature of consociational democracies and that it also characterizes majoritarian systems. For example, in Britain, the flagship of majority-rule democracy, all important decisions are typically prepared by bureaucrats and made in the cabinet in complete secrecy and, after being announced, are hardly ever changed under parliamentary or public pressure.

Boulle also draws attention to a democratic deficiency, commenting that "proportional representation based on electoral lists controlled by party hierarchies" is a "manipulative" element in consociational democracy (1984:61; see also Prinsloo 1984:21). List PR, which tends to give party leaders considerable power, is unpopular in the Anglo-American countries, but it is the electoral system of virtually all other democracies. Moreover, in Britain, in spite of its very different electoral laws, there is a comparable degree of elite dominance: party leaders have usually been able to reserve safe constituencies for themselves and to oppose the nomination of undesirable candidates by constituency organizations. If there is any difference in the extent of oligarchical control, it is minimal.

A number of scholars have criticized the rule of secrecy and other "rules of the game" that I describe in my analysis of the Dutch politics of accommodation (Lijphart 1968a:122-38) from a diametrically opposite perspective: they argue that these rules are a common element of all modern democracies, both consociational and majoritarian (Di Palma 1973:10-13; Burton 1984:54; Wolinetz 1978). Scholten asserts that "these Dutch practices are hardly unique compared with the USA and Great Britain, or the homogeneous Scandinavian multiparty systems" (1980:335). The four consociational principles of power-sharing, segmental autonomy, proportionality, and minority veto set consociational democracies apart from majoritarian ones—and, as I have already argued at length in Chapter 1, they are perfectly democratic—but I agree with the above authors that a substantial degree of oligarchy and secrecy is a common and probably unavoidable characteristic of democratic politics everywhere.*

---

*A different criticism is that consociationalism may fail to incorporate "new" minorities, like Surinamers in the Netherlands and guest workers in Switzerland (Enloe 1977:152; Nagata 1979:505). This criticism ignores two problems: most of the new minorities do not have citizenship, and these minorities are relatively

It should be pointed out that a growing number of British scholars have come to the conclusion that majority rule is not working well in Britain and that a strong injection of consociationalism would give the country both a more democratic and a more effective government. They deplore the abrupt alternations in government and its unrepresentative character. Especially S. E. Finer has forcefully called for the introduction of proportional representation and coalition government in order to end "the discontinuities, the reversals, the extremisms of the existing system and its contribution to our national decline" (1975:32; see also Finer 1978; N. Johnson 1975). I am not ready to endorse such a drastic change in the British form of government myself, but the proposals by Finer and others are significant in that they show the approbation of consociationalism and its democratic character even in the majoritarian heartland.

I hope that this discussion has undone the damage of my own earlier criticisms of consociationalism. There is nothing in consociational democracy that people who are both consociationalists and democrats have to be apologetic about.

CRITIQUE E: ADDITIONAL DECISION MODES MUST BE CONSIDERED

Consociational theory makes a basic distinction between the two contrasting decision-making principles of consociationalism and majoritarianism. This distinction does not entail a dichotomous classification: there is a continuum of possibilities between a purely consociational and a purely majoritarian pattern. The seven principal cases of consociational democracy are not pure cases, but they are close to the consociational end of the continuum. Among the seven, there are also slight variations. For instance, as already discussed, Switzerland is a clearer example than the Netherlands. Moreover, there are intermediate cases, such as Canada and Israel, which I have called semi-consociational (Lijphart 1977a:119-34).

This twofold or bipolar contrast appears to be challenged by a fourfold classification of "decision modes" proposed by Jürg Steiner and his collaborators: majority decision, amicable agreement, decision

small. What kind of representation should be provided for non-citizens has not been solved well by any democracy. The problem of the representation of small groups can, at least in principle, be solved more easily in consociational systems by means of PR than in majority-rule regimes.

by interpretation, and non-decision (Steiner and Dorff 1980a, 1980b; Steiner 1981a, 1981b, 1983; Germann and Steiner 1985). Majority decision and amicable agreement seem to correspond roughly with majoritarian and consociational decision-making; hence decision by interpretation and non-decision appear to be additional categories of decision-making. This is not the case, however. Steiner's four categories are intended for the classification of decisions in relatively small groups such as parliamentary committees, and they are based on criteria that are related to but not identical with those that distinguish majoritarianism from consociationalism.

Amicable agreement means that a decision is explicitly approved by all of the members of a group; this certainly fits the consociational pattern. A decision by interpretation occurs if, after the members have expressed their opinions, the chair summarizes the discussion and formulates a decision which is tacitly accepted by the other members.* Steiner distinguishes decisions by interpretation from amicable agreements not only in terms of whether the decisions are formalized, but also in terms of whether full agreement is reached; when decisions are "interpreted," they may represent a consensus, but they may also be the chair's judgment of what a clear majority favors. However, it is reasonable to assume that most decisions by interpretation are in fact compromises accepted by all members. This decision mode may even be thought of as the typical consociational way of arriving at decisions in meetings of small groups. Non-decisions may occur in consociations either because no compromise can be reached, for the time being at least, or because inaction is the substance of the compromise. Even decisions classified by Steiner as majority decisions may in fact be consociational—for instance, if the final proposal represents an "average" of the various views with which a small minority is still not completely happy.

The essence of consociationalism is the search for broadly acceptable compromises; it does not require that decision-makers abandon their original preferences, that they whole-heartedly support the compromises, or that they never cast a vote against a particular compromise proposal. Amicable agreement and decision by interpretation are therefore the usual consociational decision modes, but the other two modes may also occur. As Lehner states, consociationalism

---

*Instead of the chair, one of the other members of the group may serve as the interpreter of the decision, or the decision may be interpreted in the minutes of the meeting.

"refers to a situation in which interest aggregation generally is non-competitive and characterized by extensive bargaining among conflicting interests. The objective of that bargaining is to reach a compromise which minimizes conflict, but does not necessarily result in a resolution of disagreements" (1984:26). According to Lehner, not only amicable agreements but also decisions by interpretation and non-decisions "may be associated with consociational decision-making" (ibid.).

I am not arguing that there is anything defective in Steiner's fourfold scheme. It may well be a useful tool for empirical research into small group behavior. My only conclusion is that Steiner's classification does not imply that in the organization of democratic regimes there are options beyond the two specified by consociational theory. The basic choice remains between the majoritarian and consociational models.

CRITIQUE F: WHAT CONDITIONS ARE FAVORABLE OR UNFAVORABLE TO CONSOCIATIONAL DEMOCRACY?

In *Democracy in Plural Societies* I listed nine conditions conducive to the establishment and successful operation of consociational democracy, and I emphasized that these should be regarded merely as *favorable factors,* not as necessary and sufficient preconditions (Lijphart 1977a:53-103). (Each of these will be discussed and applied to the South African case in Chapter 5.)

Just as in several of the previously discussed criticisms, the critics here attack a part of consociational theory from diametrically opposite directions, and they contradict each other more than they disagree with me. On the one hand, some authors accept the conditions that I propose but then exaggerate them into absolute preconditions in order to show that consociationalism cannot work in South Africa or in other plural societies that are measured against these conditions. (I shall return to this erroneous interpretation in Chapter 5.) On the other hand, several critics have tried to show that all or most of my favorable conditions cannot be regarded as conditions at all. The basic problem is that they can think only in terms of conditions that are both necessary and sufficient. For instance, Mughan asserts that since I state that my conditions are not indispensable and not sufficient factors, "one cannot help but speculate that the relationship hypothesized by the author is spurious" (1979:516). In the most extensive critique, Adriano Pappalardo (1981) uses such rigorous standards for defining what can be accepted as a true condition that hardly any of my conditions survive. A typical sentence reads as follows: "A condition for consociational democracy must be present in all the involved countries" (p. 384). In other words, only a necessary condition can be accepted as a condition. And van Schendelen writes that "Lijphart's . . . conditions may be present and absent, necessary and unnecessary, in short conditions or no conditions at all" (1984:34).

These critics fail to appreciate that virtually all social science knowledge is probabilistic in nature. Hardly any relationships between variables can be stated in absolute terms. When I argue that a particular factor—say traditions of elite accommodation—is favorable, all I am saying is that the presence of this factor makes successful consociationalism more probable and its absence makes it less probable. This is the most common and normal approach in the social sciences. For instance, in the field of voting behavior we know that there is a relationship between age and voting turnout: younger people are less likely to make use of their right to vote than older people. This does not mean that youth is a necessary factor for the failure to vote (because there are also some older people who do not vote), nor that youth is a sufficient factor (because there are some young people who do vote), but still we have a perfectly valid probabilistic proposition.

It would require too much space to examine the objections raised against each of the favorable conditions, and it is not necessary since most of the objections consist of exceptions—which are not numerous and important enough to undermine the favorable conditions.* However, even when there are no exceptions at all, the critics have not desisted from raising doubts. For instance, the favorable condition of external threats perceived as a common danger by all segments of a plural society occurred at crucial points of the development of consociationalism—in the form of international crises, foreign occupation, or colonial control—in all seven principal cases of consociational democracy. But, the critics question, does an external threat not

*I am responsible for part of the confusion regarding a few of the favorable conditions because I changed my mind in some respects between 1968 and 1977. However, I still fully support all of the conditions specified in *Democracy in Plural Societies* (Lijphart 1977a:53-103). Another slight source of confusion is that I used subheadings in that work that do not correspond to each of the conditions. For instance, under the subheading of "Crosscutting Cleavages," I argue that such cleavages are (with one exception) *not* a favorable condition.

mean a greater burden on the decision-makers and hence should it not be counted as a negative factor (Steininger 1975:253-54; Pappalardo 1981:378)? The answer is obvious: Yes, a foreign threat does increase the decision-making load, but this disadvantage is amply compensated by the advantage of inter-segmental solidarity.

Even if some of the criticisms in this category were valid, it is worth noting that they would not weaken consociationalism as a normative model, especially in cases where few favorable factors are in evidence. If these conditions should not be taken seriously, their absence cannot be regarded as an obstacle to consociationalism either. In the next chapter, I shall emphasize that the significance of the favorable conditions should not be overrated, not because they fail to reflect empirically valid relationships, but because they are merely probabilistic instead of decisive: even if most or all of the favorable factors are lacking, it is still possible to have a successful consociation.

AN APOLOGY AND A CHALLENGE TO THE CRITICS

In spite of the length of this chapter, I have obviously not been able to do full justice to all of the objections raised by the very many critics of consociational theory. And although I have tried to be objective, fair, and reasonable, I may occasionally have been too zealous in the defense of my own ideas. I apologize for both of these limitations. I do not consider the debate closed, and I am ready to engage in further oral or written arguments.

At the same time, I should like to issue a challenge to the critics: if my counterarguments have failed to convince you and if you continue to disagree with one or more aspects of consociational theory, is your objection significant enough to invalidate the theory as a whole, and—even more important—does it invalidate the recommendation of a consociational solution for South Africa? I feel confident that most critics will reply negatively to this question. For instance, there may continue to be disagreement on the question of whether religious or ethnic differences can be settled more easily by consociational methods, but this controversy does not seriously affect the question of whether the consociational model is appropriate for South Africa. Some critics may feel that I have overemphasized external factors as causes of the 1975 Lebanese civil war, but this matter again is barely relevant to the recommendation that South Africa should adopt a consociational solution.

On the whole, I believe that this chapter has shown the great strength of consociational theory, especially as a normative model. The few criticisms that have some validity or that raise legitimate doubts may detract slightly from the empirical validity of consociationalism but have minimal relevance to its value as a policy recommendation.

Chapter 5

CONSOCIATIONALISM AS A REALISTIC
OPTION FOR SOUTH AFRICA

In Chapter 4 I demonstrated the validity of consociational theory and its relevance as a normative model to plural societies in general. In this chapter I shall try to show that consociationalism has eminent practical relevance to the specific case of South Africa and that the chances are good that a South African consociation can work well.

Those who are pessimistic about consociation in South Africa tend to make three grave mistakes. First, they exaggerate the importance of the conditions conducive to consociational democracy. I have stressed that these are merely favorable factors (Lijphart 1977a: 54-55), but several scholars have transformed them into absolute prerequisites. For instance, A.J. Venter refers to "Lijphart's requirements" (1983:286). Rhoodie writes that "there are certain modal conditions which must be met" (1983b:472). Frankel refers to rigorous "preconditions" (1980:489), and Stultz calls the favorable factors "prerequisites" (1984:364). Second, the pessimists exaggerate the unfavorable background conditions in South Africa. Stultz writes the following: "It is widely believed that the prerequisites for consociationalism simply do not exist in South Africa today" (1984:364). De Crespigny and Collins assert that "all of these [favorable] conditions are absent" (1983:442). And according to van den Berghe, "All the basic preconditions . . . are totally missing in South Africa . . . [Hence] the odds against consociation [are] at a million to one" (1983:149). The third mistake is to consider South Africa's cultural and socioeconomic differences so great as to signify a "fundamental irreconcilability" among the segments (du Pisani 1983:239). None of these claims stands up to careful scrutiny. I shall first examine the background conditions in South Africa to determine how favorable or unfavorable they are for consociation.

FAVORABLE AND UNFAVORABLE FACTORS
FOR CONSOCIATION IN SOUTH AFRICA

There are nine variables that may make the establishment and maintenance of a consociational democracy in a particular country more or less likely.* Generally a factor that is favorable for the *establishment* of a consociation will also be a positive condition for its *maintenance*. In this section I shall focus on the latter aspect. There is not enough time left for a South African consociation to "evolve" (Lewsen 1982:17); it will have to be set up by a deliberate and purposive decision of the segmental leaders. Such a decision may be encouraged by a demonstration that the background conditions for the successful operation of a South African consociation are by no means altogether unfavorable.

In discussing each of the nine conditions, I shall compare South Africa with the five consociational democracies that have ethnic cleavages—Belgium, Cyprus, Lebanon, Malaysia, and Switzerland— and that are therefore the most comparable to South Africa.

1. *No majority segment.* The most important factor favoring a consociation is that none of the segments of the plural society comprises a majority of the population. A majority segment will always be tempted to revert to majoritarian methods. In Northern Ireland a Protestant majority twice as large as the Catholic minority was the underlying cause for the failure of the brief power-sharing experiment in 1972, and it continues to be the biggest obstacle to the efforts of the British government to find a solution by means of a power-sharing executive and proportional representation. Similarly, the principal cause of the collapse of the Cypriot consociation in 1963 was the four-to-one population imbalance in favor of the Greek Cypriots.

Table 5.1 rates South Africa and the five other plural societies with regard to the nine background conditions on a five-point scale, from very favorable (++) to very unfavorable (--). On the first factor Cyprus, with its huge Greek ethnic majority, receives the most

---

*In addition to the nine conditions that I shall discuss, Adam and Giliomee (1979:287) correctly list the imposed instead of voluntary nature of group membership in South Africa and the restrictions on segmental leadership as "decisive obstacles" to the establishment of consociationalism. These policies are obviously incompatible with the basic consociational principles, and they will have to be removed before a consociational constitution can be agreed on.

Table 5.1

FAVORABLE AND UNFAVORABLE CONDITIONS FOR
CONSOCIATIONAL DEMOCRACY IN SOUTH AFRICA,
BELGIUM, CYPRUS, LEBANON, MALAYSIA, AND SWITZERLAND

Condition	South Africa	Belgium	Cyprus	Lebanon	Malaysia	Switzerland
1. No majority segment	++[a]	-	--	++	-	-
2. Segments of equal size	+	+	--	+	-	--
3. Small number of segments	-	0	0	-	++	++
4. Small population size	+	++	0	++	++	++
5. External threats	0	0	--	--	0	0
6. Overarching loyalties	+	0	-	0	0	++
7. Socioeconomic equality	--	-	-	-	--	+
8. Geographical concentration of segments	-	-	+	-	-	++
9. Traditions of accommodation	0	+	0	++	+	++
Total score	+1	+1	-7	+2	0	+8

[a]A five-point scale is used as follows:

   ++   Very favorable

   +   Favorable

   0   Neither favorable nor unfavorable

   -    Unfavorable

   --   Very unfavorable

unfavorable rating. Belgium and Switzerland also have clear ethnic
majorities (Flemish- and German-speaking respectively), but these
are internally divided by religion and ideology and can therefore be
given a less unfavorable score. Malaysia receives the same rating as
Belgium and Switzerland since its Malay segment is a majority in
Malaya and very close to a majority in Malaysia as a whole. Only
Lebanon and South Africa can be given a completely positive score:
the largest Lebanese sect comprises only about one third of the
population, and the two largest South African ethnic segments each
contain only about one fifth.

My score for South Africa is based on the assumption that the South African segments must be defined in ethnic terms. As I have already discussed in Chapters 2 and 3, this point is highly controversial, and hence it is advisable not to predetermine the segments in a consociational constitution. Here, however, I have to make a judgment on how a consociation is likely to operate, and consequently I cannot avoid a prediction concerning the kind of groups that will probably be the segments once South Africa has become a democracy with full freedom of association. On the basis of the empirical evidence in other parts of the world— especially black Africa, Europe, and Asia—ethnic groups are by far the strongest candidates for acting as segments.

The South African government has attempted to promote ethnic differences among the Africans, but this policy has largely backfired, especially as far as the well-educated and politically active strata are concerned (Tötemeyer 1984). J. Congress Mbata writes that "notwithstanding the efforts of the government in South Africa to emphasize ethnicity, this factor appears to be unequivocally rejected by Africans" (1975:211). It would be more accurate to say that this rejection has occurred not in spite of the government's policies but because of them. Without this official insistence on ethnic boundaries, they "most likely would have . . . been agreed to in a voluntary fashion" (Adam 1983c:9; see also Geldenhuys 1981: 214; Kuzwayo 1980a:135). As noted in Chapter 3, rather than ethnic segments, Adam (1983a) predicts that under conditions of free group formation three much larger "cultural heritage groups" will emerge (African, Afrikaner, and English). However, Adam specifies that the African group will probably be "split at least along Zulu and Xhosa language lines" (p. 141).

My conclusion on ethnic segmentation is supported by the results of public opinion surveys, even though such evidence is of limited value in view of the South African government's artificial and almost certainly counterproductive insistence on ethnic division and classification. The survey conducted by the Buthelezi Commission (1982, 1:264-69) found that among the Zulus living in KwaZulu and Natal, feelings of black identity were considerably weaker than feelings of Zulu identity. In both KwaZulu-Natal and the Transvaal substantial majorities of Zulus as well as members of other African ethnic groups were in favor of retaining their own languages as official languages in a future democratic South Africa, and they showed great concern about the protection of ethnic minority rights.

The white community, in which freedom of organization has long existed, is also clearly divided into ethnic segments, as I have stressed. In a comparative study of voting patterns in South Africa and three other plural societies—Belgium, Canada, and Switzerland—in the 1970s, I found a much higher level of ethnic voting among white voters in South Africa than for any of the other indices of class, religious, or ethnic voting in any of the four countries (Lijphart 1979a, 1980c). As Wiechers states, "In the White population group South Africa has . . . a truly plural society" (1978:109).

Bishop Tutu is right in just about every respect when he states the following:

> Blacks find it hard to understand why the Whites are said to form one nation when they are made up of Greeks, Italians, Portuguese, Afrikaners, French, Germans, English, etc. etc.; and then by some *tour de force* Blacks are said to form several nations—Xhosas, Zulus, Tswanas, etc. The Xhosas and Zulus, for example, are much closer to one another than, say, the Italians and the Germans in the White community (1984:30).

Only one of the two main white ethnic segments can be considered a nation—the Afrikaners. And it is indeed an exaggeration in the other direction to call the African ethnic segments "nations." It should be noted, however, that Tutu does not deny significant differences between Xhosas and Zulus. Motlana also admits these differences. Although he does not believe that "ethnicity is important at all," he is "willing to concede that the mass of the people might be swayed by such irrelevancies as tribal affiliation, for example, the fact that Buthelezi is a Zulu." And he strengthens rather than weakens this assertion by adding the qualification that "it is not certain that *all* Zulus will vote for a Buthelezi" (Barratt 1980:35-36, 41; emphasis added).

The comparative empirical evidence on the strength and persistence of ethnicity is overwhelming. In South Africa it is therefore highly probable—nay, virtually certain—that the ethnic factor will reassert itself under conditions of free association and open electoral competition. It is highly unlikely that blacks and whites will confront each other as monolithic entities (Hanf, Weiland, and Vierdag 1981:386-88; Schlemmer 1983a:490-91; Welsh 1980:161). It is therefore perfectly safe to assume that a South African consociation will have the advantage of not having a majority segment.

2. *Segments of equal size.* The second favorable condition, segments of about the same size, facilitates negotiations among segmental leaders. In none of the six countries in Table 5.1 do we find such a high degree of equality, but Lebanon may be given a mildly positive score because none of its segments is very large. This applies even more clearly to South Africa. In Belgium the majority and minority do not differ greatly in numbers. The differences are much greater in Malaysia and are the most pronounced in Cyprus and Switzerland.

3. *Small number of segments.* It is also helpful if a plural society is not divided into too many segments. As the number of participants in negotiations increases, bargaining becomes more complicated and difficult. From this point of view, two segments would appear to be the optimal number, but a twofold division entails both a majority-minority split and the inflexibility of a direct confrontaion. Consequently the optimal number appears to be between three and five—as we find in Malaysia and Switzerland. Belgium and Cyprus have a dichotomous division. South Africa and Lebanon have a considerably larger but by no means unmanageable number of segments.*

4. *Small population size.* It is a striking characteristic of all the successful consociations that they are relatively small countries. In small countries political leaders are more likely to know each other personally than in larger countries, the decision-making process is less complex, and such countries generally do not conduct a very active foreign policy. On the other hand, in very small countries— such as Cyprus, with its population of less than one million—the supply of political talent may be very limited (Lijphart 1977a:65-70, 139). Belgium's population is nearly twice as large as Switzerland's, but both are still given the highest score in Table 5.1, as are Lebanon and Malaysia. South Africa's population is larger again by a factor of about two, and it is given a lower but still positive rating.

5. *External threats.* External danger may increase internal unity, provided that it is perceived as a common threat by all of the segments. Many observers have pointed out that this factor is highly

---

*A.J. Venter's statement that the number of segments in South Africa is "nearly three times more than Lijphart's . . . maximum" (1983:286) is not only a bit exaggerated, but also implies too decisive an influence for this factor.

unfavorable in the current South African situation. The attitude of the black neighboring states is seen as threatening by the white regime but not by most blacks, and one sides's "terrorists" are the other side's "freedom fighters" (Adam and Giliomee 1979:301; Qoboza 1978:371; Schlemmer 1978b:265-66; Seiler 1974:19; A.J. Venter 1983:286-87). However, the external threat from neighboring states will disappear as soon as a consociational solution has been found. The only external tensions that may become a problem concern ethnic groups that straddle the national borders (Scarrit and Safran 1983:20). In South Africa the Tswanas and Ndebeles have fellow ethnics in Botswana and Zimbabwe respectively. However, this issue is unlikely to be of more than marginal importance. Hence foreign threats are neither a favorable nor unfavorable factor for a South African consociation—as for three other consociational democracies in Table 5.1. Only for Cyprus and Lebanon does the international situation constitute a lasting negative condition.

6. *Overarching loyalties.* It is obviously helpful for consociationalism if the divisions among the segments are counterbalanced to some extent by an overarching sense of belonging together. Of the six countries compared here, only Switzerland can boast such a shared national feeling (Schmid 1981). Lacking such sentiments, a next favorable condition is a commitment to the territorial unity and identity of the state. As formulated by Dankwart A. Rustow, this means that "the vast majority of citizens ... must have no doubt or mental reservations as to which political community they belong to" (1970:350-51). It excludes "situations of latent secession," as in many African states, and "situations of serious aspirations for merger" *(ibid.)*, such as exist in the Arab world. This less demanding condition is clearly present in South Africa. All South Africans feel that they are South Africans. Homeland partition has been accepted by many whites but only for ulterior purposes and only grudgingly, while radical partition is distasteful to everyone. Such a commitment to territorial unity does not exist unequivocally in three of the other countries, and secessionist sentiments among Turkish Cypriots qualify Cyprus for a negative score.

7. *Socioeconomic equality.* If there are large socioeconomic differences among the segments, the poorer segments will likely feel discriminated against and the more prosperous ones may feel threatened. As a result, grave tensions may develop which may endanger the viability of a consociation (see Smith 1969b). So-

cioeconomic inequality is common in plural societies, and it characterizes the South African and Malaysian situations to an especially marked degree. Only Switzerland can be rated positively on this factor.

Although there is no doubt that the most negative score for this condition should be assigned to South Africa in Table 5.1, it is important not to exaggerate this problem into an insuperable obstacle to consociationalism (Gann and Duignan 1981:300). In contrast with most of the other factors, it is not necessarily a static condition, and it can be improved by deliberate political action, including preferential treatment for the disadvantaged segments. The challenge posed by the huge inequalities in South Africa is not that they will make consociationalism impossible but that consociationalism will have to include a strong commitment to their reduction. Adam summarizes as follows:

> [If these differentials in resources] were addressed at the political level — through proportional revenue-sharing and equalization payments for less-developed regions or institutional sectors, including affirmative action programs to compensate for past deficiencies—unequal development would not necessarily present an insurmountable obstacle in a fast growing economy. In the same way as class conflicts are reduced in progressive West European countries through institutionalized bargaining and compulsory arbitration with ever fewer strikes and lockouts, conflicts about material privileges in South Africa could be settled without escalating violence (1983a:142).

A vigorous redistribution policy obviously requires that sufficient economic resources be available (Heisler and Peters 1983; Leftwich 1974). There are two reasons for confidence in this respect regarding South Africa. One is that South Africa is basically a wealthy country. The other is that a consociational South Africa will quickly regain international respectability and be able to draw new investments into the country; this is likely to stimulate the economic growth that will facilitate substantial redistribution.*

8. *Geographical concentration of segments.* If the segments are concentrated in clearly separate areas of a country, their relative

---

*For critical assessments of the need for as well as some of the drawbacks of affirmative action, see Archer (1980), Degenaar (1980), Glazer (1980), Hanf (1980), Means (1972), Savage (1980), and Weiner (1983).

mutual isolation will prevent latent hostilities from turning into conflict, and segmental autonomy can have a firm basis by means of federalism and decentralization. Again it is only in Switzerland that this advantage exists fully. In Cyprus a territorial separation of the segments was produced by massive population resettlements following the 1974 Turkish invasion, but the separation is not accepted as a permanent condition and hence cannot be regarded as a highly favorable condition. In the other four countries, including South Africa, this factor is unfavorable because while the segments have certain areas of relative concentration, they are largely inter-mixed in each country as a whole. In Belgium a special problem involves the bilingual capital of Brussels.

9. *Traditions of accommodation.* Finally, it is helpful to a consociation if it is supported by long-standing traditions of settling disagreements by consensus and compromise. Switzerland and Lebanon have been particularly favored in this respect. In Cyprus such traditions have been of negligible importance. Belgium and Malaysia are in an intermediate position. A mildly favorable score might also be assigned to South Africa on the basis of the broad consensus in favor of the consociational principle that has developed since about 1970, among whites as well as many blacks (as discussed in Chapter 3), and the much longer and stronger traditions of con-sensual decision-making in the African community. Schlemmer reports a statement by Chief Buthelezi denouncing "the competitive Westminster system as being incompatible with African traditions" (1978a:388). Schlemmer comments that the traditional style of politics among Africans was certainly not competitive, and that "the notion of debate among elders until consensus was achieved was fully entrenched" *(ibid.)*. But these encouraging elements are counterbalanced by a long history of white domination and black exclusion. I have therefore assigned a score of 0 to South Africa—the same score as Cyprus's and the lowest assigned on this dimension.

The bottom row of Table 5.1 gives the total scores for each of the six countries. Only one country—Switzerland—has a very high positive score: +8. Cyprus, with a score of - 7, is the only country with a very low rating. Switzerland and Cyprus are of course also the clearest cases of successful and unsuccessful consociationalism respectively. The other four countries, including South Africa, are in the middle, with scores ranging from 0 to +2. Thus while on the whole the background conditions for consociational democracy are not exceptionally favorable in South Africa, they are not unusually unfavorable either—contrary to what is often assumed. South Africa is roughly comparable to Belgium, Lebanon, and Malaysia in terms of overall favorable conditions.

The total scores should obviously be taken with a grain of salt—for at least three reasons. First, changes in individual ratings will affect the totals, and these ratings are matters of judgment on which different experts, who all try to be fair and objective, may well disagree. On the other hand, it is unlikely that such changes will upset the pattern in which Switzerland and Cyprus are in extreme and the other countries in intermediate positions. I invite my readers to do their own ratings, and I feel confident that their overall results will not deviate much from the pattern I found.

Second, the total scores in Table 5.1 are based on the assumption that the nine factors are of approximately equal importance. This is clearly not the case, but attaching different weights to the nine conditions is a difficult and hazardous operation. One simple possibility would be to give double weight to the factors that appear to be particularly important, such as (in my judgment) the absence of a majority segment and socioeconomic equality. This weighted rating would not change South Africa's total score of +1 at all. Switzerland and Cyprus would still be the extreme opposites with +8 and -10, and the intermediate countries would have totals ranging from -3 to +3. Again I am happy to invite my readers to do their own weighted scoring, but I very much doubt that they will arrive at startlingly different outcomes.

Third and most important, the nine background conditions discussed above are simply not *decisive* for the success of consociational democracy. Even when they are strongly favorable, as in the Swiss case, they do not guarantee the success of a consociation. Conversely, when they are largely unfavorable, as in the case of Cyprus, it may be more difficult but not impossible to have a successful consociation. (In fact, consociationalism still represents the only hope for a unified, peaceful, and democratic Cyprus.) The non-binding character of the background conditions is even clearer with regard to the intermediate cases. The really crucial factor is the commitment and skill of the political leaders. In his case study of consociational democracy in Colombia, Robert H. Dix (1980) found that a consociational system broke down in 1945-49 but operated successfully from 1958 to 1974—only a decade later—although all the background conditions had remained virtually unchanged. The critical difference between the two periods was the quality of the leadership. With regard to the second period, Dix states that "much credit should be given to Colombia's elites . . . for perceiving the road to political peace and stability (and, of course to their own survival) and acting accordingly" (p. 319).

As far as South Africa is concerned, many scholars who have tried to estimate the chances of a successful South African consociation endorse the conclusion that unfavorable conditions are not a decisive impediment: Adam and Giliomee (1979), Schlemmer (1978a, 1978b), Slabbert and Welsh (1979), and Hanf, Weiland, and Vierdag (1981). They all rate the South African situation as not very favorable, yet all of them are also convinced consociationalists. The first three were members of the Buthelezi Commission, which recommended power-sharing for KwaZulu-Natal, and (by implication) for South Africa as a whole, and Slabbert is the leader of the pro-consociational PFP.

IS SOUTH AFRICA AN EXTREME CASE OF PLURALISM?

A factor that is perhaps more fundamental than the background conditions discussed above is the degree to which a society is plural. It is reasonable to assume that the difficulties for consociational government increase as the differences among the segments increase. According to this line of reasoning, South Africa is sometimes regarded as too plural to sustain a successful consociation. I have unfortunately given some support to this view by my frequently quoted statement that "in the extreme cases of plural societies, such as South Africa, the outlook for democracy of any kind is poor," although I immediately add that "if there is to be democracy at all it will almost certainly have to be of the consociational type" (Lijphart 1977a:236). This statement does not mean that South Africa is necessarily *too* extreme a case, but the statement is nevertheless cited by the Constitutional Committee of the President's Council (1982a:38-39) to strengthen its conclusion that Africans should be excluded from the proposed quasi-consociational system: "the issues in racial conflict," especially between Africans on the one hand and whites, Coloureds, and Asians on the other, are said to be "non-bargainable."

How deeply plural is South Africa exactly? The four criteria for determining the degree to which a society is plural (outlined in

Chapter 4) do not work well in the South African case. The first two criteria—unequivocal identity and precise measurement of the segments—cannot be applied, not because of the absence of sharp divisions but because the entire question of race and ethnicity is so controversial. The third criterion—the extent to which segmental dividing lines coincide with the boundaries between political, social, and economic organizations—is rendered meaningless by the government's artificial imposition of racial and ethnic categories. The final criterion—whether segmental parties receive the stable voting support of their segments—is relevant only when there are free elections and universal suffrage.

It is possible of course to look into the extent of cultural differences in a population without precisely defining the segments, but such differences are not easy to measure and compare. Several scholars have too quickly jumped to the conclusion that South Africa is an extreme case in this respect. For instance, G. A. Rauche (1983a:577) states that the "cultural differential is much greater" in South Africa than in the Netherlands, Belgium, and Austria, but he omits Switzerland, Lebanon, and Malaysia from the comparison. In terms of religion and language, the differences in South Africa are certainly not greater, and probably somewhat smaller, than those among Malays, Chinese, and Indians in Malaysia, or between Christians and Moslems in Lebanon. Furthermore, it is doubtful that the exact degree of divergence matters much in a consociation since cultural diversity is accommodated by means of cultural autonomy for the different segments.

The question that remains is whether the cultural differences are so great as to preclude compromise and consensus at the leadership level. André du P. Louw (1979) sees black-white differences in terms of contrasting "mythological" and "rational" approaches, and Ngubane (1971:13) refers to "a conflict of minds" and "a conflict between two moralities," one individually and one group-oriented. However, such differences may also be said to exist between Catholics and Protestants in Europe or between Americans of southern European and northern European origin—where they have not stood in the way of pragmatic compromises. In comparison with Lebanon and Malaysia, the political leadership in South Africa is more instead of less culturally homogeneous because is it largely Westernized.

In addition to cultural differences, a few writers emphasize economic ones. For instance, de Crespigny argues that "many of the critical interests of Whites and Blacks are irreconcilable [because the whites want to maintain] their *economic standards*, their freedoms, their *power*, their cultural identities, their *status*" (1978:352; emphasis added). In principle, however, economic differences are exactly the ones that are susceptible to pragmatic adjustment. And there is no doubt that a South African consociation can succeed only if it is able to bring about a fairer distribution of income and wealth. Economic differences are not inherently irreconcilable, although they may be made so by the refusal of one or both sides to be flexible and accommodating.

The question of how plural a society South Africa is cannot be settled exactly by the available evidence, but two general conclusions seem justified. One is that if we divide the universe of plural societies into, say, three categories of low, medium, and high pluralism, South Africa should be placed in the high group. Second, however, there are no convincing reasons to assume that this high degree of pluralism will make it unusually difficult or impossible for a South African consociation to operate successfully. The Malaysian example is the closest parallel and is therefore particularly pertinent in this respect.

THE CRUCIAL ROLE OF POLITICAL LEADERSHIP

A central proposition in consociational theory is that a consociation can be established and maintained as the result of a self-negating prediction: the segmental leaders' realization that competitive behavior will lead to serious conflict and their desire to act jointly to avert this unhappy outcome—a rational and purposive response to the facts of pluralism and interdependence. In this book I have frequently disagreed with van den Berghe's observations and judgments, but his definition of consociationalism in terms of the self-negating prediction is excellent: it is "simply the best arrangement possible in situations of permanent ethnic pluralism and interdependence where the alternatives (e.g., à la Lebanon) are too awful to contemplate" (1981a:193; see also Rothchild 1970: 611; Rustow 1970:362-63). The critical role of the leaders is especially clear in those cases, like South Africa, where the background conditions and the degree of pluralism are not very favorable for consociationalism but not massive obstacles either.

There are some hopeful signs that South Africa may have

the kind of strong and rational leadership required for consociational democracy. The attitudes of the ruling Afrikaner elite are particularly important of course. As I have argued, the frequent portrayal of the Afrikaner leaders as utterly intransigent ideologues is certainly incorrect. As early as 1971 Adam called the Afrikaner leadership a "pragmatic race oligarchy" (1971a:53) and argued that its "flexibility . . . to adapt its system of dominance to changing conditions . . . should not be underestimated" (1971b:101). Adam's more recent explanation of President Botha's actions in terms of "instrumental considerations of pragmatic opportunism, not intransigent bigotry" can be applied to the National Party leadership as a whole. This kind of attitude means that "deals can be struck" and that "bargains can be made if it is expedient for the powerholders or [if] they perceive themselves sufficiently under pressure" (1983b:15-16). Welsh emphasizes that "historically, too, pragmatism has been more common than completely unbending ideological rigidity in the political subculture of Afrikaners" (1980:160).

Flexibility and pragmatism are more unambiguously present among South Africa's other political elites. Moderate white and African leaders, such as the PFP and Inkatha leadership, are very much open to compromises and concessions in a consociational framework. And as I have shown in Chapter 2, the ANC is by no means unbending in its preference for majoritarian government. The Study Commission on U.S. Policy Toward Southern Africa calls the ANC "nondoctrinaire" (1981:204). These are the predispositions that make a self-negating prediction possible.

Will the leaders be able to count on their followers' support if they should turn to consociationalism? A.J. Venter (1983:288) points to the National Party's loss of votes to the extreme right-wing HNP and Conservative Party as evidence that the leaders' freedom of action is constrained to a significant extent. Their latitude is indeed not unlimited, but survey evidence shows that the white electorate "is much more amenable to change than the politicians believe, or claim they believe. And there is substantial evidence that the voters would be even readier for change if they were encouraged by their leaders" (Hanf, Weiland, and Vierdag 1981:241; see also Seiler 1979:5; Rotberg 1980a:13, and 1980b:169-70). There is no reason to assume that the situation for the major black leaders is any more difficult.

If the South African political leaders, especially those currently in power, do not make a serious effort to establish consociational democracy and if they do not give it a serious chance to work, they cannot blame it either on their supporters or on unfavorable background conditions. They will have only themselves to blame.

Chapter 6

CONCLUSION: THE LOGIC AND URGENCY OF A CONSOCIATIONAL SOLUTION FOR SOUTH AFRICA

In this book I have shown that consociational democracy is the logical solution to the South African problem for two reasons. First, it is the only democratic solution that is possible, as argued in Chapters 2 and 3. Second, while it is nobody's preferred ideal, it is everybody's second best solution and hence the most logical compromise. Moreover, as I have argued in Chapter 5, it is an entirely realistic and feasible solution.

A consociational solution is also urgently necessary. The longer it is delayed, the more polarized the political atmosphere will become, the smaller the chances of setting up a successful consociation will be, and the more likely a violent confrontation will be. This does not mean that the consociational solution will gradually lose its value or that the outbreak of violence will spell the end of any consociational hopes. Consociation will remain the only possible plan for a peaceful, democratic, and unified South Africa, even when the chances of its adoption and successful operation decline. Indeed a violent crisis may well revive efforts at consociation because such a crisis may have the salutary effect of driving home the necessity of power-sharing. However, it would obviously be preferable if the South Africans accepted the consociational logic without the need of a violent lesson.

At the end of Chapter 3, I formulated a set of guidelines which I believe to be optimal for the application of the consociational model to South Africa. It is up to the representatives of the different population segments in South Africa to negotiate all of the more and less important formal rules of a consociational constitution and to run a new power-sharing government as effectively and responsively as possible. At the end of Chapter 2, I made the much more tentative proposal that a radical partition plan be agreed upon as a fallback solution. Its main advantage would be to serve as a reminder to the consociational negotiators that while power-sharing may appear to have several drawbacks, it is still vastly preferable to the next logical alternative. The details of such a fallback plan would also have to be jointly and consensually negotiated.

Setting up and running a South African consociation is therefore mainly the South Africans' responsibility. What can the United States and other Western and democratic countries do to encourage and accelerate this process? The *New York Times* (1985) has editorialized that "the lost white tribe" of Afrikaners should stop justifying and excusing itself and that "it needs now to listen." The South African ambassador to the United States, Bernardus G. Fourie, has stated his government's willingness to do so: "We listen to constructive criticism, constructive views" (quoted in Atkinson 1985:8). If we ask the Afrikaners and other South Africans to listen to us, we should have a clear and explicit message for them: we should urge them to move as expeditiously as possible toward a consociational settlement. This policy should include the following steps:

1. We should urge that negotiations be started at the earliest possible moment and that representatives of all significant groups in South Africa should participate—including organizations that are now banned, especially the ANC.

2. We should urge the participants to negotiate on the basis of a prior acceptance of the *principle* of consociational democracy, without necessarily giving up any special preference as to how a consociation should be organized or making any other concessions in advance.

3. We should try to achieve a consensus on the above steps among all of the world's democracies and jointly apply the maximum moral pressure on South Africa and all its constituent groups and segments, from the government to the ANC.

4. To the extent that it may be necessary, feasible, and effective, tangible pressures such as economic sanctions should be applied. We must also warn the South African whites that continued minority rule will inevitably lead to large-scale violence and civil war, and we must tell them explicitly that "in the face of such violence [we] will not support them" (McNamara 1982). However, more important than such warnings and negative sanctions is the following positive step:

5. We—the world's democracies—should offer our assistance both in the negotiating process and in the process of governing a consociational South Africa. For instance, it will probably be helpful

if the negotiations are assisted by a commission of mediators drawn from democratic countries and if the new consociational constitution of South Africa is protected by international guarantees.

As I have emphasized in Chapter 1, non-South Africans must not overestimate their influence on the course of South African events. But precisely because our influence is limited, we should not waste it by sending the South Africans unclear or conflicting signals. There is no certainty that the policy recommended above will work, but it is clear, fair, and realistic, and it offers the best hope for achieving the goal of power-sharing in South Africa.

BIBLIOGRAPHY

Adam, Heribert. 1971a. *Modernizing Racial Domination: The Dynamics of South African Politics.* Berkeley: University of California Press.

_____. 1971b. "The South African Power-Elite: A Survey of Ideological Commitment." In Adam, ed. 1971.

_____. 1977. "When the Chips Are Down: Confrontation and Accommodation in South Africa." *Contemporary Crises* 1, 4 (October): 417-35.

_____. 1978. "South Africa: Political Alternatives and Proposals." In Anglin, Shaw, and Widstrand, eds.

_____. 1979. "Three Perspectives on the Future of South Africa." *International Journal of Comparative Sociology* 20, 1-2 (March-June): 122-36.

_____. 1980a. "The Failure of Political Liberalism in South Africa." In Price and Rosberg, eds.

_____. 1980b. "Minority Monopoly in Transition: Recent Policy Shifts of the South African State." *Journal of Modern African Studies* 18, 4 (December): 611-26.

_____. 1983a. "The Manipulation of Ethnicity: South Africa in Comparative Perspective." In Rothchild and Olorunsola, eds.

_____. 1983b. "Reflections on Gordimer's 'Interregnum'." *Indicator South Africa* 1, 3: 14-16.

_____. 1983c. "Ethnic Politics and Crisis Management: Comparing South Africa and Israel." *Journal of Asian and African Studies* 18, 1-2 (January-April): 4-21.

_____. 1983d. "Outside Influence on South Africa: Afrikanerdom in Disarray." *Journal of Modern African Studies* 21, 2 (June): 235-51.

_____. 1984a. "South Africa's Search for Legitimacy." *Telos* 59 (Spring): 45-68.

_____. 1984b. "Constitutional Engineering and Economic Recolonization in South Africa." *Issue: A Journal of Opinion* 13: 30-34.

Adam, Heribert, and Giliomee, Hermann. 1979. *Ethnic Power Mobilized: Can South Africa Change?* New Haven: Yale University Press.

Adam, Heribert, ed. 1971. *South Africa: Sociological Perspectives.* London: Oxford University Press.

_____, ed. 1983. South Africa: *The Limits of Reform Politics.* Leiden: Brill.

Ake, Claude. 1967a. *A Theory of Political Integration.* Homewood, Ill.: Dorsey Press.

_____. 1967b. "Political Integration and Political Stability: A Hypothesis." *World Politics* 19, 3 (April): 486-99.

Anglin, Douglas G; Shaw, Timothy M.; and Widstrand, Carl G., eds. 1978. *Conflict and Change in Southern Africa: Papers from a Scandinavian-Canadian Conference.* Washington, D.C.: University Press of America.

Archer, Sean F. 1980. "Redistribution Issues and Policies in the South African Economy." In Slabbert and Opland, eds.

Atkinson, Rick. 1985. "The Ties That Bind Us to South Africa: Pretoria Produces More than Apartheid." *Washington Post National Weekly Edition* 2, 15 (11 February): 8-9.

Aunger, Edmund A. 1981. *In Search of Political Stability: A Comparative Study of New Brunswick and Northern Ireland.* Montreal: McGill-Queen's University Press.

Austin, Dennis. 1985. "The Trinitarians: The 1983 South African Constitution." *Government and Opposition* 20, 2 (Spring): 185-95.

Bagley, Christopher. 1973. *The Dutch Plural Society: A Comparative Study in Race Relations.* London: Oxford University Press.

Bakvis, Herman. 1981. *Federalism and the Organization of Political Life: Canada in Comparative Perspective.* Kingston, Ontario: Institute of Intergovernmental Relations, Queen's University.

_____. 1984. "Toward a Political Economy of Consociationalism: A Commentary on Marxist Views of Pillarization in the Netherlands." *Comparative Politics* 16, 3 (April): 315-34.

Bank, J. 1984. "Lijphart *malgré lui:* The Politics of Accommodation in the 'Indonesian Question'." *Acta Politica* 19, 1 (January): 73-83.

Barratt, John. 1980. "From South Africa to Azania: An Interview with Nthato Motlana." In Rotberg and Barratt, eds.

Barrell, Howard. 1984. "The United Democratic Front and National Forum: Their Emergence, Composition and Trends." In South African Research Service, ed. 1984.

Barry, Brian. 1975a. "Political Accommodation and Consociational Democracy." *British Journal of Political Science* 5, 4 (October): 477-505.

_____. 1975b. "The Consociational Model and Its Dangers." *European Journal of Political Research* 3, 4 (December): 393-412.

Batliner, Gerard. 1981. *Zur heutigen Lage des liechtensteinischen Parlaments.* Vaduz: Verlag der Liechtensteinischen Akademischen Gesellschaft.

Baxter, Lawrence G. 1981. "Constitutionalism, Bureaucracy and Corporatism." In Boulle and Baxter, eds.

Benyon, John A. 1978. "Constitutions as Devices for Organizing Systems of Government: An Historical and Comparative Overview." In Benyon, ed.

_____, ed. 1978. *Constitutional Change in South Africa.* Pietermaritzburg: University of Natal Press.

Beran, Harry. 1984. "A Liberal Theory of Secession." *Political Studies* 32, 1 (March): 21-31.

Bergeron, Gérard. 1971. "Commentaire de la communication du professeur Arend Lijphart." *Canadian Journal of Political Science* 4, 1 (March): 18-21.

Berg-Schlosser, Dirk. 1985. "Elements of Consociational Democracy in Kenya." *European Journal of Political Research* 13, 1 (March): 95-109.

Bhengu, M.J. 1984. "Chief Buthelezi Is an 'Intelligent Man' Says Dr. Alan Paton." *Inhlabamkhosi* 1, 10 (May): 11-14.

Billiet, J. 1984. "On Belgian Pillarization: Changing Perspectives." *Acta Politica* 19, 1 (January): 117-28.

Birrell, Derek. 1981. "A Government of Northern Ireland and the Obstacle of Power-Sharing." *Political Quarterly* 52, 2 (April-June): 184-202.

Bissell, Richard E., and Crocker, Chester A., eds. 1979. *South Africa into the 1980s.* Boulder, Colo.: Westview Press.

Blenck, Jürgen, and von der Ropp, Klaus. 1976. "Republic of South Africa: Partition a Solution?" *Aussenpolitik* 27, 3: 310-27.

Bluhm, William T. 1973. *Building an Austrian Nation: The Political Integration of a Western State.* New Haven: Yale University Press.

Boesak, Allan. 1984. *Black and Reformed: Apartheid, Liberation, and the Calvinist Tradition.* Maryknoll, N.Y.: Orbis.

Bohn, David Earle. 1980. "Consociational Democracy and the Case of Switzerland." *Journal of Politics* 42, 1 (February): 165-79.

_____. 1981. "Consociationalism and Accommodation in Switzerland." *Journal of Politics* 43, 4 (November): 1236-40.

Botha, M.C. 1970. "Staatsmasjinerie vir die bevordering van tuislandontwikkeling." In Viljoen, ed.

Botha, P. Roelf. 1978. *South Africa: Plan for the Future—A Basis for Dialogue.* Pretoria: Perskor.

Boulle, Laurence J. 1980a. "The New Constitutional Proposals and the Possible Transition to Consociational Democracy." In Slabbert and Opland, eds.

_____. 1980b. "The Second Republic: Its Constitutional Lineage." *Comparative and International Law Journal of Southern Africa* 13, 1 (March): 1-34.

_____. 1981. "Federation and Consociation: Conceptual Links and Current Constitutional Models." *Tydskrif vir Hedendaagse Romeins-Hollandse Reg* 44, 3 (August): 236-54.

_____. 1983. "The Likely Direction of Constitutional Change in South Africa over the Next Five Years." In Dean and Smit, eds.

_____. 1984. *South Africa and the Consociational Option: A Constitutional Analysis.* Cape Town: Juta. Published in the United States as *Constitutional Reform and the Apartheid State: Legitimacy, Consociationalism and Control in South Africa.* New York: St. Martin's Press.

Boulle, Laurence J., and Baxter; Lawrence G., eds. 1981. *Natal and KwaZulu: Constitutional and Political Options.* Cape Town: Juta.

Boynton, G. R., and Kwon, W. H. 1978. "An Analysis of Consociational Democracy." *Legislative Studies Quarterly* 3, 1 (February): 11-25.

Breytenbach, Willie J. 1980. "The Salience of African Ethno-Cultural Pluralism with Regard to Democratic Conflict Resolution and Intergroup Accommodation." In Rhoodie, ed. 1980.

Bridge, Susan. 1977. "Some Causes of Political Change in Modern Yugoslavia." In Esman, ed.

Brookes, Edgar H. 1973. "Minority Report." In Randall, ed. 1973a.

Brotz, Howard. 1978. "Constitutional Change in South Africa: Utopian and Practical." *South Africa International* 9, 2 (October): 65-72, 94-100.

_____. 1980. "Apartheid versus Practical Communalism." *South Africa International* 11, 2 (October): 69-80.

Brown, Eddie. 1980. "The South African Bureau of Racial Affairs (SABRA)." In H. W. van der Merwe and Schrire, eds.

Bruneau, Thomas C. 1976. "Portugal: Problems and Prospects in the Creation of a New Regime." *Naval War College Review* 29, 1 (Summer): 65-82.

Bull, Hedley. 1978. "The West and South Africa." *International Affairs Bulletin* 2, 2: 1-15.

_____. 1980. "Implications for the West." In Rotberg and Barratt, eds.

Bunting, Brian, ed. 1981. *South African Communists Speak: Documents from the History of the South African Communist Party, 1915-1980.* London: Inkululeko Publications.

Burnham, Walter Dean. 1980. "Milestones on the Road to Democracy: Electoral Regimes and Their Relevance to South Africa." In Rotberg and Barratt, eds.

Burton, Michael G. 1984. "Elites and Collective Protest." *Sociological Quarterly* 25, 1 (Winter): 45-65.

Buthelezi, M. Gatsha. 1972a. "Independence for the Zulus." In Rhoodie, ed. 1972.

_____. 1972b. *The Past and Future of the Zulu People.* Munger Africana Library Notes, No. 10. Pasadena: Munger Africana Library, California Institute of Technology.

_____. 1978. "White and Black Nationalism, Ethnicity and the Future of the Homelands." In H. W. van der Merwe et al., eds. 1978.

_____. 1979. *Power Is Ours.* New York: Books in Focus.

_____. 1984. "Extracts of an Aide Memoire from the Chief Minister of KwaZulu, Chief M. G. Buthelezi, to Dr. G. Viljoen, Minister of Co-operation, Development, and Education." *South African Digest,* 9 November, p. 2.

Buthelezi, M. Gatsha, and Phatudi, C. M. 1984. "Historic Declaration." *Clarion Call* (July-August).

Buthelezi Commission. 1982. *The Requirements for Stability and Development in KwaZulu and Natal,* 2 vols. Durban: H and H Publications.

Butler, Jeffrey, Rotberg, Robert I., and Adams, John. 1977. *The Black Home-lands of South Africa: The Political and Economic Development of Bophu-thatswana and KwaZulu.* Berkeley: University of California Press.

Cadoux, Charles. 1980. "Mutation, diversification ou éclatement du système constitutionnel sud-africain?" In *Année Africaine 1980.* Paris: Pedone.

Callaghy, Thomas M., ed. 1983. *South Africa in Southern Africa: The Intensi-fying Vortex of Violence.* New York: Praeger.

Cannon, Gordon E. 1982. "Consociationalism vs. Control: Canada as a Case Study." *Western Political Quarterly* 35, 1 (March): 50-64.

Carter, Gwendolen M. 1966. *Separate Development: The Challenge of the Trans-kei.* Johannesburg: South African Institute of Race Relations.

Carter, Jimmy. 1978. "Speech of the President on Soviet-American Relations at the U.S. Naval Academy." *New York Times,* 8 June.

Chehabi, H. E. 1980. "The Absence of Consociationalism in Sri Lanka." *Plural Societies* 11, 4 (Winter): 55-65.

Chinwuba, Felix Aneze. 1980. *Consociationalism as an Approach to Political Integration: The Case of the Federal Republic of Nigeria.* Doctoral disserta-tion, Tulane University.

Christopher, A. J. 1982. "Partition and Population in South Africa." *Geographi-cal Review* 72, 2 (April): 127-38.

Ciskei Commission. 1980. *The Quail Report.* Pretoria: Conference Associates.

Claeys, Paul H., and Loeb-Mayer, Nicole. 1984. "Le 'Para-fédéralisme' belge: Une tentative de conciliation par le cloisonnement." *International Political Science Review* 5, 4: 473-90.

Cloete, Gideon Stephanus. 1977. "Enkele implikasies van die Erika Theron-verslag vir die toekomstige staatkundige ontwikkeling van Suid-Afrika." *Polit-ikon* 4, 2 (December): 137-65.

_____. 1978. "Opvattings van Stellenbosch Universiteit-studente insake politieke verandering in Suid-Afrika (1978)." *Politikon* 5, 2 (December): 150-73.

_____. 1981. *Etnisiteit en groepsverteenwoordiging in die staatkunde: 'n Vergelijkende studie.* Doctoral dissertation, University of Stellenbosch.

Clough, Michael, ed. 1982. *Changing Realities in Southern Africa: Implications for American Policy.* Berkeley: Institute of International Studies, University of California.

Cohen, Lenard. 1982. "Balkan Consociationalism: Ethnic Representation and Ethnic Distance in the Yugoslav Elite." In *At the Brink of War and Peace: The Tito-Stalin Split in a Historic Perspective,* ed. Wayne S. Vucinich. New York: Columbia University Press.

Connor, Walker. 1972. "Nation-Building or Nation-Destroying?" *World Politics* 24, 3 (April): 319-55.

Constitutional Committee of the President's Council, Republic of South Africa. 1982a. *First Report.* Cape Town: Government Printer.

_____. 1982b. *Second Report on the Adaptation of Constitutional Structures in South Africa.* Cape Town: Government Printer.

Couwenberg, S. W. 1985. "Zuid-Afrika als multi-etnische samenleving: Constitutionele problematiek en westerse politiek." *Civis Mundi* 24, 2 (April): 39-49.

Covell, Maureen. 1978. Review of Lijphart 1977a. *Canadian Journal of Political Science* 11, 4 (December): 887-89.

_____. 1981. "Ethnic Conflict and Elite Bargaining: The Case of Belgium." *West European Politics* 4, 3 (October): 197-218.

Cowell, Alan. 1985a. "Fight Apartheid, Tutu Tells Investors." *New York Times,* 3 January.

_____. 1985b. "South African Leader Promises Urban Blacks a Greater Voice." *New York Times,* 26 January.

_____. 1985c. "Botha Sets Out His 'Agenda' for Racial Changes." *New York Times,* 1 October.

Cowen, Denis Victor. 1961. *The Foundations of Freedom with Special Reference to Southern Africa.* Cape Town: Oxford University Press.

Crocker, Chester A. 1981. "South Africa: Strategy for Change." *Foreign Affairs* 59, 2 (Winter): 323-51.

Daalder, Hans. 1971. "On Building Consociational Nations: Cases of the Netherlands & Switzerland." *International Social Science Journal* 23, 3: 355-70.

_____. 1974a. "The Consociational Democracy Theme." *World Politics* 26, 4 (July): 604-21.

_____. 1974b. *Politisering en lijdelijkheid in de Nederlandse politiek.* Assen: Van Gorcum.

_____. 1981. "Consociationalism, Center and Periphery in the Netherlands." In *Mobilization, Center-Periphery Structures, and Nation-Building,* ed. Per Torsvik. Bergen: Universitetsforlaget.

_____. 1984. "On the Origins of the Consociational Democracy Model." *Acta Politica* 19, 1 (January): 97-116.

Dahl, Robert A., ed. 1966. *Political Oppositions in Western Democracies.* New Haven: Yale University Press.

_____. 1971. *Polyarchy: Participation and Opposition.* New Haven: Yale University Press.

Daniel, John. 1978. "Radical Resistance in South Africa." In Robertson and Whitten, eds.

Dean, W. H. B. 1983. "The Government's Constitutional Proposals 1982." In Dean and Smit, eds.

Dean, W. H. B., and Smit, Dirk van Zyl, eds. 1983. *Constitutional Change in South Africa: The Next Five Years.* Cape Town: Juta.

de Crespigny, Anthony R. C. 1978. "Deriving Policy for South Africa." In Rhoodie, ed. 1978.

_____. 1981. "Democracy, South Africa and Partition." *Politics* 16, 1 (May): 7-17.

de Crespigny, Anthony R C., and Collins, P. 1983. "Evaluation of Constitutional Proposals for Southern Africa." In van Vuuren and Kriek, eds.

de Crespigny, Anthony, and Schrire, Robert, eds. 1978. *The Government and Politics of South Africa.* Cape Town: Juta.

Degenaar, Johannes J. 1978. "Pluralism and the Plural Society." In de Crespigny and Schrire, eds.

_____. 1980. "Normative Dimensions of Discrimination, Differentiation and Affirmative Action." In H. W. van der Merwe and Schrire, eds.

_____. 1982. "Reform Quo Vadis?" *Politikon* 9, 1 (June): 4-18.

_____. 1983. "Pluralism." In van Vuuren and Kriek, eds.

de Klerk, W. A. 1971. "The Afrikaner: Contemporary Attitudes." In Randall, ed. 1971b.

de Klerk, W. J. 1977. "South Africa's Domestic Politics: Key Questions and Options." *Politikon* 4, 2 (December): 178-89.

Dekmejian, Richard Hrair. 1978. "Consociational Democracy in Crisis: The Case of Lebanon." *Comparative Politics* 10, 2 (January): 251-65.

de St. Jorre, John. 1977. *A House Divided: South Africa's Uncertain Future.* New York: Carnegie Endowment for International Peace.

_____. 1981. "South Africa: Is Change Coming?" *Foreign Affairs* 60, 1 (Fall): 106-22.

_____. 1983. "A Vote to Modernize Apartheid's Edifice." *New York Times*, 7 November.

Deutsch, Karl W. 1984. "Space and Freedom: Conditions for the Temporary Separation of Incompatible Groups." *International Political Science Review* 5, 2: 125-38.

Devenish, George. 1982. "The Role of a Constitution in a Just Political Order." *Politikon* 9, 1 (June): 19-29.

de Villiers, René. 1980. "Open or Ethnic Organisations: The Case of the South African Institute of Race Relations." In H. W. van der Merwe and Schrire, eds.

Dew, Edward. 1972. "Surinam: The Test of Consociationalism." *Plural Societies* 3, 4 (Autumn): 35-56.

_____. 1974. "Surinam: The Struggle for Ethnic Balance and Identity." *Plural Societies* 5, 3 (Autumn): 3-17.

_____. 1975. "De beheersing van raciale en culturele polarisatie in een onafhankelijk Suriname." *Beleid en Maatschappij* 2, 9 (September): 226-31.

_____. 1978. *The Difficult Flowering of Surinam: Ethnicity and Politics in a Plural Society.* The Hague: Nijhoff.

_____. 1979. "The West Indian Experience: What Lessons for South Africa?" Paper presented at the annual meeting of the Caribbean Studies Association, Martinique.

Dhlomo, Oscar. 1983. "The Strategy of Inkatha and Its Critics." In Adam, ed. 1983.

Dierickx, Guido. 1978. "Ideological Oppositions and Consociational Attitudes in the Belgian Parliament." *Legislative Studies Quarterly* 3, 1 (February): 133-60.

_____. 1984. "The Management of Subcultural Conflict: The Issue of Education in Belgium (1950-1975)." *Acta Politica* 19, 1 (January): 85-95.

Di Palma, Giuseppe. 1973. *The Study of Conflict in Western Society: A Critique of the End of Ideology.* Morristown, N.J.: General Learning Press.

_____. 1977. *Surviving Without Governing: The Italian Parties in Parliament.* Berkeley: University of California Press.

Dix, Robert H. 1980. "Consociational Democracy: The Case of Colombia." *Comparative Politics* 12, 3 (April): 303-21.

Doey, François, and Bayart, Jean-François. 1983. "Entretien avec Paul Mba-Abessole, président du comité directeur du MORENA." *Politique africaine* 11 (September): 17-21.

Dogan, Mattei, and Pelassy, Dominique. 1984. *How to Compare Nations: Strategies in Comparative Politics.* Chatham, N.J.: Chatham House.

Duchacek, Ivo D. 1970. *Comparative Federalism: The Territorial Dimension of Politics.* New York: Holt, Rinehart and Winston.

_____. 1977. "Antagonistic Cooperation: Territorial and Ethnic Communities." *Publius* 7, 4 (Fall): 3-29.

_____. 1982. "Consociations of Fatherlands: The Revival of Confederal Principles and Practices." *Publius* 12, 4 (Fall): 129-77.

Dugard, C. John R. 1980. "Political Options for South Africa and Implications for the West." In Rotberg and Barratt, eds.

_____. 1981. "Judicial Power and a Constitutional Court." In Boulle and Baxter, eds.

Duncan, Sheena. 1982. "Reform: Quo Vadis?" *South Africa International* 13, 2 (October): 97-111.

Dunn, James A. 1972. "'Consociational Democracy' and Language Conflict: A Comparison of the Belgian and Swiss Experiences." *Comparative Political Studies* 5, 1 (April): 3-39.

Dunn, William N. 1975. "Communal Federalism: Dialectics of Decentralization in Socialist Yugoslavia." *Publius* 5, 2 (Spring): 127-50.

du Pisani, A. 1983. "Partition." In van Vuuren and Kriek, eds.

du Plessis, J.A. 1978. *South Africa: From Segregation to Plural Democracy.* Pretoria: Foreign Affairs Association. FAA Study Report No. 11.

du Toit, André. 1975. "Ideological Change, Afrikaner Nationalism, and Pragmatic Racial Domination in South Africa." In Thompson and Butler, eds.

_____. 1980a. "Emerging Strategies for Political Control: Nationalist Afrikanerdom." In Price and Rosberg, eds.

_____. 1980b. "Different Models of Strategy and Procedure for Change in South Africa." In Slabbert and Opland, eds.

_____. 1983. "Political Factors Likely to Influence Constitutional Change. In Dean and Smit, eds.

du Toit, Pierre, and Theron, François. 1984. "Etnisiteit en kleurlingskap." *Politikon* 11, 1 (June): 55-66.

Dutter, Lee E. 1978. "The Netherlands as a Plural Society." *Comparative Political Studies* 10, 4 (January): 555-88.

Eagleburger, Lawrence S. 1983. "Excerpts from Address on Africa." *New York Times*, 24 June.

Economist, The. 1983. "Two Cheers for Botha?" Editorial, 15 January, pp. 17-18.

Ellemers, J. E. 1968. "De Nederlandse maatschappij in sociologisch perspectief." *Sociologische Gids* 15, 5 (September-October): 326-36.

_____. 1984. "Pillarization as a Process of Modernization." *Acta Politica* 19, 1 (January): 129-44.

Enloe, Cynthia H. 1977. "Internal Colonialism, Federalism and Alternative State Development Strategies." *Publius* 7, 4 (Fall): 145-60.

Erkens, Rainer. 1983. "The Recent Discussion on Consociational Democracy and Its Importance for South Africa." *Politeia* 2, 2: 27-45.

_____. 1985. "Limits and Prospects for a Liberal Policy in a Plural Society." In Friedrich Naumann Foundation, ed.

Esman, Milton J. 1977. "Perspectives on Ethnic Conflict in Industrialized Societies." In Esman, ed.

_____, ed. 1977. *Ethnic Conflict in the Western World.* Ithaca: Cornell University Press.

Felgate, W. S. 1981. "Co-operation between Natal and KwaZulu: An Inkatha View." In Boulle and Baxter, eds.

Fennema, M. 1976. "Professor Lijphart and de Nederlandse politiek." *Acta Politica* 11, 1 (January): 54-77.

Ferguson, Clyde, and Cotter, William R. 1978. "South Africa: What Is to Be Done." *Foreign Affairs* 56, 2 (January): 253-74.

Field, G. Lowell, and Higley, John. 1980. *Elitism.* London: Routledge and Kegan Paul.

Finer, S. E. 1975. "Adversary Politics and Electoral Reform." In Finer, ed.

_____. 1978. "Power Sharing in Plural Societies." *Times Higher Education Supplement* 343 (9 June): 17.

_____, ed. 1975. *Adversary Politics and Electoral Reform.* London: Wigram.

Foltz, William J. 1980. "The Foreign Factor in New Constitutional Provisions for South Africa." In Slabbert and Opland, eds.

Forsyth, Murray. 1984. *Federalism and the Future of South Africa.* Braamfontein: South African Institute of International Affairs. Bradlow Series No. 2.

Foster, Don H. 1983. "Some Psychological Factors Likely to Influence Constitutional Change." In Dean and Smit, eds.

Fourie, Deon. 1978. "Constitutional Alternatives and Security in South Africa." In Benyon, ed.

Frankel, Philip H. 1979. "South African Consociationalism: A Dangerous Fantasy." *Sunday Times,* 14 January.

_____. 1980. "Consensus, Consociation and Cooption in South African Politics." *Cahiers d'études africaines* 20, 4: 473-94.

Friedrich, Carl J. 1968. *Trends of Federalism in Theory and Practice.* New York: Praeger.

Friedrich Naumann Foundation, ed. 1985. *South Africa: A Chance for Liberalism?* Sankt Augustin: Liberal Verlag.

Frognier, André-Paul. 1978. "Parties and Cleavages in the Belgian Parliament." *Legislative Studies Quarterly* 3, 1 (February): 109-31.

Gandar, Laurence. 1978. "Prognosis: Evolution." In Robertson and Whitten, eds.

Gann, Lewis H., and Duignan, Peter. 1978. *South Africa: War, Revolution, or Peace?* Stanford: Hoover Institution Press.

_____, and _____. 1981. *Why South Africa Will Survive: A Historical Analysis.* New York: St. Martin's Press.

Gardner, C. O. 1971. "The English-Speaking Whites." In Randall, ed. 1971b.

Geldenhuys, Deon. 1979. "Die regionale opsie in Suid-Afrika se buitelandse beleid: Die moontlikhede van nouer samewerking in die Suider-Afrikaanse subsisteem." *Politikon* 6, 2 (December): 119-36.

_____. 1981. "South Africa's Constitutional Alternatives." *South Africa International* 11, 4 (April): 190-227.

_____. 1985. "German Views on South Africa's Future." *Aussenpolitik* 36, 1: 82-100.

Geldenhuys, Deon, and Venter, Denis. 1979. "Regional Co-operation in Southern Africa: A Constellation of States?" *International Affairs Bulletin* 3, 3: 36-72.

Gerhart, Gail M. 1978. *Black Power in South Africa: The Evolution of an Ideology.* Berkeley: University of California Press.

Germann, Raimund E. 1975. *Politische Innovation und Verfassungsreform: Ein Beitrag zur schweizerischen Diskussion über die Totalrevision der Bundesverfassung.* Berne: Haupt.

Germann, Raimund E., and Steiner, Jürg. 1985. "Comparing Decision Modes at the Country Level: Some Methodological Considerations Using Swiss Data." *British Journal of Political Science* 15, 1 (January): 123-26.

Giliomee, Hermann. 1980. "The National Party and the Afrikaner Broederbond." In Price and Rosberg, eds.

_____. 1982. *The Parting of the Ways: South African Politics 1976-82.* Cape Town: David Philip.

Giniewski, Paul. 1961. *Bantustans: A Trek Towards the Future.* Cape Town: Human and Rousseau.

Gitelman, Zvi, and Naveh, David. 1976. "Elite Accommodation and Organizational Effectiveness: The Case of Immigrant Absorption in Israel." *Journal of Politics* 38, 4 (November): 963-86.

Glaser, Kurt. 1980. "Territorial and Personal Autonomy: The Austrian Formula and Its Application to Southern Africa." In Rhoodie, ed. 1980.

Glass, Harold E. 1977. "Ethnic Diversity, Elite Accommodation and Federalism in Switzerland." *Publius* 7, 4 (Fall): 31-48.

_____. 1978. "Consensus and Opposition in Switzerland: A Neglected Consideration." *Comparative Politics* 10, 3 (April): 361-72.

Glazer, Nathan. 1980. "Individual Rights Against Group Rights." In H. W. van der Merwe and Schrire, eds.

Goldman, Joseph Richard. 1981a. "Toward a New Conceptual Framework for Developing Communist Systems: Lijphart's Consociational Theory and Authoritarian Politics for Multinational Systems." Paper presented at the annual meeting of the Midwest Political Science Association, Cincinnati.

_____. 1981b. "Consociational Politics and a State of Nations: Meinecke and Lijphart and the Theory of the State in the Third World." Paper presented at the annual meeting of the American Political Science Association, New York.

_____. 1982. *The Politics of Accommodation: The Consociational Authoritarian Model and Socialist Yugoslavia.* Doctoral dissertation, University of Kansas.

_____. 1985. "Consociational Authoritarian Politics and the 1974 Yugoslav Constitution: A Preliminary Note." *East European Quarterly* 19, 2 (June): 241-49.

Good, Robert C. 1980. "An 'Outsider's' Personal Reflections on South Africa's Future." In Rotberg and Barratt, eds.

Gordimer, Nadine. 1983. "Living in the Interregnum." *New York Review of Books* 29, 21-22 (20 January): 21-29.

Graziano, Luigi. 1980. "The Historic Compromise and Consociational Democracy: Toward a 'New Democracy'?" *International Political Science Review* 1, 3: 345-68.

Grieve, Malcolm J. 1978. "Internal and International Aspects of Dependent Homelands in South Africa." In Anglin, Shaw, and Widstrand, eds.

Groenewald, Coen. 1984. "South Africa Says YES." *South African Panorama* 29, 1 (January): 16-19.

Gunther, Richard, and Blough, Roger A. 1981. "Religious Conflict and Consensus in Spain: A Tale of Two Constitutions." *World Affairs* 143, 4 (Spring): 366-412.

Gunther, Richard; Sani, Giacomo; and Shabad, Goldie. 1985. *Spain After Franco: The Making of a Competitive Party System.* Berkeley: University of California Press.

Gutteridge, William. 1981. *South Africa: Strategy for Survival?* London: Institute for the Study of Conflict. Conflict Studies No. 131.

Gwyn, William B. 1978. Review of Lijphart 1977a. *Journal of Politics* 40, 4 (November): 1093-94.

Hanf, Theodor. 1979. "We Must Not Let Democracy Die of Thirst." *Sunday Times,* 14 January.

_____. 1980. "Education and Consociational Conflict Regulation in Plural Societies." In Slabbert and Opland, eds.

_____. 1981. "Südafrika zwischen Konfliktregelung und Konfliktverschärfung." In *Konflikte unserer Zeit—Konflikte der Zukunft,* ed. Daniel Frei. Zurich: Schulthess.

_____. 1983. "Lessons Which Are Never Learnt: Minority Rule in Comparative Perspective." In Adam, ed. 1983.

_____. 1984. "The Political Function of the Educational System in Culturally Segmented States." *Zeitschrift für Erziehungs- und Sozialwissenschaftliche Forschung* 1, 2: 281-99.

Hanf, Theodor, and Weiland, Heribert. 1980. "Consociational Democracy for South Africa? On the Importance of the Recent Constitutional Debate." In Rhoodie, ed. 1980.

Hanf, Theodor; Weiland, Heribert; and Vierdag, Gerda. 1981. *South Africa—The Prospects of Peaceful Change: An Empirical Enquiry into the Possibility of Democratic Conflict Regulation.* London: Rex Collings.

Hare, A. Paul, ed. 1983. *The Struggle for Democracy in South Africa: Conflict and Conflict Resolution.* Cape Town: Centre for Intergroup Studies.

Harik, Iliya. 1984. "Toward a New National Pact for Lebanon." *Panorama of Events* 7, 32: 13-21.

Hartlyn, Jonathan. 1981. *Consociational Politics in Colombia: Confrontation and Accommodation in Comparative Perspective.* Doctoral dissertation, Yale University.

Heard, Kenneth A. 1978. "Change, Challenge and Response: A View of the 1977 South African General Election." In Anglin, Shaw, and Widstrand, eds.

Heisler, Martin O. 1974. "Institutionalizing Societal Cleavages in a Cooptive Polity: The Growing Importance of the Output Side in Belgium." In Heisler, ed.

_____. 1977. "Managing Ethnic Conflict in Belgium." *Annals of the American Academy of Political and Social Science* 433 (September): 32-46.

Heisler, Martin O., and Kvavik, Robert B. 1974. "Patterns of European Politics: The 'European Polity' Model." In Heisler, ed.

Heisler, Martin O., and Peters, B. Guy. 1983. "Scarcity and the Management of Political Conflict in Multicultural Polities." *International Political Science Review* 4, 3: 327-44.

Heisler, Martin O., ed. 1974. *Politics in Europe: Structures and Processes in Some Postindustrial Democracies*. New York: McKay.

Henderson, Conway W. 1981. "Comment: Consociational Democracy and the Case of Switzerland." *Journal of Politics* 43, 4 (November): 1232-35.

Heunis, J.C. 1981. "Stabiliteit en hervorming in Suid-Afrikaanse konteks." *Politikon* 8, 2 (December): 1-7.

Hill, Christopher R. 1972. "The Future of Separate Development in South Africa." In *Southern Africa in Perspective: Essays in Regional Politics*, ed. Christian P. Potholm and Richard Dale. New York: Free Press.

_____. 1983. *Change in South Africa: Blind Alleys or New Directions?* London: Rex Collings.

Hirsch, Morris I. 1978. "The Process of Power Sharing." In *The Road to a Just Society*. Johannesburg: South African Institute of Race Relations.

_____. 1980. "Lessons form Rhodesia for Constitutional Change in South Africa." In Slabbert and Opland, eds.

Hoernlé, R. F. Alfred. 1939. *South African Native Policy and the Liberal Spirit.* Cape Town: University of Cape Town.

Holland, Martin. 1983. "A Rejoinder: The European Community and Regional Integration in Southern Africa—A Misplaced Analogy." *Politikon* 10, 2 (December): 38-50.

Hoppe, R. 1976. "Het politiek systeem van Suriname: Elite-kartel demokratie." *Acta Politica* 11, 2 (April): 145-77.

Horowitz, Dan. 1982. "Dual Authority Polities." *Comparative Politics* 14, 3 (April): 329-49.

Horrell, Muriel. 1973. *The African Homelands of South Africa.* Johannesburg: South African Institute of Race Relations.

Horwitz, Ralph. 1978. "South African Realities and Realpolitik." *Political Quarterly* 49, 2 (April-June): 181-90.

Houska, Joseph J. 1985. *Influencing Mass Political Behavior: Elites and Political Subcultures in the Netherlands and Austria*. Berkeley: Institute of International Studies, University of California. Research Series No. 60.

Howe, Marvine. 1985. "Rival Cypriot Leaders Meet at U.N. to Seek Final Pact." *New York Times*, 18 January.

Howe, Russell W. 1978. "Prognosis: Conflict." In Robertson and Whitten, eds.

Hudson, Michael C. 1976. "The Lebanese Crisis: The Limits of Consociational Democracy." *Journal of Palestine Studies* 5, 3-4 (Spring-Summer): 109-22.

Hueglin, Thomas. 1979. "Johannes Althusius: Medieval Constitutionalist or Modern Federalist?" *Publius* 9, 4 (Fall): 9-41.

Hughes, Arnold. 1982. "The Limits of 'Consociational Democracy' in the Gambia." *Civilisations* 32, 2: 65-92.

Hughes, Christopher J. 1978. "What Is the Lesson of Swiss Solutions to Pluralist Problems for South Africa?" In Rhoodie, ed. 1978.

_____. 1983. "A Confederation of Southern African States as a Vehicle of Stability." *Politikon* 10, 2 (December): 26-37.

Hugo, P. J. 1975. "Race and Class in South Africa." *Politikon* 2, 2 (December): 140-51.

Human Sciences Research Council (HSRC) Investigation into Intergroup Relations; Main Committee. 1985. *The South African Society: Realities and Future Prospects.* Pretoria.

Huneeus, Carlos. 1981. "La Union de Centro Democrático: Un partido consociacional." *Revista de política comparada* 3 (Winter): 163-92.

Huntington, Samuel P. 1972. "Foreword." In Nordlinger 1972.

_____ 1981. "Reform and Stability in a Modernizing, Multi-Ethnic Society." *Politikon* 8, 2 (December): 8-26.

Hutson, H. P. W. 1973. *Majority Rule—Why? Co-operation Not Confrontation in Southern Africa.* London: Johnson.

Huyse, Lucien. 1970. *Passiviteit, pacificatie en verzuiling in de Belgische politiek: Een sociologische studie.* Antwerp: Standaard.

_____. 1980. *De gewapende vrede: Politiek in België na 1945.* Leuven: Kritak.

_____. 1981. "Political Conflict in Bicultural Belgium." In Lijphart, ed.

_____. 1982. "België: Een wankele natie?" In *Politieke stelsels: Stabiliteit en verandering,* ed. U. Rosenthal. Alphen aan den Rijn: Samsom.

_____. 1984. "Pillarization Reconsidered." *Acta Politica* 19, 1 (January): 145-58.

Ignatius, David. 1983. "How to Rebuild Lebanon." *Foreign Affairs* 61, 5 (Summer): 1140-56.

Irvine, Douglas McKinnon. 1978. "Plural Societies and Constitution-Making." In Benyon, ed.

_____. 1982. "Pluralism, Ideology and Analysis: The South African Case." *Civilisations* 32, 2: 153-76.

_____. 1984. "South Africa: Federal Potentialities in Current Developments." *International Political Science Review* 5, 4: 491-506.

Jackson, Robert H., and Rosberg, Carl G. 1984. "Popular Legitimacy in African Multi-Ethnic States." *Journal of Modern African Studies* 22, 2 (June): 177-98.

Jacobs, G. F. 1971. "The United Party Plan for a New Realism in South African Politics." In Randall, ed. 1971c.

Johnson, Jill, and Magubane, Peter. 1979. *Soweto Speaks.* Johannesburg: Donker.

Johnson, Nevil. 1975. "Adversary Politics and Electoral Reform: Need We Be Afraid?" In Finer, ed.

Jooste, C. J. 1983. "Proposals for Constitutional Change in Southern Africa." In van Vuuren and Kriek, eds.

Kaminsky, Elijah Ben-Zion. 1980. Review of Lijphart 1977a. *Western Political Quarterly* 33, 3 (September): 433-34.

Karis, Thomas. 1983. "The Resurgent African National Congress: Competing for Hearts and Minds in South Africa." In Callaghy, ed.

_____. 1984. "Revolution in the Making: Black Politics in South Africa." *Foreign Affairs* 62, 2 (Winter): 378-406.

Karis, Thomas, and Carter, Gwendolen M., eds. 1977. *From Protest to Challenge: A Documentary History of African Politics in South Africa, 1882-1964*, 4 vols. Stanford: Hoover Institution Press.

Kassis, Hanna E. 1985. "Religious Ethnicity in the World of Islam: The Case of Lebanon." *International Political Science Review* 6, 2: 216-29.

Katz, Richard S. 1984. "Dimensions of Partisan Conflict in Swiss Cantons." *Comparative Political Studies* 16, 4 (January): 505-27.

Kerina, Mburumba. 1978. "Plural Societies and the Application of Democracy." In Rhoodie, ed. 1978.

Kerr, Henry H., Jr. 1974. *Switzerland: Social Cleavages and Partisan Conflict.* London: Sage. Sage Professional Papers in Contemporary Political Sociology.

_____. 1978. "The Structure of Opposition in the Swiss Parliament." *Legislative Studies Quarterly* 3, 1 (February): 51-62.

Kieve, Ronald A. 1981. "Pillars of Sand: A Marxist Critique of Consociational Democracy in the Netherlands." *Comparative Politics* 13, 3 (April): 313-37.

Kloss, Heinz. 1979. "Power Sharing Versus Partition in South Africa." *South Africa International* 10, 2 (October): 49-56.

Koch, Koen. 1982a. "Lijphart." *Vrij Nederland,* 29 May.

_____. 1982b. "Naschrift." *Vrij Nederland,* 3 July.

Koornhof, P. G. J. 1979. "Creating Conditions for Peaceful Co-Existence in South Africa." *Politikon* 6, 2 (December): 93-102.

Kotzé, Dirk A. 1978. "African Politics." In de Crespigny and Schrire, eds.

Koury, Enver M. 1976. *The Crisis in the Lebanese System: Confessionalism and Chaos.* Washington, D.C.: American Enterprise Institute.

Kriek, D. J. 1976. "Politieke alternatiewe vir Suid-Afrika op soek na 'n nuwe paradigma." *Politikon* 3, 1 (June): 57-89.

_____. 1978. "Enkele gedagtes oor die teorie en praktyk van federalisme." *Politikon* 5, 2 (December): 188-205.

_____. 1982. Review of Buthelezi Commission, 1982. *Politikon* 9, 2 (December): 96-101.

_____. 1983a. "Federal Forms of Government." In van Vuuren and Kriek, eds.

_____. 1983b. "Confederal Cooperation." In van Vuuren and Kriek, eds.

Kroes, R. 1970. "Conflict en radicalisme: Een tweetrapsmodel." *Sociologische Gids* 17, 1 (January-February): 1-18.

Kuper, Leo. 1977. *The Pity of It All: Polarisation of Racial and Ethnic Relations.* Minneapolis: University of Minnesota Press.

Kuper, Leo, and Smith, M. G., eds. 1969. *Pluralism in Africa.* Berkeley: University of California Press.

Kuzwayo, Ellen. 1980a. "Ethnic or Open Organisations in the South African Society?" In H. W. van der Merwe and Schrire, eds.

_____. 1980b. "The Committee of Ten." In H. W. van der Merwe et al., eds. 1980.

Lanning, Eldon. 1974. "A Typology of Latin American Political Systems." *Comparative Politics* 6, 3 (April): 367-94.

Lefever, Ernest W. 1978. "Limits of Government in the Third World." In Rhoodie, ed. 1978.

_____. 1980. "United States and South Africa: A Troubled Relationship." In Rhoodie, ed. 1980.

Leftwich, Adrian. 1974. "The Constitution and Continuity of South African Inequality: Some Conceptual Questions." In *South Africa: Economic Growth and Political Change,* ed. A. Leftwich. New York: St Martin's Press.

Legum, Colin. 1982. "South Africa's Search for a New Political System: The God that Failed Afrikanerdom." In *The Year Book of World Affairs 1982,* vol. 36, ed. George W. Keeton and Georg Schwarzenberger. London: Stevens.

Legum, Colin, and Legum, Margaret. 1964. *South Africa: Crisis for the West.* New York: Praeger.

Lehmbruch, Gerhard. 1967. *Proporzdemokratie: Politisches System und politische Kultur in der Schweiz und in Österreich.* Tübingen: Mohr.

_____. 1968. "Konkordanzdemokratie im politischen System der Schweiz." *Politische Vierteljahresschrift* 9, 3: 443-59.

_____. 1974. "A Non-Competitive Pattern of Conflict Management in Liberal Democracies: The Case of Switzerland, Austria and Lebanon." In McRae, ed.

_____. 1975. "Consociational Democracy in the International System." *European Journal of Political Research* 3, 4 (December): 377-91.

_____. 1979. "Consociational Democracy, Class Conflict, and the New Corporatism." In *Trends Toward Corporatist Intermediation,* ed. Philippe C. Schmitter and Gerhard Lehmbruch. Beverly Hills: Sage.

Lehner, Franz. 1984. "Consociational Democracy in Switzerland: A Political-Economic Explanation and Some Empirical Evidence." *European Journal of Political Research* 12, 1 (March): 25-42.

Lelyveld, Joseph. 1982. "White South African Opposition Facing a Bind in Plan for a New Parliament." *New York Times,* 25 December.

_____. 1983. "South African 'Homeland': A Success of Sorts." *New York Times*, 16 May.

Lemarchand, René, and Martin, David. 1974. *Selective Genocide in Burundi.* London: Minority Rights Group. Report No. 20.

Lemon, Anthony. 1980. "Federalism and Plural Societies: A Critique with Special Reference to South Africa." *Plural Societies* 11, 2 (Summer): 3-24.

Levine, Daniel H. 1973. *Conflict and Political Change in Venezuela.* Princeton: Princeton University Press.

Lewis, W. Arthur. 1965. *Politics in West Africa.* London: Allen and Unwin.

Lewsen, Phyllis. 1982. *The South African Constitution: Euphoria and Rejection.* Johannesburg: Witwatersrand University Press. Raymond Dart Lecture No. 19.

Lijphart, Arend. 1968a. *The Politics of Accommodation: Pluralism and Democracy in the Netherlands.* Berkeley: University of California Press.

_____. 1968b. "Typologies of Democratic Systems." *Comparative Political Studies* 1, 1 (April): 3-44.

_____. 1969a. "Consociational Democracy." *World Politics* 21, 2 (January): 207-25.

_____. 1969b. "Kentering in de Nederlandse politiek." *Acta Politica* 4, 3 (April): 231-47.

_____. 1971. "Cultural Diversity and Theories of Political Integration." *Canadian Journal of Political Science* 4, 1 (March): 1-14.

_____. 1975. "The Northern Ireland Problem: Cases, Theories, and Solutions." *British Journal of Political Science* 5, 1 (January): 83-106.

_____. 1976. "Repliek." *Acta Politica* 11, 1 (January): 78-84.

_____. 1977a. *Democracy in Plural Societies: A Comparative Exploration.* New Haven: Yale University Press.

_____. 1977b. "Political Theories and the Explanation of Ethnic Conflict in the Western World: Falsified Predictions and Plausible Postdictions." In Esman, ed.

_____. 1977c. "Majority Rule versus Democracy in Deeply Divided Societies." *Politikon* 4, 2 (December): 113-26.

_____. 1979a. "Religious vs. Linguistic vs. Class Voting: The 'Crucial Experiment' of Comparing Belgium, Canada, South Africa, and Switzerland." *American Political Science Review* 73, 2 (June): 442-58.

_____. 1979b. "Consociation and Federation: Conceptual and Empirical Links." *Canadian Journal of Political Science* 12, 3 (September): 499-515.

_____. 1980a. "Federal, Confederal, and Consociational Options for the South African Plural Society." In Rotberg and Barratt, eds.

_____. 1980b. "Preface: Minority Rights, Autonomy and Power-Sharing." In *World Minorities in the Eighties*, ed. Georgina Ashworth. Sunbury: Quartermaine House.

154   BIBLIOGRAPHY

_____. 1980c. "Language, Religion, Class and Party Choice: Belgium, Canada, Switzerland and South Africa Compared." In Rose, ed.

_____. 1981a. "Consociational Theory: Problems and Prospects." *Comparative Politics* 13, 3 (April): 355-60.

_____. 1981b. "De theorie van de pacificatie-democratie." In *Democratie: Theorie en praktijk,* ed. J. J. A. Thomassen. Alphen aan den Rijn: Samsom.

_____. 1982a. "Governing Natal-KwaZulu: Some Suggestions." In Buthelezi Commission.

_____. 1982b. "If First It's Tried in Natal-Zululand." *New York Times,* 27 May.

_____. 1982c. "Consociation: The Model and Its Applications in Divided Societies." In *Political Co-operation in Divided Societies: A Series of Papers Relevant to the Conflict in Northern Ireland,* ed. Desmond Rea. Dublin: Gill and McMillan.

_____1982d. "Zuid-Afrika." *Vrij Nederland,* 3 July.

_____. 1984a. *Democracies: Patterns of Majoritarian and Consensus Government in Twenty-One Countries.* New Haven: Yale University Press.

_____. 1984b. "The Politics of Accommodation: Reflections—Fifteen Years Later." *Acta Politica* 19, 1 (January): 9-18.

_____. 1985. "Proportionality by Non-P.R. Methods: Ethnic Representation in Belgium, Cyprus, Lebanon, New Zealand, West Germany, and Zimbabwe." In *Electoral Laws and Their Political Consequences,* ed. Bernard Grofman and Arend Lijphart. New York: Agathon Press.

_____, ed. (1981). *Conflict and Coexistence in Belgium: The Dynamics of a Culturally Divided Society.* Berkeley: Institute of International Studies, University of California.

Lindberg, Leon N. 1974. "The Political System of the European Community." In Heisler, ed.

Lodge, Tom. 1983. *Black Politics in South Africa since 1945.* New York: Longman.

Lombard, J. A. 1970. "Die staatkundige en administratiewe beginsels van tuislandontwikkeling." In Viljoen, ed.

_____. 1980. "Multinationalism in a Liberal Society: The Case for South Africa." In Rhoodie, ed. 1980.

Lombard, J. A., et al. 1980. *Alternatives to the Consolidation of KwaZulu: Progress Report.* Pretoria: Bureau for Economic Policy and Analysis, University of Pretoria.

Lorwin, Val R. 1971. "Segmented Pluralism: Ideological Cleavages and Political Cohesion in the Smaller European Democracies." *Comparative Politics* 3, 2 (January): 141-75.

_____. 1974. "Belgium: Conflict and Compromise." In McRae, ed.

Louw, André du P. 1979. "Swart politiek in Suid-Afrika: 'n filosofiese perspektief." *Politikon* 6, 1 (June): 71-76.

Lustick, Ian. 1979. "Stability in Deeply Divided Societies: Consociationalism versus Control." *World Politics* 31, 3 (April): 325-44.

Luyt, Richard. 1978. "African Constitutionalism: Constitutions in the Context of Decolonization." In Benyon. ed.

Maasdorp, Gavin. 1980. "Forms of Partition." In Rotberg and Barratt, eds.

Mabude, M. 1983. "Perspectives on the Future of Constitutional Development in Southern Africa." In van Vuuren and Kriek, eds.

McDonald, Steven F. 1979. "The Black Community." In Bissell and Crocker, eds.

McNamara, Robert S. 1982. "South Africa: The Middle East of the 1990's?" *New York Times*, 24 October.

McRae, Kenneth D. 1974. "Consociationalism and the Canadian Political System." In McRae, ed.

_____. 1979. "Comment: Federation, Consociation, Corporatism—An Addendum to Arend Lijphart." *Canadian Journal of Political Science* 12, 3 (September): 517-22.

_____. 1983. *Conflict and Compromise in Multilingual Societies*; vol. 1: *Switzerland*. Waterloo, Ont.: Wilfrid Laurier University Press.

_____, ed. 1974. *Consociational Democracy: Political Accommodation in Segmented Societies*. Toronto: McClelland and Stewart.

McVey, Ruth T. 1969. "Nationalism, Islam and Marxism: The Management of Ideological Conflict in Indonesia." Introduction to Soekarno, *Nationalism, Islam and Marxism*. Ithaca: Modern Indonesia Project, Cornell University.

Makatini, Johnny. 1983. "Constitutional Repression." *I.D.A.F. News Notes* (December): 1-3.

Malherbe, Paul N. 1974. *Multistan: A Way Out of the South African Dilemma*. Cape Town: David Philip.

Mander, John. 1963. "South Africa: Revolution or Partition?" *Encounter* 21, 4 (October): 11-20.

Mangope, Lucas. 1979. *Trends in Southern Africa and the Role of Bophuthatswana*. Braamfontein: South African Institute of International Affairs. Occasional Paper.

Maré, Gerhard. 1983. "Africans under Apartheid in the 1980s." In South African Research Service, ed. 1983.

Marquard, Leo. 1971. *A Federation of Southern Africa*. London: Oxford University Press.

Matanzima, Kaiser. 1976. "Transkei: Its Independence and Future." *Politikon* 3, 2 (October): 2-3.

Mbata, J. Congress. 1975. "Profile of Change: The Cumulative Significance of Changes among Africans." In Thompson and Butler, eds.

Mbeki, Thabo. 1978. "South Africa: The Historical Injustice." In Anglin, Shaw, and Widstrand, eds.

_____. 1983. "Reforming Apartheid Doesn't End Slavery." *New York Times,* 18 July.

Means, Gordon P. 1972. "'Special Rights' as a Strategy for Development: The Case of Malaysia." *Comparative Politics* 5, 1 (October): 29-61.

Meer, Fatima. 1971. "Indian People: Current Trends and Policies." In Randall, ed. 1971b.

_____. 1972. "An Indian's Views on Apartheid." In Rhoodie, ed. 1972.

Mervis, Joel. 1972. "A Critique of Separate Development." In Rhoodie, ed. 1972.

Messarra, Antoine Nasri. 1977. *La Structure sociale du Parlement libanais (1920-1976).* Beirut: Institut des Sciences Sociales, Université Libanaise.

_____. 1983. *Le Modèle politique libanais et sa survie: Essai sur la classification et l'aménagement d'un système consociatif.* Beirut: Librairie Orientale.

_____. 1984. "Les Chances de survie du système consociatif libanais: D'une consociation sauvage à un modèle consociatif rationalisé." Paper presented at the International Symposium on Democratic Conflict Regulation in Plural Societies, Beirut, 17-21 December.

Meyer, Gabi. 1983. *Conflict and Conflict Accommodation: An Annotated Bibliography.* Rondebosch: Centre for Intergroup Studies. Occasional Paper No. 9.

Milne, R. S. 1975. "'The Pacific Way': Consociational Politics in Fiji." *Pacific Affairs* 48, 3 (Fall): 413-31.

_____. 1981. *Politics in Ethnically Bipolar States: Guyana, Malaysia, Fiji.* Vancouver: University of British Columbia Press.

Milne, R. S., and Mauzy, Diane K. 1978. *Politics and Government in Malaysia.* Vancouver: University of British Columbia Press.

Mironesco, Christine. 1982. *La Logique du conflit: Théories et mythes de la sociologie politique contemporaine.* Lausanne: Favre.

Moerane, M. T. 1978. "The Problems of Plural Societies with Special Reference to the Urban Blacks of South Africa." In Rhoodie, ed. 1978.

Mughan, Anthony. 1979. Review of Lijphart 1977a. *Ethnic and Racial Studies* 2, 4 (October): 515-16.

Mulder, C. P. 1972. "The Rationale of Separate Development." In Rhoodie, ed. 1972.

Munger, Edwin S. 1978. "Prognosis: The United States of South Africa." In Robertson and Whitten, eds.

_____, ed. 1980. *The Buthelezi Commission.* Pasadena: Munger Africana Library, California Institute of Technology. Munger Africana Library Notes No. 56.

Nagata, Judith. 1979. Review of Lijphart 1977a. *International Journal* 34, 3 (Summer): 505-6.

Nasir, Khalil A. 1978. "The Problems of Intergroup Accommodation and Pluralism in the Politics of Pakistan." In Rhoodie, ed. 1978.

Nattrass, Jill. 1978. "Constitutional Alternatives, Economic Growth and Equity." In Benyon, ed.

Nel, D.J. Louis. 1984. "Democracy Is the Way." *New York Times*, 17 September.

Neuman, Stephanie G. 1976. "Integration: Conceptual Tool or Academic Jargon?" In *Small States and Segmented Societies: National Political Integration in a Global Environment*, ed. Stephanie G. Neuman. New York: Praeger.

New Republic Party. 1980. *Constitutional Policy: Submission to the Commission on the Constitution*. Cape Town: N.R.P. Research Department.

New York Times. 1983. "Changing Apartheid's Color." Editorial, 5 November.

_____. 1984. "Mr. Mugabe's Politics of Hate." Editorial, 25 June.

_____. 1985. "The Lost White Tribe." Editorial, 29 March.

Ngubane, Jordan K. 1963. *An African Explains Apartheid.* New York: Praeger.

_____. 1971. "South Africa's Race Crisis: A Conflict of Minds." In Adam, ed. 1971.

_____. 1979. *Conflict of Minds: Changing Power Dispositions in South Africa.* New York: Books in Focus.

Ng'weno, Hilary. 1984. "The Lessons of Apartheid." *Newsweek* (Pacific Edition), 24 September.

Nieuwoudt, C. F. 1977. "The Structuring of Political Change in South Africa." *Politikon* 4, 2 (December): 166-77.

Njisane, Mlahleni. 1980. "Transkei's First Years of Independence: A Review of Separate Development." In H. W. van der Merwe and Schrire, eds.

Nkomo, W. F. 1972. "An African's View of Apartheid." In Rhoodie, ed. 1972.

Noble, Lela Garner. 1979. Review of Lijphart 1977a. *Journal of Commonwealth and Comparative Politics* 17, 3 (November): 316-17.

Noel, S. J. R. 1971. "Consociational Democracy and Canadian Federalism." *Canadian Journal of Political Science* 4, 1 (March): 15-18.

_____. 1977a. "Political Parties and Elite Accommodation: Interpretations of Canadian Federalism." In *Canadian Federalism: Myth or Reality*, ed. J. Peter Meekison, 3d ed. Toronto: Methuen.

_____. 1977b. "The Prime Minister's Role in a Consociational Democracy." In *Apex of Power: The Prime Minister and Political Leadership in Canada*, ed. Thomas A. Hockin, 2d ed. Scarborough, Ont.: Prentice-Hall.

Nolutshungu, Sam C. 1980. "Change and Reform in South Africa?" *International Journal* 35, 4 (Autumn): 646-62.

_____. 1982. *Changing South Africa: Political Considerations.* Manchester: Manchester University Press.

Nordlinger, Eric A. 1972. *Conflict Regulation in Divided Societies.* Cambridge, Mass.: Center for International Affairs, Harvard University. Occasional Papers in International Affairs No. 29.

Obler, Jeffrey; Steiner, Jürg; and Dierickx, Guido. 1977. *Decision-Making in Smaller Democracies: The Consociational "Burden."* Beverly Hills: Sage. Sage Professional Papers in Comparative Politics No. 01-064.

Olivier, Gerrit C. 1978a. "Plural Accommodation in South Africa: Problems, Perspectives and Solutions." In Rhoodie, ed. 1978.

_____. 1978b. "Divisive and Integrative Forces in South African Political and Constitutional Development: An Historical Perspective." In Benyon, ed.

_____. 1978c. "The Executive." In de Crespigny and Schrire, eds.

_____. 1980. "Conflict Resolution in South Africa: Policy Options Open to the Afrikaner Power Establishment." In Rhoodie, ed. 1980.

_____. 1981. "Hervormingsstrategieë in Suid-Afrika." *Politikon* 8, 2 (December): 57-69.

Olivier, N. J. J. 1981. "Implications of Constitutional Development in KwaZulu/Natal for the Rest of South Africa." In Boulle and Baxter, eds.

_____. 1985. "The Constitutional Proposals of the South African Government." In Friedrich Naumann Foundation, ed.

Olivier, N. J. J., and van Wyk, Dawid H. 1978. "Parliament." In de Crespigny and Schrire, eds.

Oppenheimer, H. F. 1982. *Chairman's Statement 1982.* Johannesburg: Anglo American Corporation of South Africa Limited.

Ormsby, William. 1974. "The Province of Canada: The Emergence of Consociational Politics." In McRae, ed.

Özgür, Özdemir A. 1982. *Apartheid: The United Nations and Peaceful Change in South Africa.* Dobbs Ferry, N.Y.: Transnational Publishers.

Pakendorf, Harold. 1980. "Can Separate Development Evolve?" In Rotberg and Barratt, eds.

Pappalardo, Adriano. 1981. "The Conditions for Consociational Democracy: A Logical and Empirical Critique." *European Journal of Political Research* 9, 4 (December): 365-90.

Parker, Frank J. 1983. *South Africa: Lost Opportunities.* Lexington, Mass.: Lexington Books.

Parry, Geraint. 1979. "Recommended Accommodation." *Government and Opposition* 14, 1 (Winter): 111-14.

Parsons, Talcott. 1978. "Cleavage and Conflict in Modern Type Societies." In Rhoodie, ed. 1978.

Paton, Alan. 1959. *Hope for South Africa.* New York: Praeger.

_____. 1968. *The Long View.* New York: Praeger.

_____. 1971. "Some Thoughts on the Common Society." In Randall, ed. 1971c.

Paton, Alan, and Mathews, A. S. 1972. "The Case for a Common Society in South Africa." In Rhoodie, ed. 1972.

Pedersen, Mogens N. 1982. *The Dissatisfied Voter as Deus ex Machina: A Critique of Arend Lijphart's Attempt to Understand Political Change and Stability in Western Europe.* Odense: Institute of Social Sciences, Odense University. Working Paper No. 16.

Peters, B. Guy; Doughtie, John C.; and McCulloch, M. Kathleen. 1977. "Types of Democratic Systems and Types of Public Policy: An Empirical Examination." *Comparative Politics* 9, 3 (April): 327-55.

Phatudi, Cedric, and Kapuuo, Clemens. 1974. *South Africa's Homelands: Two African Views.* Pasadena: Munger Africana Library, California Institute of Technology. Munger Africana Library Notes No. 22.

Pijnenburg, B. 1984. "Pillarized and Consociational-Democratic Belgium: The Views of Huyse." *Acta Politica* 19, 1 (January): 57-71.

Potgieter, P. J. J. S. 1977. *Die nuwe konstitusionele bedeling: Noodsaaklikheid.* Potchefstroom: Insituut vir Suid-Afrikaanse Politiek.

Powell, G. Bingham, Jr. 1970. *Social Fragmentation and Political Hostility: An Austrian Case Study.* Stanford: Stanford University Press.

_____. 1979. Review of Lijphart 1977a. *American Political Science Review* 73, 1 (March): 295-97.

Powell, G. Bingham, Jr., and Stiefbold, Rodney P. 1977. "Anger, Bargaining, and Mobilization as Middle-Range Theories of Elite Conflict Behavior." *Comparative Politics* 9, 4 (July): 379-98.

Presthus, Robert. 1973. *Elite Accommodation in Canadian Politics.* Cambridge: Cambridge University Press.

Price, Robert M. 1980. "Apartheid and White Supremacy: The Meaning of Government-Led Reform in the South African Context." In Price and Rosberg, eds.

Price, Robert M., and Rosberg, Carl G., eds. 1980. *The Apartheid Regime: Political Power and Racial Domination.* Berkeley: Institute of International Studies, University of California.

Prinsloo, M. W. 1984. "Political Restructuring, Capital Accumulation and the 'Coming Corporatism' in South Africa: Some Theoretical Considerations." *Politikon* 11, 1 (June): 20-42.

Prinz, Friedrich. 1978. "A Model of a Multinational Society as Developed in Austria-Hungary Before 1918." In Rhoodie, ed. 1978.

Progressive Federal Party. 1978. *Report of the Constitutional Committee of the Progressive Federal Party and Recommendations Based on the Report for Consideration by the Federal Congress of the P. F. P. to be Held in Durban, 17th & 18th November 1978.* Cape Town: Office of the Leader.

Puschra, Werner. 1981. *Südafrika: Optionen für die Bundesrepublik Deutschland.* Bonn: Forschungsinstitut der Friedrich-Ebert-Stiftung.

_____. 1984. *Schwarze Gewerkschaften in Südafrika: Neue Mittelklasse oder Massenbewegung?* Bonn: Forschungsinstitut der Friedrich-Ebert-Stiftung.

_____, ed. 1983. *Black Trade Unions in South Africa: Core of a New Democratic Opposition Movement?* Bonn: Forschungsinstitut der Friedrich-Ebert-Stiftung.

Qoboza, Percy. 1978. "South Africa: A Black Viewpoint." In Rhoodie, ed. 1978.

_____. 1980. "An Open Society—Is It Still Achievable?" In Rotberg and Barratt, eds.

Rabushka, Alvin. 1978. "Prescriptions for the Plural Society: Theory and Practice in the South African Context." In Rhoodie, ed. 1978.

Rabushka, Alvin, and Shepsle, Kenneth A. 1972. *Politics in Plural Societies: A Theory of Democratic Instability.* Columbus, Ohio: Merrill.

Rae, Douglas W., and Taylor, Michael. 1970. *The Analysis of Political Cleavages.* New Haven: Yale University Press.

Rajah, D. S.; Curry, D. M. G.; and Ngcobo, S. B. 1978. "Constitutional Proposals: Panel Discussion." In Benyon, ed.

Ranchod, B. G. 1978a. "The Restoration of Human Rights: A Means Towards Achieving Social Justice in South Africa." In Rhoodie, ed. 1978.

_____. 1978b. "Constitutions and Political Rights." In Benyon, ed.

_____. 1983. "Attitudes to Constitutional Proposals." In van Vuuren and Kriek, eds.

Randall, Peter, ed. 1971a. *Anatomy of Apartheid.* Johannesburg: Study Project on Christianity in Apartheid Society. Occasional Publication No. 1.

_____, ed. 1971b. *South Africa's Minorities.* Johannesburg: Study Project on Christianity in Apartheid Society. Occasional Publication No. 2.

_____, ed. 1971c. *Directions of Change in South African Politics.* Johannesburg: Study Project on Christianity in Apartheid Society. Occasional Publication No. 3.

_____, ed. 1973a. *South Africa's Political Alternatives: Report of the Political Commission.* Johannesburg: Study Project on Christianity in Apartheid Society. Spro-Cas Publication No. 10.

_____, ed. 1973b. *A Taste of Power: The Final Co-ordinated Spro-Cas Report.* Johannesburg: Study Project on Christianity in Apartheid Society. Spro-Cas Publication No. 11.

Rauche, G. A. 1983a. "An Adequate Model of Reform? A Critical Analysis of the Constitutional Model Proposed by the President's Council." In van Vuuren and Kriek, eds.

_____. 1983b. "Consociational Government: An Adequate Model of Reform?" *Politeia* 2, 1: 19-30.

Razis, Vincent V. 1980. *Swords or Ploughshares? South Africa and Political Change.* Johannesburg: Ravan Press.

Rex, John. 1971. "The Plural Society: The South African Case." *Race* 12, 4 (April): 401-13.

Rhoodie, Nic J. 1978a. "Introduction." In Rhoodie, ed. 1978.

_____. 1978b. "Key Socio-Political Determinants of Intercommunal Power Deployment in a South African Plural Democracy." In *The Road to a Just Society.* Johannesburg: South African Institute of Race Relations.

_____. 1980a. "Federalism/Confederalism as a Means of White-Black Conflict Resolution: Conceptual Dissonance in White Nationalist Ranks." *Politikon* 7, 2 (December): 101-10.

_____. 1980b. "Introduction." In Rhoodie, ed. 1980.

_____. 1983a. *Intergroup Conflict in Deeply Segmented Societies: An Introductory Conceptual Framework.* Pretoria: Human Sciences Research Council.

_____. 1983b. "Value Consensus as a Prerequisite for Consociational Federalism in Southern Africa." In van Vuuren and Kriek, eds.

_____, ed. 1972. *South African Dialogue: Contrasts in South African Thinking on Basic Race Issues.* Philadelphia: Westminster Press.

_____, ed. 1978. *Intergroup Accommodation in Plural Societies.* London: Macmillan.

_____, ed. 1980. *Conflict Resolution in South Africa: The Quest for Accommodationist Policies in a Plural Society.* Pretoria: Institute for Plural Societies, University of Pretoria.

Riekert, J. G. 1981. "The Requirements for Meaningful Autonomy for KwaZulu/Natal." In Boulle and Baxter, eds.

Robertson, Ian, and Whitten, Phillip, eds. 1978. *Race and Politics in South Africa.* New Brunswick, N.J.: Transaction Books.

Robertson, John D. 1984. "Economic Performance and Transient European Cabinet Administrations: Implications for Consociational Parliamentary Democracies." *International Studies Quarterly* 28, 4 (December): 447-66.

Rogowski, Ronald. 1974. *Rational Legitimacy: A Theory of Political Support.* Princeton: Princeton University Press.

Rose, Richard, ed. 1980. *Electoral Participation: A Comparative Analysis.* Beverly Hills: Sage.

Rotberg, Robert I. 1980a. "Creating a More Harmonious South Africa." In Rotberg and Barratt, eds.

_____. 1980b. *Suffer the Future: Policy Choices in Southern Africa.* Cambridge, Mass.: Harvard University Press.

Rotberg, Robert I., and Barratt, John, eds. 1980. *Conflict and Compromise in South Africa.* Lexington, Mass.: Lexington Books.

Rothchild, Donald. 1970. "Ethnicity and Conflict Resolution." *World Politics* 22, 4 (July): 597-616.

_____. 1984. "Middle Africa: Hegemonial Exchange and Resource Allocation." In *Cooperative Resource Allocation: Politics, Performance, and Policy Priorities,* ed. Alexander J. Groth and Larry L. Wade. Beverly Hills: Sage. Sage Yearbook in Politics and Public Policy, vol. 13.

_____. 1985. "State-Ethnic Relations in Middle Africa." In *African Independence: The First Twenty-Five Years,* ed. Gwendolen M. Carter and Patrick O'Meara. Bloomington: Indiana University Press.

Rothchild, Donald, and Olorunsola, Victor A., eds. 1983. *State versus Ethnic Claims: African Policy Dilemmas.* Boulder, Colo.: Westview Press.

Rustow, Dankwart A. 1970. "Transitions to Democracy: Toward a Dynamic Model." *Comparative Politics* 2, 3 (April): 337-63.

Sadie, J. L. 1978. "Demographic and Socio-Economic Projections and Constitutional Alternatives." In Benyon, ed.

_____. 1980. "The Political Arithmatic of South Africa." In Rhoodie, ed. 1980.

Saul, John S., and Gelb, Stephen. 1981. *The Crisis in South Africa: Class Defense, Class Revolution.* New York: Monthly Review Press.

Savage, Michael. 1980. "What Does Removal of Race Discrimination Effectively Mean in the South African Context?" In Slabbert and Opland, eds.

Scarrit, James R., and Safran, William. 1983. "The Relationship of Ethnicity to Modernization and Democracy: A Restatement of the Issues." *International Studies Notes* 10, 2 (Summer): 16-21.

Schlemmer, Lawrence. 1970. *Social Change and Political Policy in South Africa: An Assessment of the Future of Separate Development and of Possible Alternatives.* Johannesburg: South African Institute of Race Relations.

_____. 1977. "Theories of the Plural Society and Change in South Africa." *Social Dynamics* 3, 1 (June): 3-16.

_____. 1978a. "The Devolution of Power in South Africa: Problems and Prospects." In Rhoodie, ed. 1978.

_____. 1978b. "Social Implications of Constitutional Alternatives in South Africa." In Benyon, ed.

_____. 1978c. "Conflict and Conflict Regulation in South Africa." In de Crespigny and Schrire, eds.

_____. 1980a. "The Stirring Giant: Observations on the Inkatha and Other Black Political Movements in South Africa." In Price and Rosberg, eds.

_____. 1980b. "Change in South Africa: Opportunities and Constraints." In Price and Rosberg, eds.

_____. 1981. "An Overview: A Summary of the Major Points Emerging from the Workshop." In Boulle and Baxter, eds.

_____. 1983a. "Need and Criteria for a New Constitutional Dispensation." In van Vuuren and Kriek, eds.

_____. 1983b. "Build-up to Revolution or Impasse?" In Adam, ed. 1983.

_____. 1984. "Education and Change in South Africa." *Zeitschrift für Erziehungs- und Sozialwissenschaftliche Forschung* 1, 2: 253-65.

Schlemmer, Lawrence, and Muil, Tim J. 1975. "Social and Political Change in the African Areas: A Case Study of KwaZulu." In Thompson and Butler, eds.

Schmid, Carol L. 1981. *Conflict and Consensus in Switzerland.* Berkeley: University of California Press.

Schmitt, David E. 1977. "Ethnic Conflict in Northern Ireland: International Aspects of Conflict Management." In Esman, ed.

Scholten, Ilja. 1980. "Does Consociationalism Exist? A Critique of the Dutch Experience." In Rose, ed.

Schreiner, G. D. L. 1982. *Political Ecology in a Checker-Board Region.* Pietermaritzburg: University of Natal Press. George Campbell Lecture.

Schrire, Robert A. 1978a. "Power and Power-Sharing in South Africa." In *The Road to a Just Society.* Johannesburg: South African Institute of Race Relations.

_____. 1978b. "The Context of South African Politics." In de Crespigny and Schrire, eds.

Sedoc-Dahlberg, Betty. 1983. "The Surinamese Society in Transition: A Test-Case on Consistencies in Values and Goals in a Caribbean Society." In *Politics, Public Administration and Rural Development in the Caribbean,* ed. Hans F. Illy. Munich: Weltforum Verlag.

Seidman, Judy. 1980. *Facelift Apartheid: South Africa after Soweto.* London: International Defence and Aid Fund for Southern Africa.

Seiler, John. 1974. "Measuring Black Political Support in South Africa." *Politikon* 1, 2 (December): 19-26.

_____. 1977. "Consociational Authoritarianism: Incentives and Hindrances Toward Power Sharing and Devolution in South Africa and Namibia." Paper presented at the annual meeting of the American Political Science Association, Washington, D.C.

_____. 1979. "The Afrikaner Nationalist Perspective." In Bissell and Crocker, eds.

Selfe, James. 1985. "The State of Black Politics in South Africa Today." In Friedrich Naumann Foundation, ed.

Shaw, J. A. 1978. "The Collapse of the Lebanese State and Its Relevance to Political Developments in South Africa." *Politikon* 5, 2 (December): 206-10.

Simkins, Charles E. W. 1983. "Economic Factors and Constitutional Change." In Dean and Smit, eds.

Sinclair, Michael. 1982. "In Search of the Political Middle-Ground in South Africa." *Politikon* 9, 1 (June): 30-39.

Sklar, Richard L. 1982. *Democracy in Africa.* Presidential Address to the Twenty-Fifth Annual Meeting of the African Studies Association, Washington, D.C. Los Angeles: African Studies Center, University of California.

Slabbert, F. van Zyl. 1971. "Modernization and Apartheid." In Randall, ed. 1971a.

_____. 1983. "Sham Reform and Conflict Regulation in a Divided Society." In Adam, ed. 1983.

_____. 1985. "The Nature of the South African Problem and the Progressive Federal Party's Approach to Its Solution." In Friedrich Naumann Foundation, ed.

Slabbert, F. van Zyl, and Welsh, David. 1979. *South Africa's Options: Strategies for Sharing Power.* New York: St. Martin's Press.

Slabbert, F. van Zyl, and Opland, Jeff, eds. 1980. *South Africa: Dilemmas of Evolutionary Change.* Grahamstown: Institute of Social and Economic Research, Rhodes University.

Smiley, Donald V. 1977. "French-English Relations in Canada and Consociational Democracy." In Esman, ed.

Smit, P. 1983. "The Plural Nature of the South African Population." In van Vuuren and Kriek, eds.

Smith, M. G. 1969a. "Pluralism in Precolonial African Societies." In Kuper and Smith, eds.

_____. 1969b. "Some Developments in the Analytic Framework of Pluralism." In Kuper and Smith, eds.

Smooha, Sammy. 1978. *Israel: Pluralism and Conflict.* Berkeley: University of California Press.

South Africa, Republic of. 1983a. *House of Assembly Debates (Hansard).* Cape Town: Government Printer.

_____. 1983b. *Republic of South Africa Constitution Act: No. 110, 1983.* Pretoria: Department of Foreign Affairs and Information.

South African Research Service, ed. 1983. *South African Review I: Same Foundations, New Facades?* Johannesburg: Ravan Press.

_____, ed. 1984. *South African Review II.* Johannesburg: Ravan Press.

Southall, Roger J. 1981. "Buthelezi, Inkatha and the Politics of Compromise." *African Affairs* 80, 321 (October): 453-81.

_____. 1983. "Consociationalism in South Africa: The Buthelezi Commission and Beyond." *Journal of Modern African Studies* 21, 1 (March): 77-112.

Southern Africa Working Party of the American Friends Service Committee. 1982. *South Africa: Challenge and Hope.* Philadelphia: American Friends Service Committee.

Stadler, Alf. 1975. "Anxious Radicals: SPRO-CAS and the Apartheid Society." *Journal of Southern African Studies* 2, 1 (October): 102-8.

Stanton, Diane Ruth. 1983. *Consociational Democracy and Its Alternatives in South Africa: Constitutional Reforms 1948-1983.* Master's thesis, University of California, San Diego.

Staples, Janice. 1974. "Consociationalism at Provincial Level: The Erosion of Dualism in Manitoba, 1870-1890." In McRae, ed.

Starcke, Anna. 1978. *Survival: Taped Interviews with South Africa's Power Elite.* Cape Town: Tafelberg.

Steiner, Jürg. 1971. "The Principles of Majority and Proportionality." *British Journal of Political Science* 1, 1 (January): 63-70.

_____. 1974. *Amicable Agreement versus Majority Rule: Conflict Resolution in Switzerland.* Chapel Hill: University of North Carolina Press.

_____. 1981a. "The Consociational Theory and Beyond." *Comparative Politics* 13, 3 (April): 339-54.

_____. 1981b. "Research Strategies Beyond Consociational Theory." *Journal of Politics* 43, 4 (November): 1241-50.

_____. 1983. "Conclusion: Reflections on the Consociational Theme." In *Switzerland at the Polls: The National Elections of 1979*, ed. Howard R. Penniman. Washington, D.C.: American Enterprise Institute.

Steiner, Jürg, and Dorff, Robert H. 1980a. *A Theory of Political Decision Modes: Intraparty Decision Making in Switzerland.* Chapel Hill: University of North Carolina Press.

_____, and _____. 1980b. "Decision by Interpretation: A New Concept for an Often Overlooked Decision Mode." *British Journal of Political Science* 10, 1 (January): 1-13.

Steiner, Jürg, and Obler, Jeffrey. 1977. "Does the Consociational Theory Really Hold for Switzerland?" In Esman, ed.

Steiner, Kurt. 1972. *Politics in Austria.* Boston: Little, Brown.

Steininger, Rudolf. 1975. *Polarisierung und Integration: Eine vergleichende Untersuchung der strukturellen Versäulung der Gesellschaft in den Niederlanden und in Österreich.* Meisenheim am Glan: Hain.

Sterling, Carleton W. 1978. Review of Lijphart 1977a. *Review of Politics* 40, 2 (April): 303-4.

Stevenson, Hamish. 1983. *A Political-Strategic Analysis of a Constitutional Alternative for South Africa in the Consociational Perspective: Its Possibilities and Limitations.* Bachelor's thesis, University of North Carolina, Chapel Hill.

Stiefbold, Rodney P. 1974. "Segmented Pluralism and Consociational Democracy in Austria: Problems of Political Stability and Change." In Heisler, ed.

Stokes, Randall. 1978. "External Liberation Movements." In Robertson and Whitten, eds.

Streek, Barry. 1984. "Disunity Through the Bantustans." In South African Research Service, ed. 1984.

Study Commission on U.S. Policy Toward Southern Africa. 1981. *South Africa: Time Running Out.* Berkeley: University of California Press.

Stultz, Newell M. 1977. "Transkei Independence in Separatist Perspective." *South Africa International* 8, 1 (July): 10-26.

_____. 1979. "On Partition." *Social Dynamics* 5, 1 (June): 1-13.

_____. 1980. "Some Implications of African 'Homelands' in South Africa." In Price and Rosberg, eds.

_____. 1982. "Sanctions, Models of Change and South Africa." *South Africa International* 13, 2 (October): 121-29.

_____. 1984. "Interpreting Constitutional Change in South Africa." *Journal of Modern African Studies* 22, 3 (September): 353-79.

Stuurman, Siep. 1983. *Verzuiling, kapitalisme en patriarchaat: Aspecten van de ontwikkeling van de moderne staat in Nederland.* Nijmegen: Socialistiese Uitgeverij Nijmegen.

Sutton, William M. 1977. "The New Constitution." *Natal Witness,* 10 October.

_____. 1978. "The N.R.P. Federal/Confederal Proposals: A Unique Solution." *Volkstem* (June): 10.

Suzman, Helen. 1972. "The Progressive Party's Programme for a Multi-Racial South Africa." In Rhoodie, ed. 1972.

Sylla, Lanciné. 1982. "La Gestion démocratique du pluralisme socio-politique en Afrique: Démocratie concurrentielle et démocratie consociationnelle." *Civilisations* 32, 2: 23-61.

Terreblanche, S. J. 1978. "Moontlike fiskale strukture in 'n alternatiewe konstitusionele model in Suid-Afrika." In Benyon, ed.

Thebehali, David. 1980. "The Social, Economic and Political Future of Soweto in a Plural South Africa." In Rhoodie, ed. 1980.

Thomas, Wolfgang H. 1977. *Plural Democracy: Political Change and Strategies for Evolution in South Africa.* Johannesburg: South African Institute of Race Relations.

_____. 1979. "Südafrika zwischen Teilung und Integration." *Aussenpolitik* 30, 3: 301-22.

Thompson, Leonard M. 1966. *Politics in the Republic of South Africa.* Boston: Little, Brown.

Thompson, Leonard M., and Prior, Andrew. 1982. *South African Politics.* New Haven: Yale University Press.

Thompson, Leonard M., and Butler, Jeffrey, eds. 1975. *Change in Contemporary South Africa.* Berkeley: University of California Press.

Thula, Gibson. 1978. "The Process of Power Sharing." In *The Road to a Just Society.* Johannesburg: South African Institute of Race Relations.

_____. 1980a. "A Basis for the Constitutional Transformation of South Africa." In Rotberg and Barratt, eds.

_____. 1980b. "A Constitutional Alternative for South Africa (Inkatha)." In Slabbert and Opland, eds.

_____. 1980c. "Inkatha, The National Cultural Liberation Movement." In H. W. van der Merwe et al., eds. 1980.

Tiryakian, Edward A. 1967. "Sociological Realism: Partition for South Africa?" *Social Forces* 46, 2 (December): 208-21.

Tötemeyer, Gerhard. 1984. "Ethnicity and National Identification Within (South) African Context." *Politikon* 11, 1 (June): 43-54.

Tsujinaka, Yutaka. 1984. "A. Lijphart to takyoku shakai no demokurasii: Jiritsu kyozon to minshisei no dilemma." In *Gendai sekai no minshishigiriron*, ed. Rei Shiratori and Yasunori Sone. Tokyo: Shinhyoron.

Tuéni, Ghassan. 1982. "Lebanon: A New Republic?" *Foreign Affairs* 61, 1 (Fall): 84-99.

Turk, Austin T. 1967. "The Futures of South Africa." *Social Forces* 45, 3 (March): 402-12.

Turner, Richard. 1978. *The Eye of the Needle: Toward Participatory Democracy in South Africa.* Maryknoll, N.Y.: Orbis.

Tutu, Desmond Mpilo. 1982. *Crying in the Wilderness: The Struggle for Justice in South Africa.* Grand Rapids, Mich.: Eerdmans.

_____. 1984. *Hope and Suffering: Sermons and Speeches.* Grand Rapids, Mich.: Eerdmans.

Ungar, Sanford J. 1984. "Reagan's South Africa Policy Is a Failure." *New York Times,* 17 September.

Urio, Paolo. 1984. "Le pluralisme dans la société helvétique." *International Political Science Review* 5, 4: 507-19.

van den Berg, J. Th. J., and Molleman, H. A. A. 1974. *Crisis in de Nederlandse politiek.* Alphen aan den Rijn: Samsom.

van den Berghe, Pierre L. 1965. *South Africa: A Study in Conflict.* Middletown, Conn.: Wesleyan University Press.

_____. 1978. "Racial Segregation in South Africa: Degrees and Kinds." In Robertson and Whitten, eds.

_____. 1979a. "Introduction." In van den Berghe, ed.

_____. 1979b. "The Impossibility of a Liberal Solution in South Africa." In van den Berghe, ed.

_____. 1981a. *The Ethnic Phenomenon.* New York: Elsevier.

_____. 1981b. "Protection of Ethnic Minorities: A Critical Appraisal." In *Protection of Ethnic Minorities: Comparative Perspectives,* ed. Robert G. Wirsing. New York: Pergamon Press.

_____. 1983. "A Response to Heribert Adam." In Rothchild and Olorunsola, eds.

_____, ed. 1979. *The Liberal Dilemma in South Africa.* New York: St. Martin's Press.

Vandenbosch, Amry. 1979. "Brown South Africans and the Proposed New Constitution." *Journal of Politics* 41, 2 (May): 566-88.

van der Kroef, Justus M. 1978. Review of Lijphart 1977a. *Annals of the American Academy of Political and Social Science* 438 (July): 128-30.

van der Merwe, C. J. 1985. *And What About the Blacks?* Cape Town: Federal Information Service of the National Party.

van der Merwe, Hendrik W. 1983. "Urbanization and the Political Position of Africans in South Africa." *South African Journal of Sociology* 14, 4: 109-17.

van der Merwe, Hendrik W., and Schrire, Robert, eds. 1980. *Race and Ethnicity: South African and International Perspectives.* Cape Town: David Philip.

van der Merwe, Hendrik W. et al., eds. 1978. *African Perspectives on South Africa: A Collection of Speeches, Articles and Documents.* Stanford: Hoover Institution Press.

van der Merwe, Hendrik W. et al., eds. 1980. *Towards an Open Society in South Africa: The Role of Voluntary Organisations.* Cape Town: David Philip.

van der Meulen, J. W. 1983. *Westelijke druk en het apartheidsregime.* The Hague: Nederlands Instituut voor International Betrekkingen Clingendael.

van der Ross, R. E. 1981. "Die voorvereistes vir stabiele demokrasie in Suid-Afrika." *Politikon* 8, 2 (December): 43-56.

_____. 1983. "Perspectives on Constitutional Problems." In van Vuuren and Kriek, eds.

van der Vyver, J. D. 1978. "Prospects for the Future Political Development of South Africa." In de Crespigny and Schrire, eds.

van der Werff, J. H. 1985. "Zuid-Afrika: Op weg naar een onzekere toekomst." *Civis Mundi* 24, 2 (April): 49-81.

Van Dyke, Vernon. 1975. "Justice as Fairness: For Groups?" *American Political Science Review* 69, 2 (June): 607-14.

_____. 1977. "The Individual, the State, and Ethnic Communities in Political Theory." *World Politics* 29, 3 (April): 343-69.

_____. 1982. "Collective Entities and Moral Rights: Problems in Liberal-Democratic Thought." *Journal of Politics* 44, 1 (February): 21-40.

_____. 1983. "Legitimacy in Plural Societies." *Politikon* 10, 2 (December): 6-25.

van Jaarsveld, F. A. 1980. "From Apartheid to Incipient Democratic Pluralism." In Rhoodie, ed. 1980.

van Klaveren, Alberto. 1983. "La Doctrina consociativa como modelo de convergencia política: La experiencia europea." *Estudios sociales* 10, 36 (2d trimester): 9-40.

_____. 1984. "Instituciones consociativas: Alternativas para la estabilidad democrática en Chile?" *Alternativas* 2 (January-April): 24-55.

van Schendelen, M. P. C. M. 1978. "Verzuiling en restauratie in de Nederlandse politiek." *Beleid en Maatschappij* 5, 2 (February): 42-64.

_____. 1983. "Critical Comments on Lijphart's Theory of Consociational Democracy." *Politikon* 10, 1 (June): 6-32.

_____. 1984. "The Views of Arend Lijphart and Collected Criticisms." *Acta Politica* 19, 1 (January): 19-55.

van Vuuren, D. J. 1983. "The Unitary State." In van Vuuren and Kriek, eds.

van Vuuren, D. J., and Kriek, D. J., eds. 1983. *Political Alternatives for Southern Africa: Principles and Perspectives*. Durban: Butterworths.

van Wyk, D. 1983. "The Westminster System." In van Vuuren and Kriek, eds.

Vasil, Raj K. 1984. *Politics in Bi-Racial Societies: The Third World Experience*. New Delhi: Vikas.

Venter, Albert Jan. 1979. Review of Lijphart, 1977a. *Politikon* 6, 1 (June): 85-86.

_____. 1980a. *'n Kritiese ontleding van die konsosiasiemodel van Arend Lijphart*. Master's thesis, University of South Africa.

_____. 1980b. "Leierskapinskiklikheid in diepverdeelde samelewings: 'n Kritiese waardering van Lijphart se konsosiasieteorie." *Politikon* 7, 2 (December): 126-48.

_____. 1981. "Some of South Africa's Political Alternatives in Consociational Perspective." *South Africa International* 11, 3 (January): 129-41.

_____. 1983. "Consociational Democracy." In van Vuuren and Kriek, eds.

_____. 1984. "Lijphart." In *Die moderne politieke teorie*, ed. A. M. Faure and D. J. Kriek. Durban: Butterworths.

Venter, T. D. 1975. "Konfederale assosiasie van state of federasie as staatkundige toekomsbedeling in Suid(er)-Afrika: Teoretiese perspektiewe vir die Suid-Afrikaanse party-politiek." *Politkon* 2, 2 (December): 94-114.

Vigne, Randolph. 1978. "The Bantustans." In Robertson and Whitten, eds.

Vile, M. J. C. 1977. "Federal Theory and the 'New Federalism'." In *The Politics of "New Federalism,"* ed. Dean Jaensch. Adelaide: Australasian Political Studies Association.

Viljoen, G. van N., ed., 1970. *Tuislandontwikkeling: 'n Program vir die Sewentigerjare*. Pretoria: Suid-Afrikaanse Buro vir Rasse-aangeleenthede.

von der Ropp, Klaus Baron. 1978. "Globalteilung als Strategie friedlichen Wandels in Südafrika." In *Polarität und Interdependenz: Beiträge zu Fragen der Internationalen Politik*. Baden-Baden: Nomos.

_____. 1979. "Is Territorial Partition a Strategy for Peaceful Change in South Africa?" *International Affairs Bulletin* 3, 1 (June): 36-47.

_____. 1981. "Power Sharing Versus Partition in South Africa." *Australian Outlook* 35, 2 (August): 158-68.

_____. 1982a. "L'Avenir de l'Afrique du Sud." *Politique étrangere* 47, 2 (June): 429-40.

_____. 1982b. "Südafrika 1982: Revolution von oben—Revolution von unten?" *Liberal* 24, 11 (November): 845-56.

_____. 1984. "Die neue Verfassung der Republik Südafrika: Von 'Westminster' nach 'Southminster'." *Verfassung und Recht in Übersee* 17, 2: 194-211.

_____. 1985. "South Africa's Challenge to the Western World: A German View." In Friedrich Naumann Foundation, ed.

von Vorys, Karl. 1975. *Democracy Without Consensus: Communalism and Political Stability in Malaysia.* Princeton: Princeton University Press.

Vorster, M. P. 1981. "KwaZulu/Natal Wetgewende Vergadering." In Boulle and Baxter, eds.

Vosloo, W. B. 1974. "Pluralisme as teoretiese perspektief vir veelvolkige naasbestaan in Suid-Afrika." *Politikon* 1, 1 (June): 4-14.

_____. 1976. "Separate Development as a Framework for Peaceful Change in South Africa." *Politikon* 3, 2 (October): 19-30.

_____. 1978a. "A Comparative Perspective on Metropolitan Areas as Laboratories for Community-Oriented Local Government Reorganisation in South Africa." In Rhoodie, ed. 1978.

_____. 1978b. "The Executive." In Benyon, ed.

_____. 1980. "Consociational Democracy as a Means to Accomplish Peaceful Political Change in South Africa: An Evaluation of the Constitutional Changes Proposed by the National Party in 1977." In Rhoodie, ed. 1980.

Vosloo, W. B., and Schrire, R. A. 1978. "Subordinate Political Institutions." In de Crespigny and Schrire, eds.

Walshe, Peter. 1983. *Church versus State in South Africa: The Case of the Christian Institute.* London: Hurst.

Weaver, Tony. 1983. "The President's Council." In South African Research Service, ed. 1983.

Webster, John. 1982. "Introduction." In Tutu 1982.

Weiner, Myron. 1983. "The Political Consequences of Preferential Policies: A Comparative Perspective." *Comparative Politics* 16, 1 (October): 35-52.

Welsh, David. 1978. "The Road to a Just Society: An Overview." In *The Road to a Just Society*. Johannesburg: South African Institute of Race Relations.

_____. 1980. "Intergroup Accommodation in South Africa." In H. W. van der Merwe and Schrire, eds.

_____. 1982. *South Africa: Power, Process and Prospect.* Rondebosch: University of Cape Town. Inaugural lecture.

_____. 1983. "Evaluation and Critique of Constitutional Proposals for Southern Africa." In van Vuuren and Kriek, eds.

Wessels, D. P. 1983. "The Executive Authority." In van Vuuren and Kriek, eds.

Whisson, M. G. 1971. "The Coloured People." In Randall, ed. 1971b.

Whitaker, Jennifer S. 1983. "Pretoria's Wars." *New York Times*, 21 January.

Whitaker, Philip. 1979. Review of Lijphart 1977a. *International Affairs* 55, 2 (April): 272-74.

Whyte, Quintin. 1952. *Go Forward in Faith: A Statement of the Fundamental Beliefs of the South African Institute of Race Relations.* Johannesburg: South African Institute of Race Relations.

Wiechers, Marinus. 1978. "Possible Structural Divisions of Power in South Africa." In Benyon, ed.

_____. 1981. "The Franchise and Alternative Electoral Systems." In Boulle and Baxter, eds.

Woldring, Klaas. 1977. "The South African SPRO-CAS Study Projects on Christianity in Apartheid Society (1969-1973)." *Publius* 7, 1 (Winter): 41-57.

Wolinetz, Steven B. 1978. "The Politics of Non-Accommodation in Canada: Misapplications of Consociational Models and Their Consequences for the Study of National Integration and Political Stability." Paper presented at the annual meeting of the Canadian Political Science Association, London, Ontario.

Woodward, Calvin A. 1981. "Reform or Revolution in South Africa." *Round Table* 282 (April): 101-15.

Worrall, Denis. 1971. "The Plural-State System as a Direction of Change." In Randall, ed. 1971c.

_____. 1975. "Government in the Plural Society: The South African Model." In *Case Studies on Human Rights and Fundamental Freedoms: A World Survey*, ed. Willem A. Veenhoven, vol. 2. The Hague: Nijhoff.

_____. 1978. "The South African Government's 1977 Constitutional Proposals." In Benyon, ed.

_____. 1981. "The Constitutional Committee of the President's Council." *Politikon* 8, 2 (December) 27-34.

Young, Crawford. 1976. *The Politics of Cultural Pluralism.* Madison: University of Wisconsin Press.

Zimmermann, Reinhard. 1978. "Die Verfassungen von Transkei und Bophutatswana, der Verfassungsentwurf für die Republik Südafrika und das Konzept des 'Separate Development'." In *Jahrbuch des öffentlichen Rechts der Gegenwart*, vol. 27, ed. Gerhard Leibholz.

Zolberg, Aristide R. 1977. "Splitting the Difference: Federalization Without Federalism in Belgium." In Esman, ed.

INDEX

Accommodation, 87n. *See also* Consociational democracy; Traditions of accommodation

Adam, Heribert, 3, 25, 41n, 46, 68, 100, 119n, 121, 125, 128, 131

Affirmative action, 17, 125. *See also* Proportionality; Socioeconomic equality

African National Congress (ANC), 22, 23, 24, 77, 131, 134

Ake, Claude, 97

ANC. *See* African National Congress (ANC)

Apartheid, 33, 41. *See also* Homeland partition

Assimilation, 31

Austria: consociationalism in, 12, 84, 89, 90, 98, 100, 103-4, 110; as plural society, 94, 97, 98, 105, 106, 129

Autonomy. *See* Federalism; Segmental autonomy

Background conditions. *See* Favorable conditions

Bakvis, Herman, 108

Barry, Brian, 90, 91, 93n, 94, 96-97, 103-4

Belgium: consociationalism in, 12, 84, 89, 90, 93n, 98, 100, 107n, 110; favorable conditions in, 119-20, 123-27; as plural society, 19, 58, 94, 97, 98, 105, 119, 122, 129

Beran, Harry, 41-42

Blenck, Jürgen, 2, 42-45

Boesak, Allan, 24, 30

Bophuthatswana, 3n, 21, 34, 37, 39, 40, 41, 74

Botha, Pik, 14, 19

Botha, P. Roelf, 34

Botha, P. W., 2, 14, 33, 39, 52, 63, 68, 131

Botswana, 35, 124

Boulle, Laurence J., 22, 53, 61, 77, 80, 111

Boynton, G. R., 94-96

Brookes, Edgar H., 16, 17, 27, 51

Burnham, Walter Dean, 28, 29

Burundi, 21

Buthelezi, M. Gatsha, 22, 23, 25, 41, 122, 126

Buthelezi Commission, 9, 47, 74, 76-77, 78-80, 121, 128

California, 72n

Canada, 19, 84, 90n, 93n, 94, 112, 122

Capeland, 43-46

Capricornia, 43-46

Carter, Jimmy, 14

Chile, 84

Cillié, Piet, 62

Ciskei, 3n, 34, 74-76. *See also* Ciskei Commission

Ciskei Commission, 9, 12n, 47, 74-76, 79

Collins, P., 118

Colombia, 84, 127-28

Communist Party, 2

Confederation, 34-35. *See also* Federalism

Conservative Party, 33, 60, 62, 131

Consociational democracy: characteristics of, 6-9, 11-12, 30-31, 47, 87n; criticisms of, 11-13, 83-117; favorable conditions for, 13, 86, 87n, 114-16, 119-28; negotiations on, 15, 46, 67, 81-82, 133-34; proposed for South Africa, 9-11, 13, 15, 47-82, 83, 116, 118-35. *See also* Executive power-sharing; Minority veto; Proportionality; Segmental autonomy

Constitution (1983): characteristics of, 16, 17, 36, 47, 52-56, 76; critique of, 4, 9-10, 56-64, 65, 66

173

AREND LIJPHART is Professor of Political Science at the University of California, San Diego. He is especially interested in the comparative study of democratic regimes and deeply divided societies. His recent books include *Democracy in Plural Societies: A Comparative Exploration* (New Haven: Yale University Press, 1977), *Democracies: Patterns of Majoritarian and Consensus Government in Twenty-One Countries* (New Haven: Yale University Press, 1984), and *Choosing an Electoral System: Issues and Alternatives,* co-edited with Bernard Grofman (New York: Praeger, 1984).

INSTITUTE OF INTERNATIONAL STUDIES
UNIVERSITY OF CALIFORNIA, BERKELEY

215 Moses Hall   Berkeley, California 94720

CARL G. ROSBERG, *Director*

Monographs published by the Institute include:

RESEARCH SERIES

1. *The Chinese Anarchist Movement.* R.A. Scalapino and G.T. Yu. ($1.00)
7. *Birth Rates in Latin America.* O. Andrew Collver. ($2.50)
16. *The International Imperatives of Technology.* Eugene B. Skolnikoff. ($2.95)
17. *Autonomy or Dependence in Regional Integration.* P.C. Schmitter. ($1.75)
19. *Entry of New Competitors in Yugoslav Market Socialism.* S.R. Sacks. ($2.50)
20. *Political Integration in French-Speaking Africa.* Abdul A. Jalloh. ($3.50)
21. *The Desert & the Sown: Nomads in Wider Society.* Ed. C. Nelson. ($5.50)
22. *U.S.-Japanese Competition in International Markets.* J.E. Roemer. ($3.95)
23. *Political Disaffection Among British University Students.* J. Citrin and D.J. Elkins. ($2.00)
24. *Urban Inequality and Housing Policy in Tanzania.* Richard E. Stren. ($2.95)
25. *The Obsolescence of Regional Integration Theory.* Ernst B. Haas. ($6.95)
26. *The Voluntary Service Agency in Israel.* Ralph M. Kramer. ($2.00)
27. *The SOCSIM Microsimulation Program.* E. A. Hammel et al. ($4.50)
28. *Authoritarian Politics in Communist Europe.* Ed. Andrew C. Janos. ($8.95)
30. *Plural Societies and New States.* Robert Jackson. ($2.00)
31. *Politics of Oil Pricing in the Middle East, 1970-75.* R.C. Weisberg. ($4.95)
32. *Agricultural Policy and Performance in Zambia.* Doris J. Dodge. ($4.95)
33. *Five Classy Computer Programs.* E.A. Hammel & R.Z. Deuel. ($3.75)
34. *Housing the Urban Poor in Africa.* Richard E. Stren. ($5.95)
35. *The Russian New Right: Right-Wing Ideologies in USSR.* A. Yanov. ($5.95)
36. *Social Change in Romania, 1860-1940.* Ed. Kenneth Jowitt. ($4.50)
37. *The Leninist Response to National Dependency.* Kenneth Jowitt. ($4.95)
38. *Socialism in Sub-Saharan Africa.* Eds. C. Rosberg & T. Callaghy. ($12.95)
39. *Tanzania's Ujamaa Villages: Rural Development Strategy.* D. McHenry. ($5.95)
40. *Who Gains from Deep Ocean Mining?* I.G. Bulkley. ($3.50)
41. *Industrialization & the Nation-State in Peru.* Frits Wils. ($5.95)
42. *Ideology, Public Opinion, & Welfare Policy.* R.M. Coughlin. ($6.50)
43. *The Apartheid Regime: Political Power and Racial Domination.* Eds. R.M. Price and C. G. Rosberg. ($12.50)
44. *Yugoslav Economic System in the 1970s.* Laura D. Tyson. ($5.95)
45. *Conflict in Chad.* Virginia Thompson & Richard Adloff. ($7.50)
46. *Conflict and Coexistence in Belgium.* Ed. Arend Lijphart. ($8.95)
47. *Changing Realities in Southern Africa.* Ed. Michael Clough. ($12.50)
48. *Nigerian Women Mobilized, 1900-1965.* Nina E. Mba. ($12.95)
49. *Institutions of Rural Development.* Eds. D. Leonard & D. Marshall. ($11.50)
50. *Politics of Women & Work in USSR & U.S.* Joel C. Moses. ($9.50)

LIST OF PUBLICATIONS *(continued)*

POLICY PAPERS IN INTERNATIONAL AFFAIRS

POLITICS OF MODERNIZATION SERIES